BARRED FROM PRISON

Claire Culhane was born in Montreal in 1918. Her family were Russian Jewish immigrants. At eighteen years old she was a member of the Friends of the Mackenzie-Papineau Battalion. In 1967 she was administrator in a Canadian government-sponsored hospital in South Vietnam. Her Asian experience led to her first book, *Why is Canada in Vietnam?* (NC PRESS, 1972). By 1975 she had delivered papers at international conferences in Paris, Stockholm, Oslo, and Hanoi, and had criss-crossed Canada and the U.S. five times reporting on what she had learned firsthand about Canada's involvement in southeast Asia. In 1976 she became a member of the Citizens Advisory Committee at the B.C. Penitentiary, where she was an eyewitness to many of the events described in this book. Her work since that time as a member of the Prisoners' Rights Group has involved her in prisoners' activities throughout Canada and the U.S.

Nelson Potter

Eddie Hatmut

Harry Skinner

Trish Green

Mad Dave Foster

Editor Odyssey Newsletter

Love & Prayers
& Strength
Ron Van Bee

Peggy Swarteum

Marilyn Jn Here
Bryan Reynolds

A prisoner's days run,
the weeks a slow drawn pain,
the years standing like stone.

*   *   *

No to their NO. Yes to all else.

—Daniel Berrigan

BARRED
FROM PRISON

Claire Culhane

PULP PRESS
VANCOUVER

Odyssey,
Millhaven
Tuesday, Oct. 23ʳᵈ'79
G. Schmitz

This is a Pulp Book
Published by Pulp Press
Box 3868 MPO
Vancouver Canada

ISBN 0-88978-076-5 (cloth)
        0-88978-078-1 (paper)

Excerpts from Daniel Berrigan are from *Prison Poems* (Unicorn Press, P.O. Box 3307, Greensboro, N.C., USA 27402).
Some of the material in Ch. 8 first appeared in "Prisons in Canada," a review of *Cruel and Unusual* by Gérard McNeil and Sharon Vance, in *Our Generation,* Vol.13, No.2, Spring 1979.
Author's proceeds are to be donated to the *Prisoners' Rights Group*, 3965 Pandora St., Burnaby, B.C., Canada V5C 2A8.

Printed & bound in Canada.

Contents

The Cast

INMATE COMMITTEE—B.C.PENITENTIARY

    Ivan Horvat (J.J.)—Chairman
    Omer Prud'homme—Vice-Chairman
    Paul Leister—Secretary-Treasurer
    Gordon Duck—Entertainment
    Gary Lake—Recreation
    Lea Sheppe—Coordinator
    Jack Dow—Coordinator

CITIZENS ADVISORY COMMITTEE—B.C.PENITENTIARY

    Tom Alsbury—Delegate for Dave Barrett, MLA (NDP)
    Rev. Bob Burrows—B.C.Police Commission
    Claire Culhane—Prisoners' Rights Group (PRG)*
    Ezzat Fattah—Criminologist, Simon Fraser University*
    Gordon Gibson—MLA (Lib.)
    Reginald Grandison—Lawyer, delegate for Dr. Wallace
    Michael Jackson—Professor of Law, University of B.C.
    Stuart Leggatt—MP (NDP)
    Edwin Lipinski—Psychiatrist, Simon Fraser University*
    Frank Maczko—Professor of Law, University of B.C.*
    Mary McGrath—Lawyer, Legal Aid Society of B.C.*
    Wendy O'Flaherty—Programmer, CBC (TV)*
    Vi Roden—Delegate for Gordon Gibson*
    Don Sorochan—Lawyer*
    James Spears—Reporter, *Vancouver Province**
    Staff Sergeant Paul Starek—RCMP*
    Envoy Stevenson—Salvation Army*
    Dave Stockand—Reporter, *Vancouver Sun**
    Dr. Scott Wallace—MLA (PC)
    Bryan Williams—Lawyer*

                 (*present at first meeting, June 22/76)

CANADIAN PENITENTIARY SERVICE

    First Level (Institutional—B.C.Penitentiary)

        Directors—Dragan Cernetic
                 Herbert C. Reynett (Feb./77)
        Acting Directors—Kenneth Peterson
                 W.R. Swan (Oct./76)
        Acting Director of Security—Ev Berkey

Second Level—Regional (B.C.)

Regional Director General—James Murphy
Regional Executive Officer—Douglas M. McGregor
Regional Information Officer—Jack Stewart
Transfer Board—Al Byman
                    Jean Simonds (Nov./76)

Third Level—National (Ottawa)

Commissioners—André Therrien
                  Donald R. Yeomans (Dec./77)
Director Inmate Affairs—C. G. Rutter
Correctional Investigator (Ombudsperson)—Inger Hansen

Abbreviations

A/D—Acting Director
C.A.C.—Citizens Advisory Committee
CO—Classification Officer
CPS—Canadian Penitentiary Service*
I.C.—Inmate Committee
LMRCC—Lower Mainland Regional Correctional Centre
OWCC—Oakalla Womens Correctional Centre
PCU—Protective Custody Unit
PRG—Prisoners' Rights Group
PSAC—Public Service Alliance of Canada
PTI—Physical Training Instructor
RCMP—Royal Canadian Mounted Police
SHU—Special Handling Unit
SMSU—Super Maximum Security Unit
SMU—Super Maximum Unit
UPRM—United Prisoners Rights Movement
V&C—Visiting and Correspondence

*Name changes: Canadian Correctional Service (1978); Correctional Service of Canada (1979).

CHAPTER ONE

The B.C.Pen 'Comes Down'

"Get over here as quickly as you can."

At 1:00 in the morning my phone finally rang. A hostage taking had been announced on the radio around 7:00 p.m. that evening—September 27, 1976—and I was waiting for this call.

It was Mary McGrath from inside the B.C.Penitentiary where she and other members of the Citizens Advisory Committee (C.A.C.)—Don Sorochan, Michael Jackson, Jim Spears and Ezzat Fattah—were meeting with the Inmate Committee (I.C.).

I had been insisting with both Don and Mary earlier that evening that the C.A.C. should be at the Pen, not just sitting home listening to the news. They felt we could wait until morning, but there they were now at the B.C.Pen, calling me to join them. It took me only twenty minutes to get to New Westminster, wondering as I drove why I had not been called at the same time as the others.

It was drizzling rain and a grey fog was rolling in from the Fraser River, shrouding the grounds. I drove past the DO NOT ENTER sign at the entrance (calculated to confuse rather than direct a newcomer, since there is no way to reach the penitentiary parking areas other than past these signs). A single guard checked me through. Leaving my car in the nearest STAFF ONLY section, I climbed the outside stairway to the Board Room.

That something had been brewing at the Pen came as no surprise. In an earlier visit that week with Ivan Horvat, president of the Inmate Committee which had been elected just four months earlier (coinciding with the appointment of the Citizens Advisory Committee), he asked me if I was going to be around for the next little while—or whether I might be planning a vacation. I assured him I would be around for a long time. Talking through the telephone system and separated by the heavy plexiglass window in the well-monitored visiting area, he was obviously unable to let me know what was really troubling him.

Two days later when I was visiting Paul Leister, the Secretary of their Committee, he also appeared upset. He suggested I call Ottawa that same day and get through to the Director of Inmate Welfare, Mr. C.G.Rutter.

As soon as I left Paul I placed a call to Mr. Rutter to tell him about the tensions at the B.C.Pen—further, that Director Cernetic had left and that unless someone in authority from Ottawa came out immediately, a grim situation looked as if it were going to get much grimmer.

Mr. Rutter seemed genuinely surprised at my request, explaining that during an earlier call that day to the C.A.C. Chairman, he had been assured that everything was under control. He had therefore decided to wait and see what, if anything, developed. I would have been amazed had he reacted any other way, for the hallmark of the penitentiary bureaucracy appears to be to postpone any decision until the situation explodes into someone else's jurisdiction.

By coincidence I was placing this call from the office of Ron Stern, lawyer for several members of the I.C., who at their request had also made a similar appeal to Ottawa—this time to André Therrien, Commissioner of Penitentiaries. Ron had received the same bland assurance, consistent with the system's usual delaying tactics.

Four hours later the B.C.Pen 'came down.'

—25 of the 95 cells in the North wing were wrecked.

—50 of the 110 cells in B-7 wing were gone.

—200 cells in the East block were almost totally destroyed.

—2 hostages were being held in the kitchen area.

Except for the Protective Custody Unit (PCU), where those convicted of sex offences and those labelled 'informers' did their time, and the Super Maximum Security Unit (SMSU), solitary confinement area, the prisoners had taken over the 'joint.' They were being represented by their Inmate Committee.

I had time to think about these events for the next hour and a half as I was left to cool my heels in the outer lounge of the Board Room. The half dozen Administration people, smoking and drinking coffee around the large table, appeared to be digging in for a long siege. When I asked to be taken to where the other C.A.C. members were meeting, they put me off: "There'll be lots of time." This attitude was to prevail over the next 80 hours as the Administration repeatedly undermined the prisoners' efforts to press for a speedy negotiation before violence took over completely. I later learned that when they saw that I was not among the C.A.C. arrivals, the prisoners refused to proceed until I was called. An hour later when they realized I was probably being excluded, they refused to start until I joined the meeting. It was only then that Don Sorochan came to collect me, at 2:30 a.m.

We headed up the landscaped hill towards the Commissary where the other members of the C.A.C. were meeting with the I.C. Clanging noises and shouting rang out from the East block. Ten bed sheets were strung along ten smashed windows reading:

S   O   L   I   D   A   R   I   T   Y

Extensive media coverage during the following week would not show a photograph of, or even mention, this significant slogan.

As we made our way past the perimeter guards, Don summed up the situation. The Inmate Committee was in control. Their first demand—that the C.A.C. be called in as observers—was clearly intended to reduce any likelihood of a tragic repetition of the 1975 hostage taking. That one had ended with the murder of a sympathetic Classification Officer, Mary Steinhauser, and the wounding of Andy Bruce, one of the hostage takers.

The seven member Inmate Committee—Ivan Horvat, Omer Prud'homme, Gary Lake, Lea Sheppe, Paul Leister, Gordon Duck, and Jack Dow—had set up their headquarters in the Commissary. The atmosphere was tense. Coarse remarks flew around the table as they denounced the Administration's tactics. Horvat and I managed to calm things down so we could get on with some concrete recommendations.* Al Hadvick, the Vice-President of the Public Service Alliance of Canada (PSAC)—the guards' union, B.C. Component—was accepted as liaison with the Administration and permitted to attend the opening meeting.

J.J. outlined what had been taking place in the past few months:

> On July 7th an election was held and seven candidates were elected to be the B.C.Pen Inmate Committee. Out of 377 prisoners, 337 voted and the 7 candidates with the most votes became the Committee. Immediately after the election it became obvious that the Inmate Committee was going to have a rough time trying to establish any type of permanent and positive program in view [of the fact] that we had to start from scratch and were violently opposed by Custody at every step.
>
> Mr. Cernetic was away for the month of July, and we saw that high-ranking Custody was trying to make us ineffective. With the Acting Director not willing to accept the responsibility of the Director's office...the only thing to do was sit and wait until the Director returned.
>
> In the meanwhile, our frustrations were many. We couldn't get a place to work nor a place to meet. (The first regular Inmate Committee meeting was conducted in the gymnasium toilet.) I.C. members were threatened and constantly harassed. Access to the inmate population and Committee movement were strictly opposed by all factions of Custody staff.

*"One member of the Committee, Claire Culhane, spent considerable time with the Inmate Committee...this greater involvement...was due to the particular confidence which the Inmate Committee placed in her. Several other members of the Committee who were involved in meetings with the Inmate Committee at times when Mrs. Culhane was also present were impressed with the moderating influence which she had on the Committee members. These members are of the view that her particular role contributed to the peaceful resolution of the hostage taking."—from *Brief of the Citizens Advisory Committee of the B.C. Pen* to the Subcommittee on the Penitentiary System in Canada, Feb.15/77, p.9.

The power struggle between B.C.Pen Custody and all other departments was at its peak and we were let know that we were treading on dangerous ground. John Lakusta was leading the Custody and at the same time was President of the local PSAC.

The rest is documented history.*

Earlier in the week, the same John Lakusta had attended our C.A.C. meeting and had rejected our offer to meet with his union in an effort to help end their overtime boycott. Consistent with their resistance to the Director's support of more community programs, the strategy of the guards' union was to refuse to work any overtime, thereby decreasing the number of staff available for extra prisoner programs. Characteristically, the guards prefer maximum lock-up time, and this was their way of confronting the Administration which they felt was showing more sympathy towards the prisoners than to their own priorities.

This attitude of the guards had been generated by a combination of factors. Negotiation time for their union had once again arrived, and with it the pattern of deliberately triggering unrest to provide a useful background to their simultaneous demands for increased pay, shorter hours, earlier retirement, and so on. The public could be called upon to support them, as they could then point to still another 'riot' which 'hard-pressed,' 'over-worked,' 'under-paid' guards must cope with.

Whereas a foreman who enforces company policy is never a member of the plant's trade union, the head of Custody (the most sensitive department in the penitentiary system) is, on the other hand, a member of the guards' union. By virtue of such a position in the prison structure, one would thereby have the power to intimidate and control both prisoners and union membership. A person in this position can—and often does—use that position to institute measures which can later be used as a lever in negotiations. The boycott of overtime fell into

*from an undated paper prepared by Ivan Horvat shortly before the September 1976 events.

this category. It meant fewer guards on duty and more prisoners locked up for longer periods of time—all calculated to further increase the tensions.

As the prisoners were being 'allowed' to smash up their cells, the I.C. felt, understandably, compelled to expose what was to them by now a familiar strategy.

More Pen Violence Forecast

. . .rising tension in the segregated section of the B.C. Penitentiary is bound to create new outbursts of violence. . .prison has so far failed to meet any of the demands for plumbing changes for hot and cold running water; provision for outdoor recreation periods; installation of a T.V. area; serving of meals by kitchen staff rather than guards to end what the inmates charged was contamination of food with cigarette butts and broken glass by vindictive guards. . .(lawyers) not permitted to talk with segregated inmates although it had originally been planned for them to do so. . .

Stewart (Information Officer) said comments about inevitability of new violence were "sensationalized a little bit. . ." noted that present inmates in segregation probably won't be there for an extended period anyway.

—*The Province*, Mar.19/76

The hostage taking was consequently initiated in order to halt the growing momentum and forestall the guards from using their clubs and tear gas, to bring in the C.A.C., and to inform the public so that everyone could see that it was not just another case of prisoners acting in their stereotyped 'violent and irresponsible' fashion. This would be the first time that a group of citizens would mediate a confrontation between prisoners and administration during the actual crisis.

How Did the Citizens Advisory Committee Develop?

For me this story began when the United Prisoners Rights Movement (UPRM)* was becoming increasingly worried about the crisis that was obviously mounting at the B.C.Pen. One

---

*In early 1976, several UPRM members formed, at its disbandment, the Prisoners' Rights Group (P.R.G.).

of our members, Keith Baker (who had been one of the original eight petitioners to file the 1975 action declaring solitary confinement at the B.C.Penitentiary to be 'cruel and unusual punishment') had been released shortly after the 1975 Mary Steinhauser tragedy.

During a visit with him in April 1976, when he was again doing time, Keith mentioned having had quite a long discussion with 'the Dragon' (as Director Dragan Cernetic was known) about prisoners' rights and internal problems. When Keith suggested we follow it up, UPRM made an appointment for 8:15 the next morning.

What we tried to get across to Cernetic was that if he didn't want to face hostage taking every few months, he was simply going to have to sit down sometime with a prisoners' committee to talk to them.

A few months later, September 28, 1976, *The Columbian* would publish a partial list of hostage-taking and other violent incidents at the B.C.Pen since 1973:

1973—Oct.5. Three-day riot by prisoners led to destruction of twenty-three cells.
1974—Jan. & Feb. Two separate stabbing incidents.
    June. Overtime ban imposed by guards.
    Aug.8. Prisoner lost an eye in scuffle.
1975—Feb. Physical Ed. teacher held hostage four hours.
    June 9-11. (41 hours) Fifteen hostages held by Andy Bruce, Clair Wilson and Dwight Lucas, ending with a Classification Officer, Mary Steinhauser, shot by member of the B.C.Pen tactical squad. Andy Bruce seriously wounded in jaw by bullet. [Bruce and Lucas still held in solitary confinement, Clair Wilson transferred July 1976].
    July 4. Prison barbering instructor held hostage eight hours by one prisoner.
    July. Two day work stoppage begun by prisoners to highlight attempt to form Prisoners Union lasted one week.

1976—Feb. Two guards held for fifteen hours by two prisoners.

April. Three guards held for thirteen hours by four prisoners. Two prisoners found dead.

June. Attempt to take two guards hostage. They escaped with minor injuries.

Aug.31. Prisoner took guard hostage for ten minutes.

Sept.5. Prisoner stabbed to death—a sex offender placed in general population despite warnings and requests from prisoners to have him returned to Protective Custody Unit.

Sept.9. Twelve day state of emergency when guards refused to work overtime. Left three prisoners dead.

Six deaths in six months.

Cernetic insisted at first that he had no trouble, that all was under control. But two hours later he was still pouring out his problems and ideas for possible solutions. The interview ended with him suggesting that we set up a Citizens Committee, as there was a Divisional Instruction (No.845) dealing with matters of community relationships. When we asked if he would agree to meet with us in the event that we succeeded, he said he would, adding, prophetically, "But the guards won't like it."

We contacted Professor Ezzat Fattah, then head of the Criminology Department at Simon Fraser Univesity, who approved of the idea but regretted that he had no time to join us. Dr. Guy Richmond, recently retired Coroner and author of *Prison Doctor*, expressed similar regrets. Susan Songry of the Sisters of the Institution of the Child Jesus in North Vancouver—a Native Indian woman who had already contacted Andy Bruce's family—immediately agreed to join and even offered a donation.

All our efforts were in vain. The Canadian Penitentiary Service had been forming a Citizens Committee all along. On May 29th, Mr. Cernetic wrote us to suggest that we contact Mr. Sorochan for further information. I did, and was invited to attend their first meeting on June 22, 1976.

The timing was interesting. A 110-day work stoppage at

Archambault Maximum Institution in Québec had just ended—peacefully—with the prisoners winning their demands, mainly through the work of a strong Inmate Committee backed by a staunch prison population:

> . . .we struck to obtain respect in the eyes of our keepers and society, in the hope that this would be the origin for genuine change in a decrepit, morally bankrupt federal penal system.*

The Canadian Penitentiary Service (CPS) was now urging other prisons to encourage similar formations—citizens' committees on the outside and prisoners' committees on the inside.

At the first meeting of the Citizens Advisory Committee guidelines were laid down by Bryan Williams (who, along with his law partner, Don Sorochan, had handled the Jack McCann vs. The Queen petition, which established that solitary confinement at the B.C.Penitentiary was indeed "cruel and unusual punishment"). This C.A.C. was being set up, we were told, to help defuse the tensions at the B.C.Pen—long recognized as the most "turbulent" maximum institution in the system.

At the same time, Cernetic was encouraging the prisoners to elect their own Committee, insisting in a special Memorandum, dated August 23, 1976, that:

> Henceforth, I would very much appreciate if any documentation or correspondence sent to the Administration bears the title "Inmate Committee." Any such document-ation. . .bearing the name "Prisoners Committee" will not be acknowledged as official as Commissioner's Directives state that it shall be referred to as the "Inmate Committee."

Privately, Cernetic explained that if the men were permitted to call themselves "prisoners" instead of "inmates" they might go on to consider themselves *political prisoners*.

---

*William MacAllister (I.C. Chairman), "The Strike," in *Minutes of Proceedings*, Issue No.12, Dec.7/76, Appendix JLA-S11, p.12A-1.

The Prison System is riddled with the language of euphemism:

Language is related to power...the vocabulary coined by those who design and control the prison is dishonest because it is based on a series of false assumptions...we need to consciously abandon the jargon that camouflages the reality of caging and develop honest language...

Prisoners perceive the use of "system" language as denying them the reality of their experience.

Cage—refers to places of involuntary confinement in prisons or jails. Dishonest language calls them "rooms" or "residencies."

"Corrections"—use of quotes draws attention to the contradictions in this dishonest term, denoting programs, procedures or processes which punish rather than correct.

Guards—refers to people who are paid to keep other people caged in jails and prisons. Dishonest language calls them "correctional officers."

Prisoner—a person held in custody, captivity or a condition of forcible restraint. Dishonest language calls them "inmates" or "residents."

Prisons—places of confinement. Dishonest language calls them "correctional facilities" or "reformatories."

Segregation—units within a prison that punish by isolating prisoners from the rest of the imprisoned population. Dishonest language calls them "adjustment units" [or "Special Handling Units," "Disassociation," "Segregation," etc.]

—from *Instead of Prisons: A Handbook for Abolitionists*, p.10.

In Cernetic's opinion, that would never do. The prisoners, however, thought otherwise:

The news about a possible committee was a topic for much controversial discussion among the inmates. Everyone looked on with skepticism as memories came back of other committees which tended to end up either in the 'hole' or transferred out of the institution. Prison officials frown upon any type of prisoner organization and unity, and prisoners' leaders are usually removed as soon as it looks as though any type of program, without total custodial supervision, might be implemented.

But this time it was the Administration that suggested a committee...we knew that the Director Dragan Cernetic was under instructions from Ottawa to bring the institution back to normal. Most of us decided that after three and a half years of not having a committee, a committee might not be a bad idea—*After all, we had nothing, and 10% of something is always better than 100% of nothing.* We knew that unless we ourselves tried to bring about some type of constructive and meaningful change, it would never be done.*

Once the two Committees were established—one of prisoners and the other of citizens—the next step was to formally introduce the C.A.C.to all sections of the institution.

On July 23rd—three months before the riot—Acting Director Ken Peterson, expressing very positive feelings about the C.A.C., welcomed us in the B.C.Pen Board Room. He described the four sections of the Pen as being actually four prisons within one institution, having many administrative and operational difficulties because of overlapping budgets and staff.

General Population (approx. 450) was the largest section, representing those prisoners considered maximum security risks and who didn't qualify for the other three sections. What he didn't say, but of which many of us were aware, was that although work and study programs were supposed to be available, shortage of equipment and personnel, together with interference by Custodial staff, resulted in far longer lock-up hours then in most other maximum institutions across the country.

Protective Custody Unit (PCU) (approx. 80) which four years ago held 22 prisoners, now counted 80-90. Peterson admitted that the men were literally "stacked like cordwood" as

*from a paper prepared by Ivan Horvat shortly before September 1976.

little cell space was allocated to them. Contrary to regulations, there were many cells holding two men.

We were also told that for the most part prisoners entered PCU at their own request, seeking protection from the general population which labelled them 'finks' and 'rats,' as well as 'skinners,' meaning sex offenders.

Although prisoners in PCU were supposed to have the same rights as general population, there were no facilities to provide separate staff, kitchen, and so forth, so there was inevitably an element of discrimination. It was, in Peterson's words, "like trying to distribute unfairness equally."

(A more thorough discussion of this highly misrepresented Unit appears in Chapter Seven.)

Regional Reception Centre (approx. 80) where men sentenced in B.C. Courts to Federal time (two years or more) spend six weeks undergoing various tests and examinations to assess where they should be sent—to maximum, medium or minimum security penal institutions, depending on the nature of their crime and their social and educational background. However, these 'fish,' as they are known, should instead be held in a separate building, not in a maximum security institution. Simply having been *in* the Pen could stigmatize them at some future time, even if they have been immediately designated for medium or minimum status and are not to be retained at the Pen.

Super Maximum Security Unit (SMSU) (approx. 42). The infamous "Penthouse" or "Hole" was at that date holding 18-25 under "Administrative Dissociation"—

> Where the institutional head is satisfied that
> (a) for the maintenance of good order and discipline in the institution, or
> (b) in the best interests of an inmate
>
> it is necessary or desirable that the inmate should be kept from associating with other inmates, he may order the inmate to be dissociated accordingly...
>   —*Section 2.30(1)(a), Penitentiary Regulations.*

Note that this is not a specific charge to which prisoners can respond and defend themselves—in itself a most flagrant abuse of natural justice and due process. On the contrary, the cases of men in solitary are simply "considered, not less than once each month, by the Classification Board for the purpose of recommending to the institutional head whether or not the inmate should return to association with other inmates."

In effect, the Director can rule that the prisoner does not qualify for return to the general population for the entire duration of his sentence, leaving him in solitary for months and years—and in some instances, for the rest of his life. (This arbitrary level has not yet been reached in the Kingston Prison For Women.)

Mr. Peterson then provided us with a few statistics on the security staff. He admitted that there was a very high turnover, as much as 85% in the past year. At that point there were 335 on staff, though there should have been 363 according to their reckoning—a ratio of one staff member to one prisoner.

> *Wm. MacAllister* (prisoner)
> "Canada is the only country in the world, in the entire world, that employs more penitentiary personnel in its system than it has inmates."
> *John Reynolds* (M.P.)
> "I agree with you."*

It had been previously agreed that after Mr. Peterson's briefing, the C.A.C would divide *voluntarily*, with half going to meet with the Inmates Committee, and the other half meeting with the guards' union. Instead, the C.A.C. Chairman read a prepared list, assigning me to the meeting with the guards. My request to change was refused. There was nothing to do but join the group moving toward the I.C. meeting.

As the eleven of us climbed the outside staircase to the Administration Building, I recalled that the same C.A.C. Chairman had earlier that month classified me as "prisoners advocate."

---

*In the *Minutes of Proceedings and Evidence of the Sub-Committee on the Penitentiary System in Canada,* Issue No.12, Dec.7, 1976, p.52. Hereinafter, *Minutes of Proceedings.*

The only conclusion I could draw from his attitude was that if I were being manoeuvred into a confrontation with the guards' union, as seemed obvious, it could well result in an ugly scene which could only serve to discredit me, thereby giving the C.A.C. reason to request my resignation. As the only prisoners advocate on the C.A.C., I would have been easy to isolate. I suspected I had nearly been set up.

We finally reached the room where the I.C. was waiting for us. On behalf of their Committee, Chairman Ivan Horvat expressed pleasure at the opportunity to meet us, but felt they had to establish two points before we could proceed:

> (1) You should know that this is the first time that we, as the Inmate Committee, have had a place to sit down and meet. We have been getting together, whenever we could, in the gymnasium toilet until now. And

> (2) after much consideration, we have decided that we cannot meet with your Committee as long as there is a member of the RCMP on it—particularly, Inspector Paul Starek, who has personally booked several of us.

Almost as if they were ready for such an argument, one of the C.A.C. members offered this proposition:

> Since the other half of our Committee is at this moment meeting with the guards' union and it is very likely that there are objections being raised there to the presence on our Committee of people like Claire Culhane, are you suggesting that we accept *your* recommendation to exclude Inspector Starek *and* to accept *their* recommendation to exclude Ms. Culhane?

This parallel was not acceptable to the I.C., inasmuch as they "...weren't aware of any occasion when any member of the guards' union had been personally mistreated by Ms. Culhane, as compared with Inspector Starek's personal record of actual mistreatment of prisoners *and their families*."

A letter dated August 4, 1976, to the Citizens Advisory Committee from the Inmate Committee is more specific:

> We have also seen documented evidence of the harassment of prisoners' family members by the very detachment commanded by the man you insist on keeping as one of your Members. The Minister of Justice, the Attorney-General and others have received complaints about that very subject. File P-440-4 concerns the harassment of the 14 year old son of a prisoner in this Institution. Staff Sergeant Starek and some of the men he commands have no respect for due process of law.

Horvat repeated their regret that they would be unable to continue the meeting as long as the C.A.C. included Insp. Starek. When asked if the I.C. would accept any other member of the RCMP in his place, Horvat said, "Well, this is a bad moment to ask us as we have many problems right now. Maybe at some future date we might consider it, but we feel at this moment it wouldn't be wise."

It seemed we had reached an impasse. I suggested we postpone our decision until we determined if other C.A.C.'s elsewhere included RCMP members.

"You know damn well they don't," was the angry response from our side of the table. (Indeed, we had received a communication from Québec confirming that there were neither MP's, MLA's, nor police on their Committee. Instead, there were people from the community in general, including wives of prisoners.)

We reached a temporary compromise. Since only half the C.A.C. were present, and could not make any decision without the others who were meeting with the guards, we agreed to refer the matter ahead to the next C.A.C. meeting. We would send a firm reply to the I.C. within two weeks.

The following samples of correspondence between the two Committees indicate the problems which faced the prisoners as a result of this stalemate.

To: Ivan Horvat,
   Chairman Inmate Committee
From: E. Lipinski,
   Chairman, Citizens Advisory Committee
Date: July 29, 1976

. . . this letter is to inform you that the Citizens Advisory Committee wishes to assure the Inmate Committee that they will not be requested to meet with the RCMP member of the Citizens Advisory Committee at any future date, and request that the Inmate Committee inform the general population at the B.C. Penitentiary of our undertaking in this regard.

It is the position of the Citizens Advisory Committee that there are many areas of concern between our Committee and non-inmate sectors of the penitentiary in which the RCMP member of our Committee may be involved, thereby excluding involvement with the Inmate Committee.

To: E. Lipinski, M.D.
   Chairman, Citizens Advisory Committee
From: Paul Leister,
   Secretary-Treasurer, Inmate Committee
Date: August 4, 1976

The Chairman has instructed me to inform you that we will not be able to meet with your Committee again and maintain credibility with the 400 men we represent. . . . It is indeed unfortunate that no working relationship can be established between our two groups because the only possible way the failing, yet ever expanding prison empire will ever be turned around is for members of the public (who foot the astronomical bill) to take a sincere close look at what takes place behind the wall.

Our Committee felt that *all* matters behind the wall are prisoner-related so could not understand the rather vague reference to matters which are "non-inmate" related.

. . . a motion was made to put the issue to vote. The result: 7 to 0 that we not sit with the outside Committee as long as the police make up part of its membership. Any other organization would have been fine. Judges, Probation Officers, etc. but not the one group who continually and publicly refer to us as animals and advocate shooting us down in the street like dogs.

My personal opinion is that whoever chose Starek and his particular detachment made the worst possible choice at the very worst time.

The *Prisoners Committee Newsletter* of August 3, 1976 summarizes the contents of the above two letters and further explains their caution: the "only thing that the RCMP can accomplish with such a group is to get clearer access to B.C. Pen files, and the Committee will *not* be the vehicle used to accomplish that."

Since the C.A.C. delayed initiating any further meeting with the Inmate Committee, and since an emergency was rapidly shaping up, the subsequent resignation of Inspector Starek passed almost unnoticed.

But the main issue arose when the C.A.C. chairman asked if there were any specific areas in which we could be of some assistance. The prisoners made it clear that the validity of the I.C. had yet to be established. They explained:

> With Cernetic [Director] away, with Peterson [Acting Director] unable or unwilling to make any decisions, and with Lakusta [head of the guards' union as well as top Security] refusing to even recognize our Committee, we have no one to communicate with. In fact, Lakusta has already warned us that he'll do his best to see that every member of this Committee gets transferred back East...he has already ordered extra cell checks. One of us was found with a little mirror, which although officially considered contraband, has been seen in his cell for over a year and nothing was ever done about it.
>
> All kinds of things are coming down on us, so there is little use to discuss any specific area as long as we are living in this kind of an atmosphere—perhaps we should discuss all this intimidation before we go on to specific areas.

At this point, I suggested that a member of the C.A.C. be present whenever the I.C. met with the Administration, to ensure that the prisoners' demands were given more serious consideration. From then on, whenever other suggestions were made, the I.C. would insist that they be acted upon with some one from the C.A.C. present.

At the end of the meeting, the I.C. was removed under guard. When Custody considered the distance between the two groups to be 'safe', we were allowed to leave—the same two groups which had just spent the last few hours quietly sitting across a table from each other in a small, unguarded room. As we crossed the lawn we could see the I.C. sitting at the top of the hill, waiting to be escorted back to their cells. Gordy Duck, a member of the I.C., picked a few roses and walked across the full length of the lawn to hand them to the two women members of our group—Wendy O'Flaherty and myself. This gallant gesture took a bit of courage as he could have found himself charged with 'defacing government property.'

After this first meeting with the Inmates Committee, we were to go on a grand tour. It proved, however, to be a series of delays, put-offs, and avoidances.

First we went to visit the *workshops*. But Friday afternoons the shops are shut down. We met with the instructor but had no opportunity to see or speak with prisoners who usually work there.

From there to the *library*—which we were unable to inspect as no one could find the key.

Across the hall to the *classroom*. The same story—no key.

When we reached the *hospital unit*, the nurse walked out in a huff, leaving an ill-informed guard to explain medical routines and procedures. According to him, there were not any problems: everyone received adequate and prompt medical attention. . . .

After much insistence from the C.A.C. we were taken to the "Penthouse," as the SMSU is called when it isn't being referred to as the Hole. We were cautioned: "Stand back a few feet. They might spit on you or throw things."

I ignored the warning and stepped up to the cell doors. No one spat. No one threw things. I didn't know then, as I do now, that I should have spoken to the men through their small grill window and told them who we were, and why we were there, and asked if anyone wished to speak with us. That would have opened up a real exchange. The prisoners could then have talked about their problems. As it happened, all we saw was the dismal corridor, and solid steel cell doors, and heavily armed guards patrolling the cages. We didn't see a single prisoner.

Then we went to lunch in the officers' mess, where I had an interesting discussion with the newly appointed Assistant Director of Security, Mr. Ev Berkey. We found we shared some views regarding the bureaucracy's effects on the prison population: poor coordination between the three levels of Administration (institutional, regional and national) and the difficulties prisoners face when they try to go by the rules.

Ironically, this was the same gentleman who, caught up in the same bureaucracy two months later, would find himself having to order me out of the institution without justification. (My libel suit against the B.C.Penitentiary for that action will be heard in Supreme Court of British Columbia on Feb.18, 1980.)

We also asked to tour the Protective Custody Unit (PCU), but whenever that was mentioned, the atmosphere changed. PCU was a sore point with everyone, and the more our guide assured us we would eventually see it, the more I suspected we might not —just as earlier we saw neither the library nor the classroom.

Obviously, certain areas were not on the approved list. PCU seemed to me to be one of them. Some members of the C.A.C. were especially concerned about these men, and wanted to urge them to set up their own Inmate Committee similar to that of the general population.

Shortly afterwards, as we were approaching the Administration building, we passed the PCU exercise yard. When they saw us the men crowded to the wire mesh fence.

"Hey! Come over here—"
"Come and talk to us—"
"We have a story too—"
One voice was particularly strident, shouting about someone in the general population:

"You'd better tell that sunuvabitch the next time I see him I'll kill him. I'LL KILL HIM! The bastard slugged me from behind when I was on my way to the hospital!"

There were about thirty men walking around and around. Some were playing cards. One pointed jeeringly at the only piece of equipment, a broken weight-lift bar. No one was 'exercising.' A husky youngster with a shaved head was racing along his side of the fence, trying to get my attention.

"Come here. Come here. Please come here."

He rushed as close as he could.

"I can't read or write. . . I got ten years. . . I really want to learn how to read and write."

I stopped, ready to listen, and he calmed down.

"I come from the Island. I'm in for rape. But. . . will you get them to teach me how to read and write?"

The guard came over to see what was going on.

"What are you doing for him?" I asked the guard.

"Well, we're busy getting twenty-seven inmates through their GEC [General Education Certificate]."

"But what does that have to do with finding *him* some way to learn how to read and write?"

The guard scratched his head and repeated his story about the other twenty-seven. When I asked him again he turned to the prisoner and shouted: "Did you fill out your application form?"

"How the hell can I fill out a form when I can't read or write!"

*   *   *

Having met with the prisoners and the guards' union, we were next scheduled for August 20 to meet with the personnel and staff. Some of them were under the delusion that the C.A.C. was concerned only about prisoners.

The meeting with approximately twenty-five office personnel and security guards began with one of their senior officers declaring that he could not recognize the C.A.C. as being impartial when he had seen one of its members—pointing to me—on T.V. on August 10, carrying a banner for the *Prisoners Union Committee,* the group of prison activists which had organized demonstrations following Mary Steinhauser's death.

The Chairman of C.A.C. hastily explained that as a volunteer, unpaid committee, its members were free to hold their personal views and participate in any other groups or activities, providing there was no contravention of the Letter of Understanding. No such contravention had taken place.

I explained further that the banner I had been holding clearly read *National Prison Justice Day—August 10*—and *not* Prisoners Union Committee. I told them that August 10 is the annual day of recognition for those prisoners who have died 'unnatural deaths' inside prisons across the land. A twenty-four hour vigil and fast takes place both inside and outside penitentiaries and jails each year on that date, and that in some prisons there are work stoppages.

As with the PCU section, the staff were urged to establish their own committee to liaison with the C.A.C. so that we could better coordinate our efforts and clarify our respective concerns.

Once the preliminaries of meeting with various sections at the B.C.Penitentiary were dispensed with, the C.A.C. should have been ready to move into more serious areas of consultation and advice. Instead, on a very casual note, our meetings were arranged for every second Monday of each month. Since the second Monday in October was Thanksgiving Day, the next meeting was simply postponed to the following month— November 8—over two months away!

My objection to this delay was overruled. My insistence that there was a worsening situation inside was also overruled.

We were later to read the Memorandum forwarded that same week to the Director from the Inmate Committee, dated September 21—one week before the Pen came down:

> Hopefully this statement will not add to the present confusion.... Since September 9 and this emergency [when three prisoners were killed] we have gone through a lot of changes...not been much visible movement forward, however. The invisible forces have been gathering and the pressures have been building.
>
> Hopefully this pressure will achieve what prisoners have

been trying to achieve for hundreds of years, mainly to be heard...the local union has imposed an overtime ban, hoping the institution would close, create trouble and thus reinforce their bargaining power for their contract renewal.

...the Inmate Committee's point of view is that since these things occur every six months to a year, we should clear the issues up once and for all. We feel that the only way to do that is on a national level...only achieved through public outcry. That was through a letter writing campaign—still nothing.

The concern of the Inmate Committee lies a little further in the future than just tomorrow or next week. The present confrontation has been coming for a long time—many years—and hopefully for this institution it will be the last.

If we can show the public that they have been ripped off, very cleverly conned for many, many years, maybe for a change they will ask some questions which usually no one seems to want to raise. The main demands of the [guards] union is the cutback on recreation, more lock-up and no social activities...[whereas] the Director is under orders from Ottawa to introduce programs in this institution, and to open it up...for that reason he stands firm and the guards' demands will not be met. The Inmate Committee feels that this is an excellent opportunity to examine demands and concerns of our own.

The prisoners concluded their statement on the essential fact:

The only thing we can do at this point, since we cannot get out, is to bring the public in.

Now, six days later, we *were* in.

From that early morning of September 27, when I was called to come to the Pen, until the morning of October 2, when the last of us walked down the hill, I spent eighty hours inside.

CHAPTER TWO

The Eighty Hours

By the time Don Sorochan and I reached the others, it was close to 3 o'clock in the morning. In the Commissary the I.C. was meeting with the Administration liaison, Al Hadvick, and with five members of the C.A.C.

Horvat was demanding that a press conference be arranged in the gymnasium with the forty media people who had been waiting outside the walls since early evening.

His second request was for the installation of two telephones—one, for internal use, to maintain a fifteen-minute check with the kitchen to confirm the well-being of the hostages, the other for communication with Regional and Federal headquarters.

As a show of good faith, the I.C. offered to release one of the two hostages at the press conference—Walter Day, 50, a food service worker, or Wayne Culbert, 21, a prison guard.

At 5:50 a.m. three members of the C.A.C. went down the hill to read a press release prepared by the I.C., speaking for the B.C.Penitentiary population:

> The Inmate Committee wants it made public how this incident came about and to expose the corruption of this institution.
>
> No demands to escape have been made by anyone, including the inmates who are holding hostages in the kitchen area.
>
> The cause of this incident lies other than with the prisoners, and we want to prove this to the public.
>
> This institution will probably never function again as it was, because we stop here. The East wing will never be used again. It is destroyed.
>
> Every attempt made by the Inmate Committee over the past two months to prevent this incident. . . met with deaf ears.

There was a letter writing campaign with over 100 letters. There were appeals and telegrams to Ottawa.

The 24 PSAC (guards' union) demands were not negotiable. They gave us conditions that could only result in a riot.

The institution started getting demolished Friday but it was kept under cover for this long. There was only more agitation by a small group of guards.

On Friday (Sept.24) all of the toilets in empty cells were destroyed. On Saturday (Sept.25) all of the furniture in the empty cells was destroyed. On Sunday (Sept.26) the railings along the tiers went.

This Penitentiary is not so much the problem as it is the result of a grotesque justice and court system.

Prisoners are being used as political pawns by selfishly-motivated politicians who don't really care about the consequences.

The B.C.Penitentiary quickly took on the appearance of an armed fortification. Fifty army combat troops patrolled the perimeter. Joined by the RCMP and the New Westminster police, the security guards were well reinforced.

Grey Dawn Saw Guards Maintain Tense Vigil On Walls of the B.C.Pen

...at one point a busload of RCMP arrived and they all disappeared inside the prison. They were followed by an unmarked patrol car which carried what appeared to be a cache of weapons in the trunk.

—*Columbian*, Sept.28/76

From the Commissary door we had a clear view of more weapons being unloaded—from an ambulance!

Reporters would describe the next days' policing action as though covering a war.

The tactical squad sections of the RCMP plus a 38-man riot squad entered the prison to contain the riot.

Tuesday about 50 soldiers from the Canadian Forces Base, Chilliwack, were rushed to the prison to take over perimeter positions. These troops were relieved Wednesday at noon after Hercu-les transport planes brought in 101 men of the Princess Patricia's Canadian Light Infantry Regiment from Fort Wainright, Alta.

—*The Columbian*, Sept.29/76

That first long night exhausted everyone. Jim Spears (*Vancouver Province* reporter and member of the C.A.C.) began, as he said, to hallucinate and had to go home. It was agreed that at least one member of the C.A.C. be present at all times so that there would never be a moment when the I.C. would not be 'covered' by an observer. I offered to stay, and shared a corner of the carpeted floor with J.J., pulling some blankets around us.

There was so much to talk about, and for the first time we were able to talk normally—not through monitored telephones in the forbidding glass-panelled visiting areas. We even laughed at times, touching each other casually as people do to emphasize a point.

This was the first break in the twelve hours of the takeover, and J.J. was still very keyed up. Whenever he would break off in the middle of a sentence, or digress for a moment, I would worry that we might not get back to the subject, as our hours of talking together so freely were surely numbered.

We talked about how the Inmate Committee had handed notes to two shifts of guards as a last attempt to head off the riot, begging them to sit down and parley. He was convinced that many would have done so if they had not feared intimidation by the 'heavies' in their union.

We talked about his longing for his wife, and about our concern for negotiations to succeed before anything tragic happened in the kitchen. And we weighed the possibilities of being rushed by Security, risking another Steinhauser affair.

We talked about writing a book together when it was all over: he would describe the details of the events which had led up to that moment, and I would record all the proceedings.

We talked right through the night—what was left of it.

When daylight came, although we had had no sleep, we were ready to begin work on the demands to be presented to the press conference scheduled for 4:00 p.m. that day, Tuesday, Sept. 28. Grabbing a cup of coffee and a few sandwiches, everyone went off to assigned tasks.

Each I.C. member would get water, food or medication routines rolling, or check every fifteen minutes with the kitchen where the two hostages were held. Equally important was to report back to the prison population half-hourly and return with ideas from those who had participated in similar events in other places and at other times.

I was introduced to the 'kitchen people' on our intercom so they would recognize my voice if I had to answer the phone in the absence of the I.C. members.

As soon as the *Intent & Purposes of the Eight Demands of the Inmate Committee* was ready as a basis for negotiations, I was to type copies for distribution at the press conference. Hadvick (the liaison between Administration and the I.C.), who was supposed to be installing the two phones, was actually spending his time wandering back and forth between the Administrtion and my typewriter. Moving myself and typewriter from table to table in the Commissary didn't seem to discourage him. Waiting until no one was around, he warned that he would not install phones until I showed him the demands. Rather than argue with him, I repeated his proposition to the nearest I.C. members, who dealt with this new delay with a single ultimatum: no phones—no negotiations.

At 4:00 p.m. the media came into the gym. The Inmate Committee took their seats around the table and were prepared to start the press conference when someone noticed that the phones were not yet working. When the media people were informed of the broken promise, they agreed to wait until the head games were over.

It was 11:30 p.m. when reporters trickled [back] into the auditorium.
                                    —*Columbian*, Sept.29/76

When the phones were finally installed and tested, the first call was to the kitchen, for one of the hostages to be brought upstairs. The *Sun* sensationalized.

Hostages Held As Pen Erupts Anew

Jack Stewart, Penitentiary Service spokesman, said: "hostages appeared to be unharmed..." but he pointed out the danger of the situation when he noted that the 9 inmates have access to all the knives and other cutting instruments in the kitchen.

—*Columbian*, Sept.29/76

But the kitchen helper, Walter Day "who appeared nervous and pale, said he had been treated 'with courtesy' by his captors" (*Columbian*, Sept.29). After a few more words, he was escorted quickly to the exit by the I.C., to spare him any further discomfort.

"Thank you for being here, but where were you yesterday? where were you last week?"

With these questions Horvat opened the conference.

Many of the media people apparently had never received the releases sent out in the past two months—not even those sent by registered mail. Since the Visiting & Correspondence Office submits only its own internal registration number, but no regulation postal receipt, prisoners have no way of knowing if their mail (marked and paid for as registered) *even leaves the institution.*

Horvat read from the interim statement, stressing that it was only intended as a basis for a more serious clause-by-clause development of the issues for the following day:

While there are many other needs, immediate and urgent, the Inmate Committee is endeavouring to maintain an attitude of reasonable negotiations in order to expedite the release of the hostages, and the transfer of prisoners. It is hoped that this change will serve as a basis for improved conditions at this institution.

The clauses covered key matters such as reprisals, voluntary transfers, personal possessions to be retained intact, Super Maximum Unit, approved transfers, status of the Inmate Committee—and most important, a public enquiry.

Horvat reviewed the main points of that morning's press communiqué and then brought the conference to a close.

What neither the public nor even other members of the C.A.C. knew at that time was that only two days earlier (Sept. 26) a meeting had taken place between Horvat and *Province* reporter/C.A.C. member Jim Spears:

> Mr. Horvat warned of the tense situation at the prison, and said he was making every effort to calm inmates over the closed circuit inmate radio system. Spears was denied access [by the Administration] to the Inmate Committee as a reporter and was told that he was not permitted to take notes, *even for the purpose of informing the Citizens Advisory Committee.* *

Had the media come in two days earlier, quite possibly the hostage taking would not have happened. Negotiations could have begun, and perhaps some significant compromises been reached, once the public became more aware of the gravity of what was happening inside.

Instead, reporters only saw the end product of the wrecking spree in the East wing—a mass of torn mattresses, splintered bookcases and cupboards, smashed sinks and toilets, and two sheets hung on the bars spelling out *Under New Management.*

"We did in twelve hours what the Federal government couldn't do in fifty years," the prisoners taunted. They had a point. No one could dispute the official directives over the last *thirty* years ordering the "phasing out of the B.C.Penitentiary."

"If you ever need a demolition crew, come and see us," called out another.

Later, I saw an 18 year-old Native Indian (who seemed no more than 15) sitting in the débris. He was doing 2½ years—for stealing a color T.V., I was told.

Minutes of Proceedings, Issue No.29, Feb.15/77, p.29A:20.

The media were not to be granted this measure of access again at the Pen. During the January 1978 hostage taking, RCMP Superintendent Bruce Northorp, once again in charge, ensured as much. He restricted them to the foot of the hill as he alone described the events taking place up above in the visiting area where five prisoners, thwarted in their escape bid, had taken 13 visitors hostage. The media were reduced to holding the microphone for Northorp as he reported to the public. "We idly stand by as cherished and hard-won rights are trampled upon..." the Editor of *Quest* Magazine warns.

Before the media left the conference, the Citizens Advisory Committee and the Administration issued a joint statement warning that erroneous radio reports were causing problems inside. Prisoners with transistors were hearing false stories about further smashing up in other wings, and were getting upset about it. But CPS Regional Director Jim Murphy denied that he had been "feeding lies to the media in saying that the North wing was being torn down." (*Columbian*, Sept.29).

So that the Commissary could resume serving meals to the staff, the I.C. was moved to the Physical Training Instructors' (PTI) office in the projection room area overlooking the gymnasium. Here, too, they were to have the use of the vital internal telephone to maintain their fifteen minute calls to the kitchen, uninterrupted. K-rations were shared around; blankets and sleeping bags were found; and a night watch was set up so someone would always be awake and at the phone. Others patrolled the tiers.

While we spent another night in comparative comfort, the men in the East wing were left in their accumulating filth. Those in the B-7 and North wings were also only just managing. However, thanks to the solid communication system set up between themselves and the Inmate Committee, they remained united in their determination to see it through—with no 'accidents.'

J.J. spent this night on the tiers talking to as many as he could, to explain what was happening as we prepared for the following day's negotiations. So that the demands would genuinely represent the consensus of the 400 men involved, this became his most urgent responsibility.

There remained one area, however, where the Administration was successful in undermining the I.C.'s intentions. They could and did prevent them from reaching the Super Maximum Security Unit (solitary) although the I.C. were agitating constantly to be allowed to send a representative up there accompanied by members of the C.A.C.

The general population was equally concerned. Rumours were beginning to filter down that all was not well in the 'Penthouse.' Although I was anxious to tour that area, it was agreed that only the male members of the C.A.C. would join the I.C. when they travelled through the prison, since it could be reasonably considered an invasion of privacy if women were drifting around in areas without enclosed toilets and showers.

After some argument with Jim Murphy, Regional Director, Bob Burrows and Frank Maczko of the C.A.C. and Gary Lake of the I.C. were finally allowed upstairs—two days later. They reported back to us that they found several inches of water on the cell floors and that the prisoners were in their underwear, or nude. Murphy's reaction was, "Dammit, why did they have to take their clothes away!"

A letter from solitary, dated Oct.1, tells what really was happening upstairs:

> The screws took all their anger out on us up here cuz they couldn't do it to the rest of the guys in population. The screws went right into their pig act. They brought the fire hose on the range every couple of hours to flood our cells out, laughing while they did it...real funny...then we all got skin frisks [strip naked, bend over, spread cheeks] and all of our clothes and bedding taken away. I managed to keep a few things dry for I could hear them start at cell #1 with the fire hose and I'm in #10 so I gathered up what I could, threw it in a box and shoved it under my bed into a corner where the water couldn't get at it. This kept up for three days anyway, to everyone. A couple of guys got bad colds, getting worse. No one's got any clothes to wear, if

they do they are soaking wet. Nor does anyone have any bedding.

The nurse came up here once and seen everyone in their cells with no clothes, bedding, cells flooded. She didn't do fuck all about it. No doctors been up, no medication is coming up at all. I tell you my whole body is just numb, the screws turned the heat off and opened all the windows too. The light's on 24 hours a day now. The only thing I want is a hot shower, dry clothes, dry bedding. I just want to get warm. I could use a good hot meal too. The screws gave us instant soup and oatmeal but we got no water for it. The water's shut off.

I tell you there's enough pent up energy in these cells here to power a sub or jet! All in all, everyone is trying to cheer each other up and keep the spirits up.

...just listened to Lakusta (head of the screws union) making a statement on the radio that cons never get punished for harming a guard. Bullshit. What do they think I've been doing up here for the past year, plus I'm charged in street court.

Remember four months back I told you this place was due for a riot anytime. Call it 6th sense, but I'll tell you I can feel these things in the air. I can tell by the change in people's day to day activities and the change in a guy's personality. Anyone who has been around jails long enough can feel it in the air.

I'm going to cut off here for awhile, do some walking and exercise to get warm. I'm so god damn tired, but I'm not going to sleep in this god damn wet cold cell. I've got to get moving. My body's just numb.

The Inmate Committee was extremely frustrated at not being able to help their brothers in this area where many of them had themselves done time, knew what it was like, and so could suspect what was going on.

A second letter, written Oct.3rd, justifies their concern:

Nothing's changed up here...I've been wondering if I'll be

going to court Monday. If I do I'm not leaving here unless I get a shave and a shower. I'm not going out of here looking and smelling like this... I'll wash my clothes and hang them on my bars to dry... no hot meals or anything to talk about today. Basically the same as yesterday... I feel grubby, just rotten. If there's one thing I can't stand it's a person that doesn't keep themself clean. The screws turned on the water in our cells today, so I stripped down and sponged my body down and washed my hair. Wow was it cold. I don't want to do that too many more times. It wouldn't be bad if the heat was on. It sure woke me up...

S—— got one hell of a cold, worse than anyone else on the range. C—— should be a lot worse by tomorrow too. They are both in their cells completely nude, no blanket, clothes, fuck all. Everytime someone gives them one the screws come in and take it from them...

I've got the worst cold I've ever had. My throat feels swollen. I can't smoke and can hardly talk. I'm in bed this very moment writing. I don't plan on getting out except to shave and shower... I haven't been this sick in a couple of years. I guess getting hosed down and no heat did it to me. My nose keeps running, my throat feels raw, my whole body feels weak...

It sure felt good to have a shave and shower. I feel human again. That was the highlight of the day... the screws give everyone clothes except for S—— they really have a hard-on for him... I can well understand how he's feeling and the thoughts he's thinking... I've gone through it... the hate and the bitterness is still inside of me only I keep it to myself and try to forget it... I imagine with time it will be buried away deep inside of me and I will only think of it occasionally...

How about this: this one shift of screws that are on right now won't even give guys shit paper—they laugh when someone asks. That's what you call "Pig swine." This is what I don't understand. No one up here did anything. That's straight goods. But the screws take it out on us...

Ten days later, at a University of British Columbia prison symposium, when Solicitor General Francis Fox was publicly informed of the above situation, Murphy flatly denied it.

The C.A.C. supposedly had the authority *"to inform the public generally of conditions and issues arising within the institution"* by virtue of the Letter of Understanding (Section 4, Clause F). This document, formally approved by the Commissioner of Penitentiaries, set out the mutually acceptable guidelines when the C.A.C. was set up in June. But no amount of badgering on my part succeeded in inducing the C.A.C. to issue a press release following their first visit to solitary where they had personally witnessed these wretched conditions.

The negotiations kept dragging. Two nights and two days had passed, with many meetings between the I.C. and the Adminstration, without a final agreement. We spent hours between meetings walking up and down the gym to stretch our legs and break the tension.

The RCMP were brought in at the request of the I.C. Prisoners preferred to have *them* around when the time came to move the men out of the ruined East wing—instead of the guards, who could be expected to take their revenge when the observers had left. It was also agreed that one week after the transfer was effected, there would be another meeting of all four parties—Inmate Committee, Citizens Committee, Pen Administration and RCMP—to assess how much longer the RCMP should remain. This was of great concern to the prisoners.

Mass Resignations Threatened By B.C.Pen Guards

One guard warned: "Wait and see what happens in two weeks... [when] 100 RCMP are scheduled to leave."

—*Columbian*, Oct.2/76

When two RCMP officers informally questioned us about this request later in the week, Gordie Duck offered to introduce them to two prisoners who had survived a similar disturbance at Millhaven the previous year: "You'll find when you talk to them that their brains are scrambled. They had to run the gauntlet of two rows of guards with clubs as they were moved—naked and on their hands and knees—from the yard back to their cells. We just figured we would try and avoid that if we could. That's why we asked to have you here instead of the guards, when it ends.''

Further confirmation of this type of incident exists in the Government *Report of Inquiry Millhaven Incident*, 3 Nov. 1975, p.15:

> ...it was established beyond question that inmates have, from time to time, been restrained by being handcuffed behind their backs, shackled with their legs bent backwards and upwards in order that the chain between the legs could be pulled through the chain on the handcuffs. It was also established that inmates had been left in their cells for hours in this position and a number of officers agreed that they had witnessed inmates lying in their own excrement. This treatment should not be tolerated by any society...when questioned about these methods of restraint, the Director of Millhaven Institution [presently Director of the new Kent Institution at Agassiz, B.C.] stated that he was not aware that this was taking place.

More recently, two prisoners, Leonard Morrison and Paul Andrew Cole are now suing the authorities for $1.6 million damages (as far as I know, the first time in Canadian prison history) following a riot on May 11/79.

Prisoners at Alberta's Fort Saskatchewan Jail have filed suit against the Crown, the jail director [Terry Downie] and Alberta Solicitor General, Graham Harle. They're charging that they were subjected to brutal treatment last month that violated the Alberta Bill of Rights.

The statement of claim by the prisoners on behalf of themselves and 14 others says they were beaten, shot at with weapons loaded with wooden bullets, and forced to crawl through a cellblock and down a flight of stairs.

—*Canadian Press,* June 11/79.

The delay in finalizing the negotiations was partly due to the many postponements, some of them requested by the I.C. as sometimes they had to rush to other parts of the prison to cool down some new crisis. Men had been living in a cold, miserable garbage heap for almost a week now, and there were bound to be some who couldn't take the endless strain, especially when they learned how the Administration was up to its usual passing-the-buck routines. From the first day, the I.C. demands had been submitted up to three hours before we were to meet at the negotiation table, to provide the other side with sufficient time to study them and return with firm answers. When we did meet, Murphy's first response would often be that they still had to get Ottawa's approval about such-and-such—although they had already had three hours to do just that before coming to the table.

By this time we could see that the prisoners were more worried about the safety of the remaining hostage than were the officials. Where the I.C. was trying to speed up his release, the Administration was in effect blocking it.

A likely motive for the latter's strategy was the desire to remove the C.A.C. With us out of the way, it would be much easier for them to conduct the negotiations to suit their own purposes.

For example—during one of the joint meetings between the Administration and the C.A.C., when RCMP Supervisor Bruce Northorp was reading his draft submission for the next negotiation session, he referred to the RCMP's agreement to *be involved* in the transfer of prisoners from the East block to the gymnasium. It wasn't appreciated when I pointed out that what had actually been agreed to was that the RCMP would *take control* of the transfer, not just become "involved." To only become "involved" would leave a loophole for Security to take over, which was exactly what the Inmate Committee had specified must be avoided at all costs.

It wasn't long before the first attempt to oust our Committee:

> . . . at approximately 1:00 a.m. Sept.30, five members of the Citizens Advisory Committee while still in the prison gymnasium were preparing a press release on negotiations. Four

members of the Inmate Committee were also there... Administration representatives had left the area and a Citizens Committee member received a telephone call instructing us to leave the gymnasium immediately. It appeared as if Security forces were preparing some kind of action. The event was immediately recognized as such by a member of the Inmate Committee who said that he felt duty bound to call the...kitchen area...holding one security guard as hostage. Because of the real danger that the departure of the Citizens Committee members could produce a panic situation...and endanger the hostage, Citizens Committee members remained in the gym pending clarification of the instructions to evacuate. After about thirty minutes it appeared there had been a misunderstanding although during that period the crisis was aggravated by muffled sounds of something banging against the gymnasium roof. Only later did...[we] discover that inmates in the East wing were throwing bricks on the gym roof.*

When this ploy failed, Acting-Director Peterson's next phone call demanded that I leave the institution instead of passing another night with the Inmate Committee. He suggested that a sole woman spending the night with seven men could lead to "scandal." The further inference that there had been subversive acts on my part, such as secretly remaining overnight without Security's knowledge or permission, was equally absurd, since *all* C.A.C. members were escorted on and off the grounds at all times and had to sign at the front gate as they passed through. This was simply an attempt to get me off the premises. It could hardly have been a secret that I had remained in the institution continuously since my arrival two nights before.

Since it was already about 3:00 a.m., and I would have to be at

*Minutes of Proceedings, Issue No.29, Feb.15/77, p. 29A:21.

the 8:00 a.m. meeting anyway, when Don Sorochan offered to replace me, I agreed to leave.

The second attempt was made the following night—just hours before the actual signing of the Agreement (around 2:00 a.m. Oct.2). Again the C.A.C. was offered the opportunity to leave before Security moved in "...as your group is nearest the exit." They were definitely trying to frighten us off.

Again we refused.

Again nothing happened.

One must keep in mind that these 'offers' were being made in the same prison where only one year earlier a tactical squad had rushed another hostage-taking group, resulting in the death of Mary Steinhauser and the wounding of Andy Bruce. Therefore, when the Prisoners' Rights Group presented its Brief to the Parliamentary Subcommittee four months later, I was instructed to

> ...strongly urge that this Committee investigate the reason why these attempts were made to remove the Citizens Committee from the prison grounds while the hostage was still held, and what was being planned in the event that we did leave. Could this [departure of outside observers] have placed the life of the hostage in danger....

To this day that question has not been answered, either formally by the Subcommittee, by its Chairman, or by any of the individual Members of Parliament who have been repeatedly reminded of it since then.

Two years later I was to learn from a reliable source that when these two attempts failed, the decision was made to remove us physically—one by one to be carried out of the gym area. For some reason the plan failed to materialize. (Who was assigned to cart out the "prisoners advocate," one wonders.)

Minutes of Proceedings, Issue No.28, Feb.15/77, pp.48-49.

Hospital Alert For Teargas Victims

Prison authorities apparently planned to tear gas those rebellious prisoners inside the B.C.Pen sometime Thursday afternoon (Sept.30) but then called it off...request made at approx. 4:30 p.m. but a stand-down of medical staff came at 8:00 p.m. when the teargas plan was apparently dropped.... Royal Columbian Hospital medical director, Dr. Ladislav Antonik said today that the hospital had been asked to take in teargas victims...Regional Director Jim Murphy denied any knowledge of the plan...it appeared common knowledge at the Royal Columbian Hospital located just a few minutes away from the Pen— that a teargas attack was being contemplated against the rioters inside the prison...nurses were lining the windows of the nurses' residence waiting for the first casualties to arrive...one shouted down: "What time are you expecting the teargas victims...?" A man drove into the parking lot and an attendant told him to move on as they "were expecting traffic from the Pen."

—*Columbian*, Oct.1/76

There was never a moment in the eighty hours that we were not aware of such a possibility. At one of the I.C. meetings, Jack Dow admitted that he was worried about my presence there. "We don't want another Mary Steinhauser, and we should start to think about that."

I asked them to consider the event of them 'coming down' on us. Would my being there make any difference? In other words, did *my* presence make it more, or less, dangerous for them? They all granted, "If they're going to come down, they'll come down anyway—whether you're here or not."

At that I was left to make my own decision about whether to stay on.

I chose to remain.

Finally the Memorandum of Agreement was presented, in four copies, ready for the signatures of each of the parties present during the negotiations—the Inmate Committee, the Citizens Advisory Committee, the RCMP, and the Administration of the B.C.Penitentiary.

Seizing the pretext that he was not being handed the original copy—that it had probably been seen by the whole prison population before ever he saw it—Murphy still balked at signing. As the person who had typed the Memorandum, I had no difficulty in gathering up all four copies to prove that they were not 'circulating through the prison.'

The last attempt to delay the signing had failed.

The Memorandum covered the following: responsibilities of the RCMP; transfers from the "uninhabitable areas of the Pen ...to habitable" ones or to other institutions; no reprisals, physical punishment, or double jeopardy; permission for transferred prisoners to take with them their personal effects intact; conditions for contact between Inmate Committee and Super Maximum Unit; and, most important, a public enquiry.

The Citizens Advisory Committee had been particularly involved in the preparation of the recommendation of an Enquiry. It was to be "full and open with broad terms of reference to enquire into the particular and general causes of the disturbances at the B.C.Penitentiary, the resolution of the demands made by the inmates, the implementation of the settlement, and the future role of the B.C.Penitentiary in the prison system."

Unfortunately, this is not what happened.

Another study of Canadian penitentiaries was launched Tuesday night when 13 M.P.'s were named to do a country-ranging investigation of prisons and all things connected with them.

...There was some political bickering and fears were expressed there would be more. It was noted that a similar sub-committee in 1973 achieved nothing and that the results of many inquiries and Royal Commissions have been ignored by government.

...Conservatives...said an impartial approach is only possible through a non-partisan committee made up equally of government and opposition members.

The Liberal majority insisted on an absolute majority on the sub-committee and added that partisanship would disappear when MP's got down to work.

—*Vancouver Province*, Oct.27/76

The predictable difference between the reactions of the prisoners and the guards to the Agreement was well displayed by the media.

Inmates Claim "Victory" as Revolt Ends
Hostage Free Unharmed

"You guys won the war for us," shouted one inmate from the battered cell block...as they [the 'kitchen people'] turned themselves in to the RCMP and were taken to the Burnaby detachment cells.

"Anytime we can get an agreement in a place like this it has to be a victory," said Horvat. "A lot of people were making decisions but it wasn't the people who were being forced to spend their whole life here. We are people too, you know."

—*Columbian*, Oct.1/76

Guards Have Lost Faith In Leader

...because he, André Therrien, Commissioner of Penitentiaries, has failed to recognize the explosive situation that has developed over the last year...personnel were forced to work excessive overtime because management refused to operate the institution in a safe manner and was yielding to both inmates and outside pressure groups.

Management would rather give in to pressure from inmates regardless of the safety of their own personnel.

—*Vancouver Sun*, Oct.1/76

Prison Staff Pleads Exhaustion

A spokesman for the Solicitor-General's component of the PSAC said guards have been complaining about lack of security measures for more than two years but management has 'adopted the philosophy of looking after inmates before staff.'

"We're heading toward a situation in Canada like Attica if correctional measures are not taken," said Paul Caouette....

—*Columbian*, Oct.2/76

Riot Force Remains at B.C.Pen

Murphy said the disturbance showed that while the system has improved in the last few years, the change is still too slow for some people.

—*Columbian*, Oct.1/76

Meanwhile the Quebec Civil Liberties Association called for the release of all prisoners in federal penitentiaries convicted of non-violent crimes, saying the move would relieve over-crowded conditions in prisons. . . .

But the union representing Canada's 7,000 prison guards called for more stringent security measures for maximum-security prisoners and blamed the 'incompetence' of top federal penitentiary officials for the incidents....

—*Columbian*, Oct.2/76

The next order of business was the release of the remaining hostage.

B.C.Pen hostage Wayne Culbert did not look like a man who had spent 81 hours cooped up with between six and ten hardened criminals when he was released today...uniform looked as if it had been freshly pressed.

—*Columbian,* Oct.2/76

We were then notified about "the safe removal of the inmates who had held Mr. Culbert to an RCMP lockup. . . ."

These men had acted in what they thought were the best interests of the institution and its occupants. They had taken hostages, whom they later released unharmed, only to ensure the signing of an Agreement which everyone hoped would correct a deplorable internal situation. I therefore sent the following letter to the press.

...revelations being exposed by the present Parliamentary Committee investigating the Canadian penitentiary system cannot but bring some useful results.

Would it not, therefore, be a measure of justice that those who initiated this inquiry should not be punished for having done so?

The seven prisoners who took hostages...did so for only one reason—to bring the public in to see what had become unbearable. They now face additional years of imprisonment as punishment for their efforts. It is to be hoped that sufficient public pressure will induce Solicitor General Fox to intervene on their behalf.

—*Province*, Feb.17/77

Two months later, it was gratifying to learn they only received a total of 45 years, concurrent.

...only one inmate will serve extra time (three months) because the terms are to run concurrently

....All pleaded guilty to two counts of illegal confinement.

—*Columbian*, Apr.27/77

*   *   *

5 a.m. The last hostage had been released. The media was packing up their equipment, and the C.A.C. was getting ready to leave when the Inmate Committee asked us to meet one last time with them in a corner of the gym. Rounding up as many of the two groups as we could, we gathered in a little circle.

"We just want to thank every one of you for what you've done. To tell you how much we appreciate that you came out, gave up your time to help us the way you did. You have to know that we don't think we could have done it without your moral and physical support. Just the fact that you were here meant everything," was the way Gordie Duck began.

"But there is still one thing more. You know as well as we do that when this is over we're marked men. We're not going to ask for transfers out. We're going to stay here because this is a political job, and we won't take off right now. Maybe later, but not now.

"So, we're asking you, would you please stick around. Not 24 hours at a stretch as you've been doing, but will some of you come in every day to see us. Don't lose touch. We're really going to need you for what's going to happen next."

At this point, Envoy Stevenson of the Salvation Army, visibly moved, offered his support: "I've been coming in for twenty years, and I certainly don't intend to stop now."

"Well, thanks, I'm very grateful and I thank you. But maybe I should just add that once when I spent a long time in the hole the only people I ever saw for those twenty months were guards. You may have been coming in, but I sure didn't get to see you," Gordie replied.

I commented on the fact that this was the first time in the history of the Canadian Penitentiary System when prisoners holding hostages confronted the authorities *with an outside group bearing witness from the first moment to the last.* Also, this was an Agreement negotiated by prisoners who not only won improved conditions for their fellows, but in the process laid themselves open to further harassment and reprisals by virtue of being considered the 'ringleaders.'

We could and did agree to maintain regular daily contact with them.

RCMP Move In To Take Over Pen Duties

Mary McGrath, of the Citizens Advisory Committee, said the Committee acted as an observer throughout the negotiations. "We obviously committed ourselves to carrying out the agreement...."

She added that members of the Committee would be present in shifts to observe the transfer of inmates and would set up liaison groups elsewhere to observe the treatment of inmates being transferred to other prisons.

She said she hoped the agreement would be the beginning of "some sort of constructive change in the system."

—*Vancouver Sun*, Oct.1/76

Mary and I witnessed the first "change in the system" within an hour, although it was hardly an acceptable or "constructive" one. The courtesy which the RCMP had shown me during the 80 hours before the Agreement was signed changed to impudence when the prearranged tour of B-7 wing for Mary and myself was suddenly modified to include only Mary. "*You* are not going anywhere near B-7," I was told.

Predictably, the antagonist view appeared in print the next day.

Pact "Dangerous": Union Official

Ottawa (CP)...an agreement ending the hostage taking at the B.C. Penitentiary "is very dangerous to the public," said an official of the union representing Canada's 7,000 prison guards.

Paul Caouette, Executive Secretary-Treasurer...said the agreement in effect allows the Inmate Committee and the Citizens Advisory Committee to run the B.C. prison...allows the prisoners and citizens committees to supervise the RCMP.

"Where is the law in that? It's irresponsible," said Mr. Caouette.

—*Province*, Oct.1/76

The eighty hours were over.

Early in the morning of October 2nd, the Citizens Committee walked out.

CHAPTER THREE

The Log

Sept. 17—8:00 a.m. I told Konig that Herbert would like to be let off 2A tier to check the radio system as he was locked behind the barrier. Konig said he didn't care if the radio was screwed up. I told him that's how riots and hostage takings occur. He said: "I don't give a fuck if you guys riot or take hostage!" *(Gary Lake)**

A week before the riot the *Log* begins.

The Inmate Committee had set up their log anticipating events that came all too soon. It would be maintained not only during the riot and hostage taking, but through a difficult and prolonged aftermath. Over a three-month period, I.C. members regularly made entries to record the events as they unfolded. The *Log* was intended as a document which would serve as both a true history and as evidence, should any of the I.C. members be charged when it was all over.

This chapter presents entries from the prisoners' *Log* alongside media reports, official memoranda, and correspondence—all describing the same events. Short profiles of the I.C. members are given following their first entries.

A handful of prisoners had succeeded in their main objective: to bring the problems of the general prison population to the attention of the public. But now there were 240 men shut into a basketball-court-size gym. That first week in October, no one expected that they would be there for *two months*. Two months penned in a garbage heap—no privacy, no visitors, no outside exercise, grossly inadequate medical care. These men would find a way out only by 'slashing up.' (To illustrate how health care was administered, relevant log entries have been edited as a separate unit.)

---

*Other than the I.C. members, and "George W.," Miller, Surette, Andy Bruce, Clair Wilson, Dwight Lucas, Clarence Johns, and Tom Shand, the names of all prisoners have been changed.

Everything centred around getting *transferred*. Yet, what the Memorandum had agreed to do 'quickly' dragged on and on, draining the prisoners' endurance as if by a preconceived plan. What may prove to be a wearisome and frustrating account for the reader was much more so for the men who had to live through it.

Ultimately, it took a fire to get them out.

GARY LAKE: kept the Committee hopping. He was everywhere at once. Little escaped his notice. Since he was Recreation representative on the I.C., his goal was to be allowed to organize proper recreational programs. When parole time came around (Spring 1978), although the Board had approved his release to Langara College where he was registered for a Fall recreational course, when he applied for transfer to a Medium institution for his last three months—to help adjust to his coming release after close to six years of Maximum—the Transfer Board turned him down. Their reason: too dangerous for transfer to Medium.

Gary was the one who prepared and hung out the banner for the prisoners in the gym: ONE FOR ALL AND ALL FOR ONE.

Statement:

I, Gary Eugene Lake, do solemnly swear under the penalty of perjury that the following is true to the best of my knowledge.

On or about the afternoon of Tuesday, Sept. 28/76 at approximately 3:00 p.m. I was handing out drinking water near the front entrance of B-7 Living Unit. Several guards were posted on the road area and looking into the building. Norm Jensen (his rank—CX4 or CX6) turned his attention toward me and said: "I'll get you for this, Lake. I know you only have five years left in this place, but I will get you when you get out. That is a promise." [Jensen was referring to the hostage taking which had taken place the previous evening.]

A number of people witnessed the incident and heard what Mr. Jensen said. Some of them were John Dow [I.C.

member], Guard Swanson and others, including a lawyer, Mr. Jim Hogan.

As Mr. Jensen made his threat he was holding a shotgun in his hand and shaking the weapon in what appeared to be a dangerous manner. Following the threat, I called Mr. Hogan over and asked Mr. Jensen to repeat the threat in his presence. Mr. Jensen ignored the request and walked away.

Mr. Hogan advised me to avoid all the guards including Mr. Jensen. After leaving the B-7 area I immediately went to the gymnasium and reported the incident to Mr. Murphy (Regional Director). Mr. Murphy advised me that he would take care of the matter. Later that evening, Mr. Murphy informed me that he had removed Mr. Jensen from the institution.

I realize that this declaration/affidavit has the same effect as though it had been sworn to in a court of law. (Signed: Gary Eugene Lake; witnessed, Paul Leister, Committee Secretary.)

Everyone Tired at Midnight Talks

"If we sound tired it's because we are tired," said Horvat. "There are about 7 guards that are causing all the problems...it's a clique who like things the way they were 30 or 40 years ago...if the new guards don't follow their advice they get pushed out."

—*The Columbian,* Sept.29/76

Inmates Want Guard Replaced

"We want someone on the tiers who won't pepper the place with shotgun blasts...the inmates fear for their lives on a mass scale. The situation is desperate...control of the prison must be taken away from the custodial staff," said Horvat.

Since the rebellion all water supplies to the cells throughout the prison have been shut off. Horvat said the cells are "stinking and filthy...tremendous potential for an epidemic. Also some of the prison floors are ready to fall in on our people. A building inspector would condemn the place if he was to see it."

—*Vancouver Sun,* Sept.30/76

Talks On Hostage Still Held. No Reprisals Inmates Warn.

200 prisoners in East Wing... said they had no intention of attempting an escape. RCMP... were reportedly equipped with tear gas...a truck carrying barbed wire arrived...280 BURN CELLBLOCK IN QUEBEC.

—*Province,* Oct.1/76

*   *   *

The Memorandum of Agreement was signed at 4 a.m. on October 2nd, and the last hostage was released. The transfer of prisoners from the wrecked East wing to the gym began as efforts were made to phase out the B.C.Penitentiary.

*   *   *

Fox Pressing for Pen's Phase Out.

...as quickly as possible... prefers not to rebuild the damaged parts of either the B.C.Pen or Laval ...said no force will be used unless it is cleared with him first...blamed overcrowding as one of the major reasons...facilities for providing them meaningful things to do are just not adequate...problems compounded by the fact that fewer prisoners are being released early...parole board now paroles 35% of applicants compared to 60% a few years ago.

—*Sun,* Sept.30/76

Demolished Cellblock Should Not Be Replaced

Says Stu Leggatt, M.P., "It's quite obvious the East Wing should not be rebuilt or re-established. It would be a waste of taxpayers' money."

"Now is the time to accelerate the plan of building smaller maximum and minimum security institutions elsewhere," says Mayor Muni Evers of New Westminster.

—*Columbian,* Oct.1/76

Riot Force Remains at B.C.Pen

Prisoners place great hope on the results of the Hearings to force changes in the system. Stewart (Information Officer) said the

East wing is "pretty well destroyed." There had been reports of dysentery because of lack of toilet facilities...Horvat: "There are still people willing to lay down their lives for what they believe in."

—*Columbian*, Oct.1/76

Mixed Up Jail Will Always Breed Unrest

The attitude of benign political neglect—rationale of "why pour good money after bad when the prison is soon to be phased out?" has led to tragedy before and promises new tragedy in the future...the B.C.Pen will be with us for years to come, and as long as it is, there will be riots and there will be hostages."

—David Stockand (C.A.C.)
Sun, Oct.1/76

*　　　*　　　*

Despite the arrangements for C.A.C. members to maintain a continuous presence from 8:00 a.m. to 8:00 p.m. in four hour shifts, at noon on October 2, the Acting Director refused me admission to the gym. He claimed there were five prisoners missing, and until they were located no one was going to get in.

Two hours later Michael Jackson (C.A.C.) and I were finally allowed in. The problem had been solved when it was discovered that someone had forgotten to record the three prisoners transferred to another institution the morning of the hostage taking. The other two 'missing' were 'located' when the I.C. themselves supervised the count.

*　　　*　　　*

Oct.2: Once the RCMP are satisfied that the count can proceed, one Committee Member will direct traffic one by one to the diagonal opposite corner [of the gym]. At all times, the area of vision will be kept clear to the RCMP satisfaction that it indeed is a one by one count. *(Unsigned)*

*　　　*　　　*

After listening to a Classification Officer (C/O) describing the work he was doing for a certain prisoner, one of the I.C. reminded him that this particular prisoner had been transferred about two months earlier. The next day the C/O came by with a new list of prisoners for the I.C. to check off for him—to make sure they were still around.

"When you want statistics about the prison system, get them from us," the prisoners always insisted. "You'll never get accurate figures from the front office."

*   *   *

Oct.2—3:00 p.m. Phoned for Assistant Director Technical Services to provide necessities—mattresses, blankets, etc. Mr. Nichols told us Woodside has not been in the institution at all. This is his responsibility to look after these needs. *(Gary Lake)*

Oct.2—8:00 p.m. Attached delivered by member of C.A.C., setting out procedures for transfers—I was given a list of names, then told that those people move tomorrow. I am amazed.* *(J.J.)*

> IVAN HORVAT: The media called J.J. the "charismatic Chairman of the Inmate Committee" and "the twenty-two year old convicted murderer" (although he had an Appeal pending at the time).
>
> J.J. accepted his duties as Chairman of the negotiations with great seriousness. When he would quietly order Administration members to return to the table within half an hour, with certain information, the room would bristle with fury. But J.J. would carry it off with an aplomb which matched his latest escape attempt, when he cut a hole through the gym wall during an ear-splitting performance by visiting musicians—the last time the B.C.Pen has invited a Rock Band. Throwing a basketball net (secured with a ball at one end) over the wall, he climbed to his freedom—all thirteen hours of it.
>
> The C.A.C. was quite impressed with his chairmanship during those difficult hours. He set up a chain of command so that there would be no break in the negotiations should anything happen to him. Whenever a quick, unilateral decision had to be made, J.J. would gather the rest of the Committee to explain what had

---

*"I am amazed" can be interpreted as either sheer delight or cynical disbelief. That a list was provided and a guarantee of movement made was just too unusual to be accepted at face value. This reaction will be better appreciated as the true pattern of transfers unfolds.

happened and the reason for having dealt with it on his own. He would then ask for comments and criticisms to avoid potential mistakes in future.

His graffiti went up on the gym wall directly beneath the guards cage in the North-East corner:

THERE ARE NO KINGS IN OUR CASTLE
BECAUSE WE'RE ALL KINGS.

Three years later J.J. writes that he is still denied transfer from Maximum Security (Archambault) to a Medium: "even now their revenge isn't over...a check into sudden disappearance of all the evidence in my [B.C.Pen] files [to prove] that I *was* considered for a Medium....Sure enough. Nothing there...no record. So not only do they say I am and always was a Maximum case, but now I am also a liar. Incredible." (Feb.22/79)

Oct.2 "PLEASE KEEP AREA CLEAN." *(J.J.)*

Oct.3—12:30 p.m. No food, towels, mattresses, toilet paper have been sent down since before East Wing movement to gym. *(Unsigned)*

*   *   *

When I arrived Sunday morning, Oct.3—after the typical game-playing delay of being made to sit for 1½ hours in the waiting room for no apparent reason—I found the Inmate Committee still asleep. They had been up all night because of an emergency meeting with the thirteen men who had been cleared for transfer prior to the disturbance.

They had decided they would not go unless they could take fifty 'lifers' with them—their logic being that once all the short-timers were out of the way, and with the bargaining levers gone (hostages had been released by this time), what was to prevent the Administration from keeping the rest of them in the gym indefinitely? George W., spokesman for the group of 13, wanted to use their "all of us go or none of us go" position as a way of making sure that at least 50 lifers got out too.

However, remembering how eager the A/Director was to use the mistaken count the day before as an excuse to tear up the Agreement, I felt they would be walking into a trap. Everyone would lose if the Administration were given the slightest justification to renege on the Agreement. I argued that George

W. had to be persuaded to abide by the original Agreement: the 13 should go as pre-scheduled and leave the I.C. in a stronger position to fight for its full implementation.

I.C., which had been won over by George's plan, was not prepared to switch its decision, but did agree to call a meeting for 10:00 a.m.—even though most of them had only just gone to sleep.

*   *   *

Oct.3. A meeting of the full I.C. was called to order by Chairman J.J. Horvat....Those present included the following: Claire Culhane, visiting by invitation of the I.C. and representing the C.A.C.; regular members: J.J., Gordie Duck, Lea Sheppe, Jack Dow, Gary Lake, Omer Prud'homme, Paul Leister.

Chairman: It is extremely important at this point that we all be together. Following this meeting we are going downstairs to see those we represent for a major decision.

Omer: The Committee did not make the agreement [alone]. We have discussed about 13 men who are scheduled to leave. That decision was made by the floor. I feel if the decision is that the 13 leave we should immediately demand a meeting with the Administration.

Chairman: Claire, we must have you talk to George W. and the others. I feel that after they hear what you have to say the right decision will be made.

Claire: We must convince the 13 to leave as scheduled. They will be showing strength not weakness. If they are still not persuaded by the Inmate Committee, permission would have to first be obtained from the Administration—for me to speak to them, assuring them of my intention to urge that the contract be respected.

Jack Dow: I've seen men stand firm but sometimes stand too firm, and bring down too much punishment. The important factor is not to leave a loophole where the bargaining of good faith isn't violated. The Administration is obviously waiting for *any* good reason to show justification as to why they should suddenly use force. At this point, we're the first men to show refusal, the public would be sold as to the Administration having justification, and our cause is lost.

Our position is the welfare of the inmates first and foremost....But now without a hostage there is *NO* barrier to protect our people, so we must comply with the first move. People in the past have been too stubborn at times on principle, and have all become extinct. A slight compromise at this time of moving a few people to illustrate a good faith on inmates' behalf is a well calculated move.

Gordie: Beautiful. We're here also because of the kitchen people. We must be careful to protect their interest as well.

Gary: But they won't allow Claire down.

Chair: We'll contact Berkey and try to arrange it. Also at this point before we vote on anything, be certain why we're casting our vote the way it is cast. A lot of wars have been lost over minor mistakes. If anyone of us are not in shape to be responsible we must remove ourselves from the situation.

Gordie: We must point out to population also that a trial is coming up. We must protect Tommy and the others [hostage takers].

Chair: Unanimous decision has been reached by the Inmate Committee, with the advice from Claire Culhane, member C.A.C. That our number one priority is to follow the Agreement with the Administration, and that includes the fact that we must do all in our power to expedite transfer procedures including the 13 men who have been approved. These people should get on their way. Agreed?

All Members: Yes. Move we adjourn.

*   *   *

Fortunately, Gordie and Gary were able to persuade George W. and the rest of the group to transfer to Matsqui as arranged—with one exception. George insisted that an elderly sick prisoner go in his place. Berkey agreed, even as he had already agreed to the earlier request that I be allowed to join Gordie and Gary if they couldn't change George's mind.

Shortly after that meeting, Mary McGrath (C.A.C.) joined me to check off against our list of names the 13 prisoners as they stepped into the two waiting cars. They were also to be checked on arrival at Matsqui by other C.A.C. members there.

This may seem an exaggerated precaution, but not for anyone who has ever had to spend a month trying to locate a "transferred" prisoner.

*   *   *

It Can Happen Again Any Time Inmates Say Word

Prison inmates are generally willing to serve their time in peace unless pushed to the breaking point. They know that if they tear a prison apart it means the possibility of being killed...and the high probability of serving extra time. They don't want a riot....

The inmates of B.C.Pen tried to tell the public something this week. This time it ended without human injury and with the fortunate destruction of half of the institution... *no sane person who has been inside would rebuild it.*

There were long delays because Horvat and his committee had to walk among the general inmate population to calm them and inform them that all was well. For the first two days they also supplied inmates with water. They also calmed the hostage takers.

—Jim Spears (C.A.C.)
Province, Oct.3/76

Oct.3-4, 6 a.m. There are all these RCMP people supposedly looking over the most notorious vicious bunch in the society—and this gym is probably the most peaceful place in town. *(J.J.)*

Oct.4—7:10 a.m. John T. was hassled, cursed, etc. all night by one young RCMP officer and causing the general population to become a bit nervous. One con was talking about firing a can of beans at him. I asked to see the NCO in charge of that area and explained the situation. The Corporal removed the man from the (RCMP) gun cage. *(Paul Leister)*

PAUL LEISTER: secretary-treasurer of the Inmate Committee. 44 year old American of 'poor white trash' background. At the age of 17—the usual story of stolen car for a joy ride, girls picked up to head for a movie. Unfortunately they picked the wrong movie—the one across the bridge. Caught, charged with stolen car, crossing the state line, and kidnapping minors. Received a 15 year sentence.

By coincidence he found himself in the same prison as David Greenglass—the man who turned state evidence which sent his sister, Ethel Rosenberg, and her husband, Julius, to the electric chair for allegedly turning over atomic secrets to USSR. David Greenglass was also serving 15 years.

Paul soon became the jailhouse lawyer, drafting and typing documents for fellow prisoners. When I delivered one of the I.C.

press releases to UPI (United Press International) the local manager asked who had typed it? I pointed to the signature at the bottom.

"Yes, but who *typed* it?" he asked again.

"The secretary did."

"Do *prisoners* know how to type?" the man asked again, genuinely incredulous.

The last visit I had with Paul was towards the end of November 1976. He looked ghastly—seemed to have lost ten pounds in the week since our last visit. He warned me never to visit him again. A week later he broke the prison code, by naming and accusing two prisoners of participating in an alleged 'gang rape' during their time in the gym. The alleged victim later refused to testify when the case came to court, and today Paul is incarcerated in the hated Protective Custody Unit (PCU) in another Maximum Security Institution.

Oct.4. Berkey was called by Gordie who requested permission to give PTI's television set to the population in the gym. Refused. Gordie then asked Berkey to authorize the two sets to be brought in that had been removed for no reason. Refused. *(Gordie Duck)*

GORDON DUCK: had a record of being on prisoners' committees in almost every prison across Canada where he had spent the last eleven years. He was the musical one—he and six others (mostly 'lifers') were all into music. They tried to get a room where they could do some theory, and play together. They weren't asking for a $20,000 a year instructor. All they wanted was a room. Finally, after turning down some cupboard space in the gym where the mats were stored, or a corner of the gym itself where they would have to compete with handball games, they had the use of a real room, with table and chairs, door and window—twice—before it was taken back.

Soft-spoken and hot-tempered, Gordie has finally done his time and is home free, working and keeping in close touch with us. There is a bond which holds fast when people have been into 'social actions' together—some call them prison riots.

Oct.4—7:15 a.m. Telephone is not working—gives out a consistent busy signal. I need to report to the hospital that Joseph E., who is dying, should be called up and examined by the Doctor. I will report it through the RCMP. *(Paul Leister)*

Oct.4—10:20 a.m. Berkey said mail would be here today. This is the third day in a row they told us this.

People in the gym said they would not move until they heard from the recent transfers to Matsqui to assure them it was done properly. *(Gary Lake)*

*   *   *

But prisoners still couldn't get their mail out to reassure their families. I wrote names and numbers up and down my arm as they were called out to me from the gym, to phone their homes.

*   *   *

Oct.4—12:10 p.m. Rachel, V&C Department, passed gymnasium doorway and was asked about the mail. She said in reply: "It's down there."

She was then asked when the mail would be coming in?

"It won't be," she said. *(Paul Leister)*

Oct.4—11 p.m. All inmates in the gymnasium agree that the list of 45-50 people that we asked the Administration to review and deal with on transfers, is *extremely* important because if any double-cross is coming we will know it the minute they do *not* deal with that list. Many men on that list are hated by Security and if they're left behind, Security is going to slam them hard, perhaps kill a few.

If the Administration is sincere and plans to move *everybody who wants* to be moved, it will not alter anything. . . . What difference does it make who goes first if we're all going? All we're asking is for the Administration to show their honesty and sincerity in their selection process. Once they do that, the problem is over.

But—if the Administration *is* planning one of their little games that we all know they're famous for, then none of us will move. *(J.J.)*

Oct.5—4 a.m. Get hold of Jean Simonds, Transfer Board, state case: inmates request that when they appear before Transfer Board, the people in the gym should get top billing. Phone Custody to have other belongings of Joseph E. be brought up to hospital. Sammy H. has the belongings.

Reminder: Not to forget Canteen. *(J.J.)*

*   *   *

Frequent references to "belongings" are significant. A clause in the Memorandum of Agreement deals with that problem. Prisoners have so few personal things, yet even these are often "lost"—meaning stolen or destroyed.

One prisoner's family photo album, supposedly "lost," was discovered in the garbage with every picture torn up.

*   *   *

Oct.5—7:30 a.m. Reminder: food shortage up here, take care of canteen in the morning. In same time (hopefully) when telephone call gets to transfer board. *(J.J.)*

Oct.5—10:00 a.m. Visiting compound phoned by John Dow. Mr. Newton (Guard) answered phone. Request by Dow was that the outgoing mail be picked up when incoming mail was received.

Mr. Newton stated that he "does not talk to cons."

He then hung up the phone to end conversation.

At 10:00 a.m. Gordon Duck phoned Mr. Berkey explaining event and making same request...Mr. Berkey was cooperative and confirmed that it would be undertaken. *(John Dow)*

Oct.5—10:20 a.m. Mail (new system). Vi (Roden) says Parkinson will set up a new mail system for outgoing mail. *(Gordie Duck)*

Oct.6—8:00 a.m. Claire Culhane arrived at side door. Mr. Berkey said she could not stay there but had to move to bottom of stairs where RCMP are. She suggested that we set up a meeting with C.A.C. as soon as possible...telephone cut off. Omer notified RCMP of this matter. *(unsigned)*

*   *   *

While waiting at bottom of stairs chatting with Gary Lake, we watched as breakfast was served. I wondered aloud what kind of breakfast would come in brown paper bags? Gary joked: "Probably letter bombs...." I cautioned him to hush up as one of the guards jumped at those words.

*   *   *

Oct.6—Noon. Claire went to Mary's office, and Mary phoned Berkey. Vi Roden backed Claire as there was no question about [her taking] letters [out of the institution, as accused by Berkey]. [Berkey said there were] "other things" [against Claire].

Ed Lipinsky has gone on TV [and] radio to clarify [what the] "other things" [might be]. [It is obvious] she has been abused, [and they are also making an] attempt to discredit the committee.

Lipinsky said Union should name guilty persons [when they accused members of the Citizens Advisory Committee of being involved in a conspiracy to bring down the prison system].

Lipinski regretted Dr. Wallace chose media to express his opinion [when he called for the resignation of Claire Culhane].

...Phone Berkey about B-7 and five name pack [package for transfers] to Jean Simonds. *(Paul Leister)*

...Claire Culhane—barred from the prison Wednesday for acting as a courier for inmate letters....

According to the inmates, Mrs. Culhane was given about seven letters for mailing because no procedure has yet been established for sending mail out of the prison.

...subsequently heard in a news broadcast that the letters had been seized as "contraband" and Mrs. Culhane had been ordered to leave the prison and not come back.

—*Sun,* Oct.8/76

A "dear folks" letter written by the Inmates Committee in defence of Citizens Advisory Committee member Claire Culhane..."wish to state in the most emphatic manner that Mrs. Culhane, although firm in her stand against brutality and corruption, has never, at any time, entered into any scheme with any prisoner at this institution to violate the rules...demand that the ban be lifted and an appropriate apology made to Mrs. Culhane at the earliest possible moment."

—*Sun,* Oct.8/76

---

*   *   *

On two separate occasions in the first week of October, when I came by to meet with the Inmate Committee, J.J. was nowhere to be seen. I was told that he was just catching up on his sleep, which was understandable. But something seemed wrong. He later told me that he seemed to have been given an extra dosage of medication.

*   *   *

Mr. Jim Murphy,   Oct.8/76
Regional Director, C.P.S.
Vancouver, B.C.

Dear Mr. Murphy,

It is respectfully requested that Ivan Horvat, Chairman of the Inmate Committee, be given a complete physical examination by Dr. Scott Wallace at the earliest possible moment. Dr. Wallace has agreed to provide the examination if your permission is forthcoming.

Sincerely,
Ivan Horvat,
Chairman, Inmate Committee

More than 200 prisoners complained of lack of toilet paper and clean laundry and said that more than a ton of "rainsoaked putrid garbage" has accumulated at the side door of the gym. Jack Stewart: "If there are hardships, it's unfortunate, but I can't sympathize with them a great deal."

—*Columbian*, Oct.9/76

Oct.10—8:45 p.m.
Inmate Committee Support Asked By a Few in the Gym
Read by Gary Lake:

Some of the guys have asked us to run down what's happening...

Now that we're in the gym, our living conditions are not the best by any means. Our visits are curtailed, games are being played with our mail, medication, etc. We're eating out of paper bags—but even though we *are* suffering a bit, there's going to be a day when the full truth is going to come out about this dump, and the way the cons here have been used for political reasons.

So far we've done fine. No one was killed. No one was even injured, but the first test is *now!* Here in the gym we get bored. We miss our privacy. We miss our visits. We miss a lot of things. But one thing we must *never* miss, and that's the point of why we're here in the first place.

The mistake we must not make now is to start bickering or fighting among ourselves, no matter what the reason. We're in here together.

We've got to stay together. We must not give anyone the slightest excuse or opportunity to break the agreement the Solicitor General has promised to keep—and the main point of that agreement is the transfers. There are scores of men in the gym who want out of B.C.Pen. If we stand together, quietly, no fights, no violence, those men will leave. Each of us needs the support of each of us.

Because of other riots that have erupted across Canada, transfers have slowed down a bit, but we must *still* stand firm and together.

If you get a bit bored and pissed, think of the guys right above B-7 in the hole. Some of them aren't even allowed clothing to wear. They get harassed, water thrown on them, cursed, the works. Guys at Millhaven are being beaten and gassed right now while we watch television. There are other guys at Laval lying on cold wet concrete, suffering a lot more than we are. Some of them have been starving for over a week.

All we ask, guys, is to stand together no matter how fucking long it takes. If we have to, we'll sing Christmas carols in the gym.

It's our duty as people and brothers to support one another and the guys who are not with us—Tommy Shand and the others. (Into Log, *Gordie Duck)*

Oct.15—9:15 p.m. B.C.Pen staff has taken over institution. X6 Konig is in charge of gym area. We feel this man is dangerous to this situation. He told me a week prior to the riot that he didn't care if we took hostage or rioted. From past experience I feel this man should be removed. *(Gary Lake)*

Mr. Ken Peterson, Acting Director,   Oct.18/76
B.C.Penitentiary

Dear Mr. Peterson,

Because of the emergency conditions in the gymnasium, a serious potential health hazard, and an almost complete breakdown in communication between various departments in the institution, the Inmate Committee respectfully requests an emergency meeting with you and your Staff, including Mr. Woodside, Technical Services, Mr. Berkey, A/D Security, and a member of your Medical Staff.

Respectfully,
Ivan Horvat

*   *   *

The prisoners' Log shows, among other issues, frequent reference to their concern about obtaining vital medical care. I have excerpted just a small portion of these entries. If the reader finds this wearisome to read, it is because it *is* wearisome to have to fight even for an aspirin, despite the fact that one of the few rights they have—Medical Care—is written into the Regulations:

> Every inmate shall be provided, in accordance with directives, with the essential medical and dental care that he [she] requires.*

*　　　　*　　　　*

Oct.8—8:08 p.m. . . .an inmate in B-7, Richard S., was under stress, also threatens to cut his throat, and did make a small attempt at cutting or slashing his arm. . .Inspector White says he would check it out. *(Gordie Duck)*

Oct.15—11:50 a.m. Have been trying to get emergency dental treatment for Tom L. for four consecutive days. The hospital has insisted on sending oil of cloves. He has stuffed the tooth with a roll of toilet tissue and keeps the paper saturated. . .but the tooth is broken almost to the gum and the nerve is completely exposed. Mr. Berkey, A/D Security, just assured me that (1) pain killers would be sent to him and (2) he would see the dentist tomorrow morning.

Tom is in such pain that he is threatening to rip the tooth from his own mouth. *(Paul Leister)*

Oct.18—5:20 p.m. Have telephoned "Operations" (Tel.#248) and told them that Richard S. from B-7 was in really bad physical shape and should see the doctor. *(Ivan Horvat)*

Oct.21—10:15 a.m. I phoned #248 and requested to be put on the hospital list because I have an eye infection. Need eye drops. *(Ivan Horvat)*

Oct.21—10:15 a.m. Inmate Doug A. went to see the dentist about staying on antibiotics for his abcessed tooth because it is still abcessed. The dentist wanted to pull the tooth anyway but Doug wouldn't let dentist pull it because the abcessing is still bad. So Doug and the dentist

*Penitentiary Service Regulations, (PC 1962-302), Part II, Section 2.06.

had a bit of a disagreement. All Doug wants to have is be put back on antibiotics until abcess is gone. I called #116 and talked to Nichols about calling the Doctor and putting Doug back on antibiotics. Nichols said he would tell Berkey about it and call the Doctor and would call back and let me know the doctor's decision. *(Lea Sheppe)*

> LEA SHEPPE: who cleaned and swept and checked supplies and heated up his K-rations for me when I had to sit at the top of the PTI stairs to talk through the bars to them, from the outside, when I made my evening visits. Guards would come over to check the contents of the three cups lined up at the bars for me, two with spaghetti (the space too narrow to slip a bowl through) and one with coffee. They missed the warm socks which Lea had provided.

Oct.21—11:52 p.m. Nurse says she doesn't know anything about eye drops for my eyes. I've already called twice about it . . . and was told that eye drops will be forthcoming. *(Ivan Horvat)*

Oct.21—11:53 p.m. Mr. Hadvick telephoned to inform me that the nurse was thrown water at when she was delivering medication to the gym. He also informed me that the nurse refused to come back to the gym and finish her medication round. Mr. Hadvick also told me that it would take a duty officer or the Warden to order medication delivery after the nurse's refusal. . . .

I in turn informed him that there were prisoners in the gym, some of them epileptics, who need their prescribed medication. Also, I asked Mr. Hadvick to tell me how can he or a custody officer take a man off medication when it takes a doctor to prescribe it? Mr. Hadvick told me that we should have thought of that problem before the water was thrown on the nurse. I asked him what did he mean by *we,* when the committee was all (almost) up in the office and cannot know what thoughts go through the minds of 200 angry people. *(Ivan Horvat)*

Oct.21—midnight. Talked to Mr. Havelin in "Operations" and he told me that he would call Mr. Woodside and/or the Director. I stressed that men in gymnasium needed their medication, and that we were concerned with medical emergencies throughout the night.

P.S. Also, I forgot to mention that Mr. Hadvick when I talked to him, he told me that I can take his word—that no one will die throughout the night if they don't get their medication—a point which is pure bull-shit. *(I.H.)*

Oct.22—4:00 p.m. . . . problems getting medical attention for Joseph E.

who has internal bleeding and lengthy medical trauma. In fact, he is dying. Omer and Gordie called hospital several times, with very little response. *(Ivan Horvat)*

Oct.22—4:30 p.m. Joseph E. went to the hospital after the Committee telephoned many times and finally got results. The guys in the gym tried to get medical attention for Joseph since 9 a.m. *(Ivan Horvat)*

Oct.23—12:00 noon. Phoned operations for Inmate Pat O'Brien who was given only half of regular prescription. Requested remainder to be sent down. *(John Dow)*

> JOHN DOW: When he wasn't searching for a doctor or a nurse for one of the prisoners, he was worrying about his sick wife in Prince George, and their year old daughter being cared for by his mother.
>
> When he started describing the medical atrocities he had witnessed during his many prison years, he would become agitated. For example, about the two prisoners, slumped over a table in the upper exercise yard, obviously impaired and in no condition to move. Fifteen minutes after the order to report to the gate by the tower guard, one of them was taken to medical aid and pronounced dead—drug overdose.
>
> And the story about the cripple with a wooden leg, found unconscious on the cell floor. His neighbour who held an Industrial First Aid Ticket begged the guard to let him through to his friend. The man died while they were arguing the 'security regulations.'
>
> And the one whose styrofoam mattress—a perfect incendiary bomb—burst into flames. Twenty minutes of screaming before the key could be found to get him out of his cell—by which time his flesh was falling off. No fire extinguishers.
>
> "We actually had one inmate in the past year," he recalled, "who was improperly diagnosed, sent to hospital, and had the wrong operation performed, removing a vital organ as a result of the mistake."
>
> These were the kind of tragedies that fired John up.

Oct.24—2:00 p.m. Phoned "Operations" concerning Inmate Joseph E. States that his symptoms make him aware that he requires blood transfusion for his condition. He is having a problem getting to hospital as attending nurse in gym states it's not time for his transfusion, even tho, by date, he is past due. His needed intake of blood is not always consistent, but according to...stress, and he does require more as his disease progresses. The nurse has taken it on her own to deny him medical aid and overrule the doctor's duties. Lola was one of the 2 attending nurses. *(John Dow)*

Oct.24—4:00 p.m. Phoned #130 & #116 re. inmate Joseph E....his body reaction is acting up and feeling very sick. Mr. Magnuson stated he would get in touch with hospital. *(Gordie Duck)*

...4:05 p.m. P.S. As yet he has not left. Apparently as soon as escorts come back with Bob B. they'll take Joseph to hospital.

...4:27 p.m. Inmate Joseph E. has left for hospital at 4:26 p.m. *(Gordie Duck)*

Oct.24—4:45 p.m. Phoned Mr. Russell #130, regarding Myer M. He is in very bad mental condition and was requesting cell in B-7 and/or North wing. I explained to Mr. Russell that Myer is in no condition to be put into cell and I suggested at least 2 day hospital observation. Tomorrow we will call and request psychiatric examination, because Myer is in state of passiveness where he doesn't care if he lives or not, and in fact is ready to just sit and let nature take its course.

Myself and several others had to talk him into going to hospital. Actually we showed him that hospital was his best alternative in order for him to get couple nights of sound sleep. He left the gym at 5:00 p.m. and went to hospital. Will check his condition and whereabouts tomorrow. All of his personal belongings are in the gym in two boxes and are tagged with his name. *(Ivan Horvat)*

Oct.24—5:00 p.m. Joseph E. returned from hospital. *(Ivan Horvat)*

Oct.24—5:05 p.m. Further requested that inmate Brian I. be seen by psychiatrist and moved from gym because of mental problems. Concern is that the forceful removal of undesirable inmates (example other night) might repeat itself. Mr. Russell assured me that they would look into it tomorrow morning. *(Ivan Horvat)*

Oct.24—5:30 p.m. Myer M. just returned to gym to pick up his personal belongings and said that he is going to North wing. Tried contacting Mr. Russell but he is out eating?? I was assured that Myer would go to the *hospital* for at least a night. Also Mr. Swan and Mr. Byman assured us at last meeting that no inmates from the gym would go to North wing. Checking further. *(Ivan Horvat)*

Oct.24—7:00 p.m. Phoned operations and tried to find out who authorized or sanctioned Myer to move to North wing (3C—according to Guard's Log). Could get no answer. *(Ivan Horvat)*

Oct.24—7:15 p.m. Mr. Russell called regarding Myer and told me that Mr. Swan made exception in his case and did put him into North wing after hospital checked him out. I questioned why and how, seeing that Myer's problems are psychological and not physical. I told him that only a psychiatrist is qualified to say whether or not it's safe for him to be in a cell. The man is suicidal and also in a very dangerous self-orientated psychotic state.

Aside from that, the original agreement under which Myer M. went out of the gym was that he would be checked in to the hospital for couple of days or until proper psychological help was available. *Also, we were promised that no one would go to North wing. (Ivan Horvat)*

Oct.24—7:25 p.m. Mr. Russell called again and told me that he just talked to Myer, and that Myer is satisfied with North wing and feels that he will get the rest and quiet needed there. Fine and dandy. But that's not the fucking point! I don't think that, at this point, Myer is really responsible for what he says, and I think that he got the short end of the stick. Will take it up with Berkey and Swan tomorrow. *(Ivan Horvat)*

Oct.26—3:10 p.m. Doug up on visit with Dr. was told that if he wished to have medication for an abcessed jaw then he would first have to move to B-7 cell. This would appear that man is being levered as to being given proper medical attention and the Dr. is going out of the medical field into custody!! Gordon Duck phoned Mr. Scott about 3:30 p.m. to correct problem. *(John Dow)*

Oct.26—1:35 a.m. Phoned "Operations" re. Pat. We didn't receive his medication when the nurse made her rounds. I was told that the nurse would be around to the gym in about ten minutes. *(Ivan Horvat)*

Inmate Committee B.C.Penitentiary

RCMP Supervisor,   Oct.27/76
B.C.Penitentiary

Dear Sir,

Following a visit to the B-7 living unit, it was determined that the following medical problems were in existence in that area:

2-F-5   Lee W. Needs his medication both AM and PM but has not been receiving it;

2-H-2   Roger C. Has attempted to see the physician for a number of days to no avail;

4-F-5   Bill D. Has attempted to see the physician for a number of days to no avail;

4-F-9   Donald P. Needs his prescribed medication at night but has not been receiving it.

Will you kindly take whatever necessary steps to correct this situation. Your assistance, as always, is deeply appreciated.

Sincerely,
Gordie Duck,
Inmate Committee

Oct.28—9:00 p.m. Mr. Russell phoned stating that inmate Gary Y. had arrived in hospital and was being treated for lacerations self-inflicted, that he would be returned as soon as the stitching was complete. *(John Dow)*

Oct.28—9:50 p.m. Gary Y. back to auditorium door to tell the rest of the guys that he is OK and would be back by 10:00 p.m. The reason for him coming back was that the guys in the gym said that unless he was back by that time they were going to demand a reason as to why he wasn't back. The treatment of Gary's legs was going to take longer then expected, so he came back for reassurance. *(Ivan Horvat)*

Oct.29—5:40 p.m. Inmate Gary Y. was taken to hospital with self-inflicted lacerations. Stated that he needed medication and slashed when not allotted. *(John Dow)*

*   *   *

Not all prisoners go in for self-mutilation. Some see it as a cheap device to get attention. They feel they are 'slashed' enough by the system without doing it to themselves, too.

However, it also demonstrates the dehumanizing prison atmosphere which reduces men and women to take such desperate measures. When a person feels they can no longer cope with their mental suffering, by inducing physical pain they are then able to create a situation which *can* be eased. Bleeding wounds are relatively simple to treat. Staring at four walls for twenty years is not.

Dr. Korn, when asked a question about comparing solitary confinement with whipping, or other forms of physical punishment, stated: "The evidence simply is that if you keep people long enough, they will engage in self-torture, simply to focus the pain. So obviously, if the inmate chooses the infliction of...physical punishment, they have indicated the answer to that question. Physical pain which is definite, which I can control...is much more bearable than a torment that I can neither understand nor control."*

*   *   *

Oct.29—6:45 p.m. Just phoned "Operations" for assurance that Gary Y. would return from the hospital after his self-inflicted leg wounds are looked after. The reason of concern was that if he doesn't come back within a certain time span, several other prisoners will slash up... apparently Gary told the RCMP corporal that at precisely *6:30 p.m.* he would further cut his leg unless the B.C.Pen doctor starts to act in a professional manner and prescribes the medication necessary to keep the gym prisoners up to date with their prescriptions and sleeping medications...at *6:28 p.m.* RCMP Corporal returned and said that Mr. Flanigan (B.C.Pen keeper) advised him that the Dr. said that he would not prescribe any further medication and whatever medication that is already prescribed would be forthcoming, but no more...I passed on the message to people in question...*6:30 p.m.* Gary came to the gym gate bleeding profusely, and the B.C.Pen staff told him that until the escort gets there he would have to wait. RCMP Corporal came back and Gary went to hospital with him.... *(I.H.)*

Oct.29—7:20 p.m. Asked about Larry L.'s medication for migraine, 692's. Previous answer was that he'd get night medication but nothing for migraine. Larry claims that on his file it clearly states that he must have 692's whenever he needs them because of migraine headaches.

...7:30 p.m. Mr. Haines called to inform me that they still hadn't had time to check into Larry L.'s files and further that if Gary Y. keeps on occupying so much of their time, they will never get around to getting the other guys' medication straightened out. I asked if it might be more convenient if I called the hospital direct or if they might call me. Mr. H. checked and informed me that if I phoned direct they wouldn't much appreciate it because it will take up more of their time. My reply—"Since none of the committee members are worried about medication it is nothing personal..." etc. *(Ivan Horvat)*

Minutes of Proceedings, Issue No.29, Feb.15/77, pp.29A:52.

Oct.29—8:00 p.m. Gary Y. on his way to hospital with new slashes. *(Ivan Horvat)*

Oct.29—8:30 p.m. Gary Y. left for hospital with two escorts....

...9:15 p.m. Dr. Lipinski here. Talked to Gary Y. before coming down here...was asked to advise medical authorities about the medical problems and conditions here. Gary back from the outside hospital about midnight. Everything coposetic. *(J.J.)*

Oct.30—3:00 p.m. Phoned operations and talked to Mr. Hamer with regards to inmate Harry A. who has what appears to be an inner ear infection...requires immediate medical attention...requested he be taken to hospital and medical aid without delay. Attending nurse offered the alternative of coming to the bars of the gym and checking the patient through the bars. This seemed...a very inefficient method. For ear infection only a doctor is qualified. *(Paul Leister)*

Oct.30—6:05 p.m. After inspection of inmate Harry A. medication promised for treatment of ear. Nurse Sharon came to gym at 6:05 p.m. and knew nothing of medication, ear drops...or even aware of condition of inmate Harry A. Common occurrence...as many patients have been left neglected through lack of cooperation and exchange of information from shift to shift, and by people who are paid as responsible staff. Often...wrong prescribed medications are administered.

...6:30 p.m. ...medications arrived. Ear treated....*(John Dow)*

Oct. 31—11:00 p.m. Operations contacted...re. Bob S....has been out of crutches a very short time as of a long prolonged injury to his leg...many operations and marrow replacement...pain unbearable... obviously required medication more so than for someone obtaining it for pleasure...Nurse Marie was observed on the stairway talking to B. He politely requested that she go back to the hospital and check his medical file and she would realize he was not giving her a story, but had to have it due to severe pain...she gave a definite "NO" to him, refused to discuss it or check his file...due to a hostile feeling developing amongst the remaining inmates in the gym, the Committee members feared reprisals and requested the presence of the RCMP...to avoid further outbreaks and trouble...Committee feels that Nurse's judgment is irrational and non-competent, unfair and that she personally dislikes the patient and has allowed that to be the ruling factor of her decision...how many inmates have been kept awake endless nights by the moaning of an 'alleged' sick inmate who cries out in pain in his sleep. Inmates can and do in fact suffer pain just as other animals and patients in other hospitals outside of prisons. *(John Dow)*

Nov.1 HAPPY BIRTHDAY, JACK.

Nov.1—11:20 a.m. Inmate Committee member Omer Prud'homme #5766 phoned hospital at 10 a.m. requesting medication...been suffering from a throat infection for 3 days...nurse said "No...I only administer medication for flu and sore throats in the morning and at nights. If your throat is sore at any other time you're out of luck." Omer has been bringing up blood in his sputum and is not addicted to any drugs. Mother Nature doesn't work on a time schedule as to when sickness is applied and it seems very absurd and assinine that the nurse should react this way to a legitimate sickness. Jean is the acting nurse. *(John Dow)*

Nov.1—3:30 p.m. Called operations 248—and asked the officer there to phone the hospital and see if he can get in touch with the doctor. Reason being that the doctor's patient list for today was quite lengthy, and the doctor saw only 3 people this morning...called back that the Dr. saw a "few" people this morning then he got called away to a meeting...comment: Doctor sure receives good salary for seeing three patients a day. I foresee trouble tonight. *(Ivan Horvat)*

Nov.2—2:50 a.m. Gary Y. on his way to the hospital again. New slashes. *(I. H.)*

...3:30 a.m. Gary returned from hospital and told me that he would be going back there at 3:45 a.m.

...3:47 a.m. Called Operations (Mr. Adams) to inform him that we need an escort for Gary Y. who slashed again. *(I.H.)*

Nov.7—10:00 a.m. ...Andy W. had been received in hospital and given medical treatment after slashing. *(John Dow)*

Nov.7—3:05 p.m. Mr. Hadvick called to inform us that Tommy G. was being taken to Royal Columbian Hospital in order to receive treatment for slashing. *(I.H.)*

Nov.8—1:45 a.m. Keeper on way down to gym. Don D. wants to go to the hospital and wants committee member to go with him. Possible concussion. *(I.H.)*

Nov.10—3:05 a.m. Called hospital re. Howard M. wishing to check in to the hospital because of heavy depression. He wants to stay there for a couple of days to straighten his head and then come back. *(I.H.)*

Nov.10—10:30 a.m. I was assured again by "Operations" that Howard M. and Larry L. would get prompt medical attention. *(I.H.)*

Nov.13—3:40 a.m. The following note and list was received by me at 3:40 a.m.
"We would appreciate some sleeping medication before things get out of hand. If we got the right dosage first of all, there would be no need for extra lists...most of us have had two days sleep out of seven. (eleven names on list) *(Paul Leister)*

Nov.14—4:15 a.m. Clarence P. just slashed. *(Paul Leister)*

Nov.14—4:20 a.m. Mr. Macbeth just called to say the men at the gym entrance wanted more medication to calm their nerves after what happened, and the nurse refused. *(Paul Leister)*

Nov.15—2:00 p.m. Checked as to when Clarence P. will be released from hospital and the answer was?? Some guys concerned that they are going to start *kidnapping* hospital cases. P.S. Clarence P. was subsequently taken from hospital to the 'hole.' *(I.H.)*

Nov.15—2:00 p.m. Tommy G. is being admitted to hospital. *(Lea Sheppe)*

Nov.15—3:00 p.m. This log entry refers to last night. Gary Lake and myself went around the gym talking to several groups of inmates regarding our present situation, prolonged stalemate, medical situation and the aggressions that the over-abundant medications causes.
The observation was that there is very little we can do regarding the solution of B.C.Pen problems because we aren't given a chance to offer constructive solutions. As for medication, the problem with it is that Chloral is a hypnotic and its effects are that the more a man takes the more of it he wants. What we need is night tranquillizers which will relax and induce sleep, rather than "opiates" now being distributed. The suggestion was Nembutal or Mandrex. Will suggest to doctor. *(Ivan Horvat)*

Nov.15—3:10 p.m. Phil L. just slashed. Being taken to hospital. *(Paul Leister)*

Nov.19—11:10 a.m. I went to the hospital and as I was going up the stairs one guard shouted to another, "Get a couple of big guys up the hospital and prepare an SMU cell." I thought it was just a crack at me, but when I came back I found that Phil L. was next going to the hospital. I suspect foul play. Phil has been threatened many times. *(Ivan Horvat)*

Nov.19—11:50 a.m. Phil L. just returned from the hospital. *(Lea Sheppe)*

*　　　*　　　*

Lack of medical care was only one of many problems the men faced in the gym:

Riot In Cell Block Canada

"This is not a normal riot," one of the inmates explained, "there has been no demand for escape. This is a movement."...the movement seemed to have spread...Québec's Laval Institution...246 prisoners rioted setting fire to main cell block after embarking on a prolonged hunger strike to back demands to be transferred...in four year old Millhaven Maximum in Ontario inmates wrecked 100 cells in 2 days of uprisings before they were finally quelled by tear gas. In Saskatchewan Penitentiary, Prince Albert, a lone inmate psychiatric patient held a doctor hostage for an hour while he demanded and received a transfer...*extremely well-organized...surprisingly self-controlled members demanding* (at the B.C.Pen) better living conditions, access to media, and no physical reprisals for their actions.

Fox toughly announced government would not tolerate prison disturbances, and would move quickly to dispel them with RCMP, with army, with tear gas and with anything else needed to convince inmates "there is nothing to gain by that type of action."

Cons are not trying to get out of paying their dues but are only trying to maintain their dignity. Michael Jackson: "...demands prisoners are making coincide with an emerging pattern in society in which people on the lowest rungs—welfare recipients and prison inmates—whose lives are totally controlled by the system are saying: 'Look, we're people too.'...in that respect it's all part of a civil rights movement."

One of the ways to defuse tension in the prisons, argue Jackson and others, is to "share power with the cons—let the cons run it." Why not make the B.C.Pen a pilot project? he asks.*

Together with such medical problems, the prisoners had to deal with one another, the administration, and the guards.

Oct.18—5:15 p.m. Heard telephone being dialed from the gun-cage. Since it is the same extension as ours it is obvious that the guards had it off the hook all the time. Lake and myself went and talked to them about it, and all they said was "Sometimes it works and sometimes it doesn't." *(Ivan Horvat)*

Oct.18—7:00 p.m. Telephone not in working order again. Sabotage suspected. Fear of emergencies high. *(I.H.)*

Oct.18— Some inmates in B-7 were complaining about not being able to shower for 3 or 4 days at a time. They are getting 30-45 minutes a day exercise in the corridor. 6 inmates at a time are allowed to exercise in corridor. *(Lea Sheppe)*

Mr. Ken Peterson,   Oct.18/76
Acting Director,
Dear Sir:
    Because there seems to be constant confusion regarding the status of the Inmate Committee, whether meetings between your office and others in the situation are permissible, will you kindly authorize the Committee to telephone Mr. C.G. Rutter, Director Inmate Affairs, Ottawa, or to Mr. Therrien, Commissioner, so we can get a clear outline as to our function and status now and for the immediate future?
    I'm sure you will understand and agree that the emergency condition in the gymnasium—the fact that out of the 200 plus men living there, over 40 of them have the flu and other medical problems, the lack of exercise, fresh air, hot food, etc.—that clarification from Ottawa is quite justified.
                                      Respectfully, Ivan Horvat

*McLean's Magazine, Oct.18/76.

To Whom It May Concern:

...inmates who advocate moving Security out to the perimeter of the prison are quick to point out how successful the University of Victoria program has been without Security input. For the first time in Canadian history, prison inmates will graduate this year with Bachelor of Arts degrees.... We could never have done it if Security had been involved...the rest of the prison would work just as well if the Solicitor General would take Security out of the inner workings of the prison. Security has gone beyond its normal function. They have taken over every facet of operating the prisons. The Directors do not run them anymore. Security does.

If you want a bar of soap to take a shower, you have to see Security.

What does Security have to do with taking a shower?

...Now that Security is unionized, it has become politically expedient to intentionally create turmoil behind the wall. Otherwise the Union could not justify additions to its staff. And turmoil can easily be created by even one Security (Union) Supervisor if he intentionally delays the count at Recreation time, fails to call a prisoner waiting for a visit, delays feedings, etc.

Security has become the biggest evil in the prison system.*

*Canada Doesn't Have to Execute People Any More
    Just Sentence Them to Neglect*

...Since 1970 there have been 62 suicides in Federal prisons. There is the disaster of the guards' situation. Underpaid, undertrained...at war with the progressive elements in the penal system, they are even more cynical than the public towards their prisons. At B.C.Pen the turnover rate among senior security people reached 75% to 80% in 1974...[when] they put on a crash program to

*from a Statement prepared by the Inmate Committee of B.C.Penitentiary, Oct.18/76.

recruit and train new guards...they got 50 people. Within two months half of them had quit.

Dragan Cernetic, Director of the B.C.Pen...a progressive in prison reform but concedes that guards run his prison...each time the guards locked prisoners in their cells and reported that "tension" within the prison forced cancellation of Cernetic's plan.

Since hope is all a prisoner has, the warfare inside and suicide are bound to increase...puzzling why we have to put more people in jail (per capita) than England, Denmark, Sweden, France, Italy, Japan, Spain, Norway and Holland...it is remarkable that our prisons are now wiping out the reputations of Sing Sing and Alcatraz and are approaching Attica.*

Oct.18/76

To Whom It May Concern: *Re. Current Conditions in S.M.U.*

Gentlemen:

The following letter has just been received from the general inmate population. Copies of it will be going to the RCMP, the C.A.C and to Ottawa:

The prisoners in the auditorium have been made aware of the situation now prevailing in SMU and everyone is extremely concerned. The conditions that we refer to are as follows:

1) The severe beating of prisoners Miller and Surrette;
2) Fire hoses being used on certain prisoners;
3) Guards tampering with and stealing allotted food rations;
4) The lack of eating utensils of any kind—necessitating the use of hands to eat cold tinned foods;

*Allan Fotheringham, *Maclean's Magazine*, Oct.18/76.

5) Mail being improperly and illegally held up;
6) Lack of exercise and fresh air;
7) Lack of proper medical attention and general dereliction of duty by the Medical Staff.

We, as a group, feel it is very important that the above conditions cease immediately! We have all seen that the filing of complaints through "proper" channels is of no avail. It is exactly the conditions described above (and complaints, pleas, writs, requests) left unheeded that lead to extreme frustration and anger among prisoners in both the general population and SMU which further leads to hostage-taking incidents, riots, violence against guards and further disruption of all descriptions.

We feel it is obvious that the Penitentiary Administration is solely responsible for the prevailing conditions and should be held responsible and accountable for their change.

It should also be obvious to the public when they are made fully aware; consider it is a *fact* that the only incidents of violence against prisoners during the "riot" and the weeks following the riot have been in the only area of the institution where penitentiary guards were and are in control (in SMU where the prisoners are locked securely in their cells). In all the rest of the institution under RCMP and Army control there has been NOT ONE incident of violence, either on behalf of the prisoners or their temporary keepers. It should also be pointed out that the Pen guards are in custody of only ten prisoners in SMU and TWO OF THEM HAVE BEEN SEVERELY BEATEN!! while in the rest of the institution over 400 prisoners have been handled and controlled with not so much as a wrestling match!

—Inmate Population

The Inmate Committee, of course, unanimously endorses, supports and joins the general population in the

above-described complaint. We also firmly suggest that
brutality in SMU be brought to an immediate standstill.

Respectfully, Ivan Horvat,
President, Inmate Committee

cc. RCMP Supervisors (Northorp and Neils)
    RCMP Corporal Reid
    André Therrien, Commissioner
    Director of B.C.Pen
    Acting/Director of B.C.Pen
    Inmate Committee file.

*   *   *

The Inmate Committee continued to try to meet with the
Administration in order to head off trouble:

Director Regional Transfer Board,   Oct.19/76
B.C.Penitentiary.

Dear Sir,

Following the recent disturbance at the B.C.Pen, and
after all inmates were moved from damaged areas of the
prison (including the Regional Reception Centre) to the
gymnasium, lists were prepared by all inmates as to where
they wished to be transferred, as per the Memorandum
of Agreement.

The institutions of choice were collected by the Inmate
Committee and forwarded to the Transfer Board. The
reason for the lists is obvious: that primarily no inmate
would accept transfer where it would take him far from his
family and loved ones.

Today, Oct.19/76, we were informed by Ms. Jean
Simonds, Chairperson, Regional Transfer Board, that *no
such lists were received* by the Transfer Board. The lists
were typed and forwarded on the 3rd and 4th of October
via the Department of Security.

Duplicate copies are attached.

Sincerely,
Ivan Horvat, President.

*   *   *

Oct.19—10:45 a.m. Michael Jackson and another C.A.C. member were just here....We were told that they would go to SMSU and interview prisoners up there.

We gave them the Agenda for meeting with the Administration tomorrow and Jackson said he would try to be present...[They] talked to prisoners in the gym. All in all, they *expressed dissatisfaction with the way transfers are being handled—just on paper and not in actuality. (Ivan Horvat)*

*   *   *

The longer the men were held in the gym under these intolerable conditions the more likely there were to be "incidents." The accumulation of such events was calculated to create an 'explosion.' The Log, I feel, shows this inevitable build-up of pressures, hour by hour, and day by day.

*   *   *

Oct.20—4:20 p.m. While six of the I.C. members were walking up centre stairs and around to rear door of dome...two Security guards had firearms pointed directly at them. Officer Butcher cocked the firearm he was holding three times while weapon was still pointing at men. It occurs to one that the weapon could accidentally discharge and seems a very unnecessary manoeuvre. We suggest that this man not be allowed to handle firearms if he can't display more competent use of same, such as doing so only when situation calls for. *(John Dow)*

Arthur Lee, M.P.   Oct.20/76
Office of the Solicitor General of Canada.

Dear Mr. Lee,

Further to our lengthy conversation on October 17 and a meeting of the Citizens Advisory Committee on October 18, the Committee has asked me to communicate our sense of urgency that the B.C.Penitentiary be normalized rapidly...to further de-escalate the...flammable situation.

...believe that the *most expeditious way to normalize activities*...and to minimize further confrontation *is to resolve the transfer process.*

From an initial number of approximately 250 inmates

contained in the gymnasium area almost three weeks ago, the number has been reduced to [only] approximately 200.

Very truly yours,
Edwin Lipinsky, M.D.
Chairman, C.A.C.

Mr. W.R. Swan,   Oct.20/76
Acting Director,
B.C.Pen

Dear Mr. Swan,

Based upon your comment at today's meeting that you desire the inmate population and Staff to work a bit closer together, or words to that effect, and our own numerous requests to previous Executive of the Institution including the president of the local PSAC, and others, may we respectfully request that at some time in the near future, the Committee with members of the Citizens Advisory Committee in attendance, sit down with you, members of the Union, and Security Staff in an effort to open an intelligent avenue of communications.

In that way, we feel many of the problems that now seem impossible to overcome, will eventually be diminished and vanish.

We look forward to your reply.

Sincerely,
Inmate Committee

*   *   *

With no open, sensible, intelligent communication, the situation continued to deteriorate.

*   *   *

Oct.22. At about 8:00 a.m. two officers at the side gate of the gym threatened to urinate in the soup. Another officer in charge of the 'hole' told Rick W., "Wait until I get you upstairs." Because of these threats and other comments made that the medication "should not be brought down," someone threw water through the shower door at the officer on duty at the gym entrance. The Committee is taking steps to stop the water throwing. *(Paul Leister)*

Oct.22—2:25 p.m. Mr. Berkey called and told me the "sounding like rock throwing" on the gym roof was...seagulls picking up the empty food cans and dropping the cans on the gym roof.... *(Lea Sheppe)*

Oct.22—2:45 p.m. I was called to the auditorium window and was informed that the side door to the gymnasium was barricaded by the Security and that the guys, due to heat and lack of fresh air, pushed the door out which resulted in a bent bar and some insults thrown at Mr. Lakusta [head of the guards' union] who was at the scene.

I subsequently called Operations #248 and asked why was the door barricaded in the first place. I was told that Mr. Berkey issued the order to barricade all doors, the side entrance especially because he said that canned food was thrown at his officers. We weren't informed about the barricade nor when it was going up.

In turn, I told the duty officer that the side door must remain open because the men need fresh air, because now the fans aren't working and there is lots of smoke in the gym. He informed me that he would pass that on to Mr. Lakusta who is in charge of the institution.

Since the door is already busted, for tonight it will lay until we talk to Mr. Berkey tomorrow. *(Ivan Horvat)*

Oct.22—3:00 p.m. Talked to Chief Engineer and he asked me if he can put wire-mesh on the front door of the gymnasium (because of last night's incident). We suggested he put plexi-glass and plywood and be done with it. *(Ivan Horvat)*

Oct.22—3:30 p.m. Went to see Ron Stern [lawyer]...to get the negotiating transcripts for us...saw Marie Resanovich [classification officer] and she said she had seen Cernetic and he was pleased with the way we have been operating. She said if she is called to the inquiry she will tell the truth about everything. *(Omer Prud'homme)*

OMER PRUD'HOMME: took his vice-presidency of the Inmate Committee very seriously. He followed up every complaint and irregularity as they were reported to him. Omer was also the one who made sure that whenever food and smokes came our way in the PTI they were shared around.

The following September, I had a fifteen minute 'visit' with him in the lobby of the 7th floor of the Federal Court—the only way I was able to see any of the prisoners, once my visiting rights were cut

off, was when they came to court. He was at Mountain Prison,
Agassiz at that time.

Omer later signed an Affidavit describing what had occurred that
particular afternoon after I had left him:

At the Federal Court on the aforesaid date (8 Sept. 1977) I was
approached by D. McGregor...(Regional Director, Canadian
Penitentiary Service, Western Region), who inquired of me if I was
aware of a "rumor" going about to the effect that during the
events of September 1976 at the B.C.Penitentiary Claire Culhane
was having an affair with the aforementioned "Gordie Duck," and
inquired if I knew whether or not such a "rumor" was true.

That I was shocked to hear that such a rumor could even exist,
that in my view there had been no such affair, that there had been
no opportunity for such an affair to take place, that custodial
surveillance was always close by, that Claire Culhane did not strike
me as the type of person who would take part in any such affair,
and for these reasons expressed my doubts to D. McGregor, that
such a "rumor" could exist in fact.

Upon assurance that such a "rumor" existed, I then replied to
the effect that it had been suggested that inmates have "dirty
minds" but in fact it would appear that if custodial staff or any
other member of the Penitentiary Service gave origin to such a
rumor, they would have dirtier minds than inmates generally, and
walked away from the said D. McGregor, terminating our
conversation. (*excerpt*)

Oct.22—4:00 p.m. On my way to the legal visit I was handcuffed and
the escorting officers...told me that handcuffs were not an order from
Mr. Berkey but that it was discretional power of the escorting officer
and can be practised at will. The committee member who went to legal
visit before me was not handcuffed. *(Ivan Horvat)*

Oct.23—2:30 a.m. Mr. Havelick just phoned and asked me about
several fights that broke out in the gym. I informed him that there were
only two instances where blows were exchanged and that they were
personal beefs. I told Mr. Havelick that I didn't think there was any
reason for B.C.Pen Security Staff to get excited or trigger-happy. *(Ivan
Horvat)*

Oct.23—4:20 a.m. I suggest strongly that the Committee call an
emergency meeting with Acting Director Swan to push for outside yard

immediately. We have to eliminate this growing restless energy. I demand this action quickly. *(Unsigned)*

Oct.23—4:40 a.m. At approximately 4:30 a.m. Inmate Peter C. was injured in a scuffle and was taken to hospital with what appeared to be a broken nose and facial lacerations. Shortly after another inmate Matthew G. was also injured and taken to hospital suffering bruises and facial lacerations. . . . Some inmates who wish to sleep at night are irate with inmates who don't and prefer to make noise. The entire population of the gym seem to be in a state of apprehensiveness and unrest due to the lack of exercise and fresh air. Many are suffering from the virus and tempers are simply short. *(John Dow)*

Oct.23—4:50 a.m. Samuel H. was taken from gymnasium with bruises and in a state of shock. At 5:45 a.m. Inmate Colin J. was removed from gym to hospital site with bruises and facial lacerations. *(John Dow)*

Oct.23—6:00 a.m. Inmate John Z. left gymnasium, by request. *(unsigned)*

Oct.23—6:15 a.m. Omer Prud'homme, Gordie Duck and myself were called to the main dome [where the three wings—East, North and B-7—converge] by Mr. Swan and Mr. Berkey who told us to relay to the population the following:

It was their opinion that the inmates in the auditorium have violated the Memorandum of Agreement by committing physical violence on each other, and if this continues, they would use whatever force necessary to remove inmates from the gym.

Further to that, Mr. Swan said that threats and violence from inmates towards guards must stop, and that he issued same orders to the guards in regards to their threats to the inmates.

Inmate Committee members summed up the situation and attempted to analyze the reason for tonight's violence (no yard, close quarters for such length of time, no transfers, etc.). Mr. Swan said that his staff and himself would meet with the Inmates Committee later in the day. On the way out of the dome, Committee members expressed that the Inmate Committee can hardly take responsibility for individual persons under such conditions. Mr. Bradley CS-2 jumped up and said: "You guys are supposed to control the mob." Inmate Committee member Duck replied that it is not the function of Inmate Committee to control anyone. In short, Mr. Bradley, who is known to have big mouth at the best of times, started his bullshit and Mr. Swan told him to shut up, and the meeting ended.

The population in the gym was informed. *(Ivan Horvat)*

P.S. RCMP Corporal was present in the dome, had evidence to most of what took place. *(Gordie Duck)*

*   *   *

In response to the Director's orders, the Inmate Committee offer their analysis and propose remedies:

From: Population (Auditorium)   Oct.23/76
To: B.C.Penitentiary Administration c/o C.A.C.

The prisoners in the auditorium would like to point out to the B.C.Pen Administration and to the Citizens Advisory Committee that the reason for the violence in the auditorium this morning was and is caused by the rapidly deteriorating conditions in the auditorium. These conditions are as follows:

1. Medical Attention: There are persons in the auditorium who are diabetics who are not receiving proper diets and medication. There are persons with heart disease who have not been able to see the doctor. Epileptics are not receiving proper medication; persons with serious respiratory ailments, coughs, colds, not receiving proper attention. There are persons with severe nervous conditions who are unable to see a psychiatrist or Medical Officer to receive proper tranquillizers and sleeping medication. There are persons who go without sleep for 3 or 4 days at a time because of anxiety, etc. caused by the overcrowded conditions, lack of fresh air and exercise, etc. Tension has been building for the past 3 weeks and we believe that the result of this build up was viewed this morning. We believe that it should have been (and is) quite obvious to the Administration that this or other violence was bound to occur eventually. Any dime store psychologist could have predicted this, and we can only conjecture what motives were and are behind allowing conditions to exist as they are.

(There is enormous speculation on this point which only adds to the frustration of the prisoner.)

2. Transfers: There have been no serious attempts to relieve the overcrowded conditions by transferring at least some of the prisoners. We are told that there is "no room anywhere" though many persons have appeared before the Transfer Board and have been cleared to go to various other institutions. Inmates from the North wing and B-7 have been given preference over prisoners in the auditorium for transfer to the institutions where there is room. This fact quite obviously further increases tension and frustration among the prisoners in the auditorium.

3. Visits: There have been no visits allowed for any of the prisoners in the auditorium with the exception of lawyer visits.

In summation, we would point out that although none of us is quite sure what "agreements" have been made and are or are not being carried out, we are all quite sure of our situation and the conditons we are living in and we do not feel that we have broken any "agreement." We know that we are living in very unhealthy conditions and those conditions are deteriorating both mentally and physically as a result. The violence of this morning is evidence of that. The wonder of it is that it has not occurred before this.

We say, unanimously, that if the conditions here begin to improve dramatically, in a short while, then we can talk about "agreements," etc. Until then, human nature shall take its course.

*   *   *

Oct.23—6:00 p.m. RCMP Inspector Northorp asked Committee members (present in auditorium, John Dow and Lea Sheppe) if conditions of men's attitudes were at such a state that could come to further fights or uprisings. That he was there to evaluate the situation. Due to the present move or transfer allotted to some of the inmates to B-7 cells and the classifying of those for transfers commencing, it was felt that the chances of outbreak were greatly decreased. It gave the inmates assurance that there was and is eventual hope of either being transferred now or later, and not being locked up in a cell and forgotten...consideration of being transferred to out-of-province has been totally abandoned, and no further considerations would be made...it was made clear that no guarantee of mild eruptions not occurring, since people cooped up without recreation and proper facilities can only tend to become irritative, and often unruly, but that the probability of keeping the situation at a controlled level was more assured. *(John Dow)*

Oct.23—8:10 p.m. After finally trying to get to the gym and being told that only two I.C. members can go downstairs at a time, I called operations trying to confirm Mr. Berkey's orders of two days ago, that any number of I.C. members can go to the gym floor provided that they go through the door one at a time.

They checked in operations and told me (Mr. Russell) that they never heard of new orders and that no more than two I.C. members would be able to go down to the gym. At *8:25 p.m.* Mr. Russell called back to tell me that I was indeed right and that any number of us can go and stay on the gym floor, but one at a time movement must be observed when going through the doors...he would also inform officers on duty... *(Ivan Horvat)*

Oct.23—6:30 p.m. Received some disinfectant for PTI office and asked about getting a five gallon bucket of it for the washroom in the gym. I told them that a five gallon bucket was given to the guards a week ago to be refilled but hasn't been done yet. The guard said he would try and get it today. *(Lea Sheppe)*

Oct.24—10:37 a.m. Inmates Andy W., Jones, Brown, Sweeney—ask that I call transfer board and check new list to see if they are being transferred prior to this transfer...new list came down stating names of people...above were not on the list...I was to check. I did. Party at #281 said he would phone back, but as yet has not done so. He would pull their file...take an hour. Hour long gone. Check in the morning if Transfer Board still in effect. *(Gordie Duck)*

Oct.24—Noon. Called Mr. Byman re. problems regarding Don D., Garry W., Floyd W., Keith C., Sweeney. All to do with transfers. Mr. Byman made note...and indicated he would personally see that they received a reply to their problem. *(Paul Leister)*

Oct.24—12:10 p.m. We understand that Michael Jackson (C.A.C.) is in the institution and that he couldn't get down to the gym door because of transfer procedure. He came anyway but was there for only a minute or two before a B.C.Pen officer came and told him that he had to leave. We suggested that Mike goes to see Mr. Swan and ask about seeing us at the back door where there will be no interruption. He went to do just that . . . . *(Ivan Horvat)*

Oct.24—12:35 p.m. Mr. Swan called and said that he'll permit Mr. Jackson to see us at the back door but only this one time. *(Ivan Horvat)*

Oct.24—8:00 p.m. Mr. Russell called and expressed concern over guys throwing ropes to the gym ceiling. I told him that it probably is nothing more than supporters for tents which are being built because the men realize that they might be in the gym for awhile. All OK. *(Ivan Horvat)*

*   *   *

The Inmate Committee issued many press releases, but had no way of knowing if they even made it out of the institution. Few were published.

Oct.24/76
Press Release to All News Outlets From Inmate Committee

The recent riot at the B.C.Pen along with scores of hostage taking incidents, mysterious deaths, murders, suicides, deaths from drug overdoses, etc. were caused by circumstances some of which were political. In the appointment of a political body to investigate a serious situation such as exists at the B.C.Pen, some of which is caused by political matters, the new Solicitor General is obviously not interested in the true reasons for so much difficulty and turmoil at B.C.Pen and other Canadian prisons. He is more interested in making a political highway, not a factual highway.

As well, the prisoners continued to carefully spell out their needs to the Administration:

Mr. W.R. Swan, Director,   Oct.25/76
B.C.Penitentiary

Dear Sir:
1. The primary concern of the men in the auditorium is that no definite program has been established for the ones who

must remain here and eventually be returned to B-7. We would like to have a program established and ready to be put into effect immediately when the men agree to return to cells:

- *a)* How much fresh air exercise will be allowed? (We suggest as little time as possible to be spent in cells.)
- *b)* What will night recreation consist of? (We suggest that if the TV lounge is not acceptable, that TV's and card tables be placed in B-7 corridors.)
- *c)* When visiting privileges are restored we suggest since there will be a considerable decrease in population, that the open visit program be expanded to one per week for approved inmates. (When?)
- *d)* Will we have free access to the library? When?
- *e)* Will we have access to the hobby shop to order materials available before the disturbance? When?
- *f)* Will inmates not satisfied with the decision rendered by the Classification Board have the opportunity to appeal their decisions?
- *g)* If any members of the present committee are transferred, will an election be held immediately to fill those vacancies?
- *h)* Will the men have the opportunity to continue their university courses? How soon?

2. Another major concern is that the men in the auditorium who have been cleared for reduced security feel there has not been a sincere effort to reduce the overcrowded conditions and move the men.

- *a)* When will the transfers begin in earnest?
- *b)* When will Mission (institution) open?
- *c)* Why have inmates in Regional Reception Centre been receiving priority when actually we are the ones living in an uninhabitable area of the prison?

d) It is anticipated that the Transfer Board will finish today. Could we be *issued with a list that will be adhered to in the order the men will be transferred?*

e) What will be the procedure for visits for men housed in the gym? Will we be allowed our open visits?

3. Why are the balances not shown on our canteen slips which has always been the procedure?

*　　　*　　　*

Oct.25—8:34 p.m. Mr. Russell called regarding a break into music room (from the stage). I told him I was about as informed as he was, and that I could hardly predict how much trouble it might cause. Also, I told him that the Committee will do what it can to prevent any possible trouble. *(Ivan Horvat)*

P.S. Mackenzie?? went to hospital. Slash—check on him. *(I.H.)*

*　　　*　　　*

By this time the authorities could no longer ignore the gravity of holding the men in the gymnasium for so long.

---

17 B.C.Pen Inmates moved from prison gym following a minor disturbance in which three were injured, one with a suspected skull fracture. Jack Stewart: ''The inmates inside the gym are to be commended for keeping the peace as long as they have. They have been very responsible under difficult conditions.''

...202 inmates spending 24 hours a day in a basketball court size gym and none have been outside the gym for three weeks.

—*Province,* Oct.25/76

Oct.26—3:30 a.m. Operations phoned and it was stated they were disturbed over what appeared to sound like digging in the lower gym washroom area. A message was passed down by Gary Lake to cease any digging and notified the security guards at gym door who were satisfied that digging had ceased. *(John Dow)*

Oct.26—10:15 a.m. CX-2 Bradley sitting in the gun cage pointing a shotgun into the gym for no reason. Men antagonized by this unprofessional action and Mr. Bradley refuses to withdraw the shotgun.

I've called Mr. Nicholson at #116 requesting to talk to Mr. Swan. Also reporting on Mr. Bradley's bullshit trip. *(Ivan Horvat)*

Oct.26—3:15 p.m. At 2:30 p.m. Acting Dir. Swan spoke with inmate population in gym through intercom at which time he attempted to give answers to various questions laid forth by inmates. No definite commitments were made or clarifications...to the situation. The inmates were concerned with visiting privileges, work programs... general consensus of opinion was that no gains were made and that only lockup was guaranteed. *(John Dow)*

Oct.26—4:20 p.m. Mr. Swan phoned about the concern we felt on the water hose being left running and water running into the gym...stated he would have it turned off. *(Gordie Duck)*

Oct.27—12:45 p.m. Inmates on 1 and 2F have not had showers since last Thursday. Informed Mr. Scott. *(Lea Sheppe)*

Oct.27—1:30 p.m. Mr. Scott called to inform us that the library books which were promised to be here a week ago—that no one had done anything about it. I asked Mr. Scott to look into it again and take it as a new request rather than wait until Mr. Berkey is back at the end of the week. *(Ivan Horvat)*

Oct. 27. Inmates in B-7 on 4-F, 4-G and 4-E are saying that they are only getting to showers twice a week. *(Lea Sheppe)*

Oct.28—12:40 a.m. Just come from (gym) floor—have talked to subcommittee chairman and they are getting material together for the Committee meeting with Mr. Fox later today. Suggestion was to try to get one or two of *them* into the meeting, primarily because they are better informed of current turbulences in the gym. *(Ivan Horvat)*

Oct.28—8:45 a.m. Guard asked me to have tent removed from doorway...I said I'd doubt if they would move it. They said no food or anything would go to the gym to feed the guys until tent was moved from doorway. We came up with the agreement that if the fellows would lift flap and the guards could see into tent, that would do...guys lifted the flap, guard observed and approved. Meals went on as before. *(G. Duck)*

Oct.28—1:30 p.m. Went to B-7. Was there not five minutes and was chased out by Custody. Same thing happened to another I.C. member yesterday. I called Mr. Swan and told him not to give me any bullshit and if that's the fucking game they should just tell us that we can't go to B-7 and end it at that. Mr. Swan called back and told me that they are making arrangements to get me back to B-7 right now. (???) *(Ivan Horvat)*

*   *   *

The men in the gym wanted to tell their own story. Even though the Inmate Committee theoretically represented them, they were kept segregated in the PTI area and had difficulty even getting into the gym to collect their grievances.

*   *   *

Oct.28—1:35 p.m. Mr. Swan informed me that the Sol. Gen. will meet *only* with the Committee and not with any subcommittee members [from the gym]. *(Ivan Horvat)*

Oct.28—2:30 p.m. Went to B-7 again and this time I never even got further than B-7 gate. Got fucked again. Called Mr. Swan and told him that I don't appreciate being called twice to another wing of the institution just to be told to come back to the gym, especially after it was agreed that I.C. Members will have access to B-7 once a day. (Liberal access!). Swan told me that he will make arrangements for a special time once every morning for such B-7 tours. Also he told me that the morning is the best time to go.

I have informed Mr. Swan that I have nothing against mornings and in fact I called Mr. Scott yesterday and asked him to arrange just that. Since it became obvious that Mr. Scott didn't do anything about that request I started calling this noon and afternoon. Disorganization of B.C. Staff is very obvious. *(I.H.)*

Oct.28—3:30 p.m. Regular meeting of Inmate Committee called to meet with Sol. Gen. Fox—all present except for Lea Sheppe, left on duty at the gym...meeting opened by *Mr. Fox admitting he had not received the minutes which the I.C. had sent to him*...Jack Dow pointed out that when communication is broken between the I.C. and the men in SMU, B-7, etc. the danger of more trouble erupts...Mr. Jim Murphy, Reg. Dir...[said] it will be solved by tomorrow. Gordie Duck asked what is going to happen after things go back to 'normal'?...J.J. replied that since Mary Steinhauser had been killed this institution has NEVER been normal...Gordie Duck commented on the CX-8's who caused the riot [in the first place] and wondered if they would have the same power and authority to cause trouble again. [Many are still at the B.C.Pen in 1979, with same power.]

Mr. Fox asked for suggested solutions...members of the I.C. [said]...give authority back to the Director. [Not done.] Move Custody out of the inner workings of the prison. [Not done.]...also presented Mr. Fox with a carefully drawn paper suggesting a way in which, over the next few years, to CLOSE prisons rather than build new ones...but gym must be cleared first...men needed assurance that their transfers will be honoured....Mr. Byman said he and his staff never "screwed" anyone (!)...then pointed out to Mr. Fox that often times men are sent to camp, then kidnapped and sent back for no apparent reason...Mr. Byman said a transfer list would be posted....Committee pointed out that it had never been done in the past. Mr. Byman said it would be done in the future...(?)

Mr. Fox, when asked about the Parliamentary Commission [when] all parties had requested a judicial public inquiry...stated that he felt [it] would be the most public inquiry ever held...in the end be made fully public and not be shelved as many others [had been]....J.J. then described no open visits at least "for awhile"...Mr. Fox seemed surprised that there had been NO VISITS SINCE THE RIOT BEGAN...seemed reluctant to embarass the Director....

Oct.28/76

Inmate Committee
B.C.Penitentiary N.W.

Dear Mr. Solicitor General Fox,

You are in a position few men ever reach in a lifetime. You have the opportunity to take positive steps in curing the illness that has ravaged Canadian penology for decades....Any brutality, physical, psychological or otherwise, can easily be justified by stating that those who violate the law deserve nothing more. On the other hand, each time a person is consumed in the fire and evil of Canadian penology, a tiny bit of the social structure is ripped away forever....

If an individual, for whatever irrational reason, brutalizes society by the execution of anti-social conduct, and society retaliates by brutalizing the offender, *two* brutes are the result. Increase the number of brutes to a high enough number and the environment...will be torn asunder as were several prisons in recent weeks.

If Society is to turn back the tide of crime, stop the prison war that exploded into the headlines last month (and will explode in the headlines again) the alternative...*MUST* be adopted....

We hope you will consider seriously...not in the interest of politics, but in the interest of Canada as a whole. In the meantime, we wish you well in your new position.

Respectfully,
Inmate Committee

Oct.29—3:00 a.m. The regular nightly obscene phone call which we receive about two fucking o'clock in the morning was on time and prompt. *(Ivan Horvat)*

Oct.29—3:15 a.m. Some goof called and said he is going to call every half hour to make sure that we are O.K. I told him that we are fine and to let us sleep. I also asked him to identify himself and he said that he was Bugs Bunny, so I told him to go and fuck himself. *(I.H.)*

Oct.29—12:30 p.m. Went to B-7 at 10:45 a.m. Came back now. Everything was OK with one exception. When I was almost finished with the tour...on my way to the bottom floor an officer (Mr. Clayton) shouted and screamed from the PCU area, behind the bars. He said that if I understood anything at all that I should understand that *he* doesn't want me down there, and after repeating that about three times, he said that I can tell that to Swan too, but that I am not getting to those tiers.

Realizing that Mr. Clayton is obviously not a well man, I went back to B-7 dome and explained to Mr. Brown (the keeper) that there seems to be a problem down there, and that the Warden agreed that we (I.C.) would have an opportunity to see every inmate in B-7 and since there are inmates in those three tiers—it is imperative that I see them. Mr. Brown agreed and I proceeded to that area. When we got there, Mr. Clayton freaked out again and told my escort to get me out of the area. The escort with me ignored him totally and the B-7 tour was finished shortly thereafter. *(Ivan Horvat)*

Oct.29—1:10 p.m. Mr. Swan called, told me that he is aware of some tunnel building and brew drinking in the gym. I told Mr. Swan that we've done all possible and that everyone in the gym is aware of the fact that no one can go anywhere without getting their heads blown off. Also, as far as brew is concerned—what can one expect. The committee is busy with trying to keep guys from killing each other, and are doing what we can.

Mr. Swan layed a trip on me how we are supposed to be in control. . .we suggested that Mr. Swan himself tell the guys that he is aware of the tunnels, and to tell "them"—whoever "them" might be—what the consequences of such actions will be. *(I.H.)*

Oct.29—1:25 p.m. Called Swan re. B-7 move. He didn't know anything about the 25 prisoners in the gym who are packed and ready to go. He does now. *(I.H.)*

P.S. . . .B-7 problems are numerous. Most people not yet seen by the Transfer Board, hot water delivery not due, B-7 population wants to see Inmate Committee more often.

*   *   *

A month has passed. Over 50 prisoners are still held in the gym—still with no exercise, no visits, no programs, and transfers still dragging . . . .

*   *   *

Nov.1—1:00 p.m. While Michael Jackson (C.A.C.) was here, Berkey himself came down to the gym door, we enquired about an officer with a camera who was taking pictures of the gym. (Mr. Jackson witness). Berkey informed me that they were just taking pictures for the purpose of engineers—re. *fire hazard.* I reminded Mr. Berkey that no pictures can be taken of inmates without their permission (including release forms). . . .*(I.H.)*

Nov.1—1:35 p.m. Have called Mr. Berkey re. Mr. Swan's public statement that the guys in the gym were digging a tunnel. Mr. Berkey said that what had happened was that somehow the initial story leaked out and before publication the newspapers called. Swan checked. . . apparently told them there was no reason to believe that there was tunnel under construction but after he talked to the inmates in the gym—it supposedly stopped. I commented on the fact that press releases like that make guys paranoid—they think that it is a set up to justify any violence that may occur.

Also I commented on the fact that the same B.C.Pen officers that were most troublesome before the riot are still here and in fact are put right on the gym door duty. Berkey said he has to rotate his people, etc. He also said that he just came back from Ottawa and that he is confident that some good changes are on their way. *(I.H.)*

Prison System a Failure

...says Sol. Gen. Fox at a symposium on Canadian Prisons at U.B.C....Offenders must be provided with program opportunities that will help them develop daily living skills and confidence....

During a question and answer period, Claire Culhane, former member of the C.A.C., asked Fox if he was heading towards a more repressive system. He replied that his first task is to ensure order in the institution.

—*Comox District Free Press*, Nov.2/76

Nov.2—2:25 a.m. J.J. & Leister were called to the gym and told in no uncertain terms that if something isn't done soon, [if] a number of them aren't moved out of here [there will be] slashing on a major scale. J.J. telephoned Mr. Mangelson, the officer in charge of the institution. *(Paul Leister)*

Nov.2—2:45 a.m. Talked to RCMP Corporal Reid and Mr. Mangelson regarding the main problem in the gym. It was suggested that the RCMP brass and the Director B.C.Pen be awakened and called to B.C.Pen.... We feel that the solution to the problem is an immediate transfer of Floyd W., Gary Y., and Phil L. would quell most of the hostility in the gym. *(Ivan Horvat)*

Nov.2—2:45 a.m. Telephone off the hook in the gun cage....Got Mr. Jensen from the gym gate to radio to outside patrol and instruct them to tell the gun cage to put the phone back on the hook. Apparently it worked because the phone is now in functioning order. *(Ivan Horvat)*

Nov.2—8:50 a.m. At around *8:15 a.m.* while going downhill, Mr. Jensen stopped at gym side door and said to inmates, "Your meal this morning has been prepared by PCU inmates and will be served by them." Other abusive statements made to inmate population who are at a state of unrest and at nerves end, for the situation has been and is explosive. Mr. Berkey phoned at 8:40 a.m. stating that inmates were throwing cans, etc. at side door entrance and he was ordering installation of a slot in door to serve hot food through...no meals,

period, would be served at all unless can throwing, etc. stopped...
inmates would prefer to go without...at *8:55 a.m.* four inmates went
through inner gate for court purposes but were hesitant to do so until
clarification was given that they would be later returned to gym. Mr.
Elmes and Mr. Berkey assured them they would be. *(John Dow)*

Nov.2/76

Mr. E. Berkey, A/D Security,
B.C.Penitentiary

Dear Mr. Berkey,

I request permission to go up to SMU and see the inmates there. If it
is not possible for me to attend this area I request to have Louis R.
brought down. If convenient could this meeting be set up for the
afternoon or morning of Friday, Nov.5. Thank you. *(*Into Log,
Gary Lake)

*   *   *

The I.C. sent a letter to Ron Stern, the lawyer who
represented them during the hostage period.

Stern was later refused admission to the B.C.Pen on the basis
that the I.C. had no right to engage a lawyer. He could enter
only as the attorney of a prisoner, not of a committee of
prisoners:

Dear Ron,   Nov.2/76

The situation at the B.C.Pen does not look very
encouraging...the government is not really prepared to
seriously regard post-riot prisons, nor is it prepared to
utilize most of the resources at its disposal. It appears to be
mobility backwards rather than forward—the usual display
of irresponsibility.

Best regards,
Ivan Horvat

*   *   *

Nov.5—10:45 a.m. Omer just came back from B-7 but J.J. is not back
yet because the guards wouldn't let J.J. bring back his Committee files
so he stayed in B-7 until he can get to bring back his files. *(Lea Sheppe)*

Nov.5—11:20 a.m. Just back from B-7 after going through heavy hassles with Oliver. Pat Shaw (senior security) came to get me, still not allowing me to take any personal belongings from my cell, on Swan's orders. *(Ivan Horvat)*

Nov.5—12:20 p.m. After speaking to the RCMP officer in charge, Norman D. came to me and claimed two of his children burned to death a few days ago, that he had not slept in three days and needed something to sleep. He appeared very distraught and showed me a letter that referred to the tragic loss of two children. I called Mr. Havelick who said he had contacted the nurse on duty who refused to administer any further medication to Norman who had been given 1000 mg. Chloral Hydrate. I asked Mr. Havelick if Mr. Mangleson, Keeper in charge, would attempt to intervene. Mr. Havelin said he would pass the word on and Mr. Mangelson would get back to me.

Mr. Mangleson phoned back a few minutes later and said the nurse would not alter her position but suggested Rev. Speed be contacted later this morning and ask him to intervene. I notified the inmate who threatens to slash himself. *(Paul Leister)*

Nov.5—12:50 p.m. Norman D. just slashed his leg with a razor blade. Dr. O'Donnell notified and requested RCMP to monitor his move to the hospital. The way of the "Civilized" world is insanity! *(Paul Leister)*

Nov.5—2:15 p.m. Just returned from B-7 after visit from Louis R. from SMU. He told me they were notified that they were not allowed mail from Claire Culhane anymore...things seem to have cooled off in SMU and they are also getting hot meals. *(G. Lake)*

Nov.7—11:45 a.m. Paul Leister phoned Mr. O'Connell about the hose running at gym side door. It was engaged and flooded over into the gym again dampening and soaking the inmates. This situation has occurred previously and was to have been corrected. However the problem persists. *(John Dow)*

Nov.8—11:20 a.m. Omer and Paul talked to Swan who said that B-7 would get no ration box food, and that the gym would not be getting it for too much longer either. He also said that if anyone in the B-7 wing broke any more cell fixtures that they would be gassed and left in the cell.

Mr. Swan was reminded that we've been trying to get the gym problem solved since Nov.4 but it is obvious that Mr. Swan doesn't have any solutions. He said that he sees no point in meeting with the Committee. He said that he has a list of names of guys in the gym (he read some names out) who want to be leaders and thereby cause trouble.

It is my opinion that Mr. Swan is full of same old ideas—the cause of this riot—and that the only way to accomplish anything will be to completely bypass him in our quest for peaceful settlement and constructive progress. We should rap more about it and start doing. *(Ivan Horvat)*

Nov.8—1:35 p.m. Mr. Swan was on inspection and I got in conversation with him at the bottom of the gym office stairs. Again he laid out his trip about how 40 prisoners should move from gym to North wing, and I asked him what difference will that make when there will still be men left in the gym. He then said that he is not ready to tell me his plans, etc. except that he could deploy some of his men from the perimeter.

I told him that the gym will not be any more or less secure if only some of the men move—they should all leave thus solving the entire problem and not just part of it. Again I asked Mr. Swan to recommend B-7 corridors to Ottawa because it is obvious that we won't peacefully move to the North wing. Oakalla will soon start sending people over and the North wing will be full anyway.

Mr. Swan then said that we could be in the gym for a long time (no yard, visits, etc.) because he will not recommend B-7 corridors to Ottawa, reason he gives is that there are men in the gym who he would never put into the corridors for security reasons. (Last week he said that the only reason for not moving to B-7 corridors was that Ottawa has a directive against dormitory living in maximum institutions.) *(Ivan Horvat)*

Nov.8—2:45 p.m. I called Mr. Adams (Operations) and asked him if he can ask his crew on the bottom of the stairs (gym) not to point their shotguns directly at I.C. heads when we go through the doorways between the gym and PTI office.

Few minutes later the phone downstairs rang and I overheard a conversation to the effect that both the downstairs crew and the main hall custodial crew found it very funny that they (I.C.) should be concerned about shotguns pointed at their heads. *(I.H.)*

Nov.8—6:00 p.m.

Inmate Committee B.C.Pen

A regular meeting of the Inmate Committee was held, Nov.8/76 in the PTI area of the gymnasium. All members...present. Meeting opened at 6 p.m.:

President: First of all, as we all know, the minutes (of previous meeting with the administration) are inaccurate. . .Director refuses to alter or correct them and I signed them with an appropriate notation on the face of them.

. . .Page 4, under heading *Security of the Gymnasium,* for example, states Director ordered immediate cessation of the alleged digging of a tunnel but neglected to record the Director's threats about if it was not stopped. . .as recorded in our letter to his office dated Nov.4/76, indicating that his twice verbalized threat to use gas and force had been omitted from the minutes prepared in his office.

Our final paragraph of that letter (to Mr. Swan) read as follows: ''. . .it was stated that the 'riot act' was read to inmates, when, in fact, the riot act has never been read to anyone. In an effort to cooperate, however, the President of the I.C. has signed. . .(although) the current minutes are much too one-sided to be signed. Thank you. (Signed: Ivan Horvat, President, Inmate Committee.)

The main problem now is the transfer of prisoners housed in the gymnasium back into a cell situation. On this, the Administration has used deception, passed the buck, shuffled us around, and in short, offered no practical solution.

. . .on the 2nd Nov. we were told that there are 51 cells in the North wing and until they are filled there will be (1) no hot food (2) no re-instatement of fresh air and exercise in the yards (3) no re-instatement of visiting privileges. . . .

. . .we were assured by Mr. Byman. . .on Oct. 23 that no inmate would be transferred into the North wing. . .makes little sense to transfer 30 or 40 bitter prisoners to a wing which is in much worse condition than the one recently devastated. . .[which] in the past century has been condemned and closed on more than one occasion and only re-opened for ''induction'' of [new] prisoners [with] strict assurance given that the North wing would not be used for the men in the gymnasium.

. . .must also keep in mind that Mr. Swan promised all those [previously listed] things if we fill B-7. B-7 has been full over a week and now the same empty promises are being made again to fill the North wing, while we have already done our part and filled B-7.

...suspicion is high in the gym that the real motive for moving only half the prisoners out is to weed out certain [ones]...leaving a small group...to receive the full blast of Security's reprisal.

Jack Dow: ...what bothers me is that the alternative to move to the North wing is free and not a damned soul has blocked any prisoner who wants to move there; yet the Administration, including the Director, has stated the Committee is not performing its function and is preventing men in the gym from moving to North wing, which is not true....

Paul Leister: In the past few days I've noticed the same old tactics being used to create this situation....Jensen removed...for threatening to kill a member of the Committee when the uprising first erupted...known...as hating inmates and trying to cause trouble, yet in past few days someone has intentionally placed him right at the gym entrance where he can curse and heckle inmates. The same thing with Butcher...notorious for cocking his rifle... threatening...inmates. Someone puts *him* on the gym door with a rifle! This morning officers came to the side entrance of gym to pick up garbage and had the words "RAT PACK" stuck to the front of their uniforms...putting it all together it sure looks like the same small handful...once again....trying to trigger trouble in order to prove the I.C. can't properly do its job.

Jack Dow: ...it's pure harassment. Now about the stalls on movement to the Transfer Board. Six escorts (on duty) and only three guys get up there in the [whole] morning....

Lea Sheppe: How about the meals? B-7 now gets two meals a day prepared in the kitchen while the guys in the gym still get K-rations. We should (and could) all get the same food.

Omer Prud'homme: I'm highly suspicious of the motive

for the sudden increase Friday night [Nov.5] in the sleeping medication. Many have been ill with the flu, sleeping hardly at all, everyone on short tempers, even slashing themselves to get medical attention, yet they were all, for the most part, ignored until Friday night. Why the sudden increase in medication?

President: ...it took over a month of frustration, slashings, telephone calls...to get proper medication. Now if it is suddenly cut off again, what will happen?

Lea Sheppe: We'll have *another* Administration-induced incident...could that be the reason?

Omer: It sure looks funny...no medication at all in B-7 ...can't even get an aspirin down there without an argument. Yet the gym has plenty. Why?

Gary: I think it's suspicious enough that we should make the Citizens Committee aware of it.

President: ...everyone in the Region is making public statements except us; we're not even allowed to say a word. Our letters to Editors...articles...never seem to reach their destination...very unfair...can't even challenge a lie if it's fed into the media...isolated from the public and have no chance at equal time...result: public only learns the one-sided part of the Administration viewpoint.

Paul: We've also got reason to believe that our mail to Ottawa, especially our Minutes and Committee correspondence is not getting out either.

President: What we have to come to terms with is that the people here at B.C.Pen will not do anything to better the situation...like things as they are and not susceptible to change...conversations with Mr. Swan indicate that it's not here nor there to him what happens down here...my conversations are in the Log....

Let's change the subject and get on to the [Parliamentary] enquiry because there are some things we must do in preparation....

Leister: First thing we need are *all* the tape recording transcripts from Regional Headquarters [Pacific] and the RCMP.

Omer: We requested them from Mr. Murphy, Regional Director.... He said some of them were 'damaged.'

Paul: ...just had recollections of Nixon and the 18 minute Watergate gap in the tape recordings....

President: [We] should most definitely have meeting [with the C.A.C.] before we meet with the Administration...by the way Mr. Swan scolded me for going directly to the C.A.C. to request the meeting without doing it through his office...if we want a meeting with the C.A.C. we should ask him to request it for us, to which I replied that we were under the impression that C.A.C. was a part of a working trinity and not a party working for the Staff at B.C.Pen.

Paul: ...strongly urge that we attempt [again] to contact Mr. Rutter [National Inmate Welfare Committee] to travel here to meet with us alone and following that meeting to sit in on a meeting with the Administration....

Nov.8—10:50 p.m. I.C. member Sheppe refused to go to B-7 tonight because the Guards wanted to put handcuffs on him. It has never been done in the past so I refused to have it done now. Macbeth gave the orders to have the handcuffs put on. *(Lea Sheppe)*

Nov.12—11:30 a.m. A young blond officer stationed in the gun cage turned two spotlights on and threw them down into the face of several prisoners. I asked him to please cut them off. He became extremely arrogant, cursing, etc. causing a very dangerous situation in the gym. Several cans were hurled at the cage and threats were being made to set the cage on fire. I called Mr. Berkey who ordered the lights turned off. *(Paul Leister)*

Nov.14—3:45 a.m. Several inmates suddenly began yelling and when we looked out into the floor, it was obvious the trouble was once again being caused by someone stationed in the gun cage. I went to the PTI window closest to the gym cage and asked the inmates gathered there what the problem was. They said a guard in the cage had cocked a rifle three times and had called out Bruce's name, which immediately brought forward screams and curses from below. I looked over toward the cage (about 5 feet away) and saw the officer who had been pointed out as the instigator (young, early 30's, black moustache) leaning up against the opened cage window (as close as he could get to the inmates) smiling down on them in an effort to agitate them further. I also recognized Mr. Hamer standing in the background along with 4 other officers I did not recognize.

I asked the inmates to cool it and telephoned Mr. Payne who said he would investigate. *(Paul Leister)*

Nov.15—noon. Have been trying to contact I.C. Liaison officers. Can't contact external liaison. Apparently at a meeting. No one knows where internal liaison can be found. Director is incommunicado. In short, cannot get any action regarding external matters. Reason for urgency—need to contact C.A.C. and pursue matters as established at last I.C. meeting.*

Nov.16—9:10 a.m. Mr. Swan called to advise that there would be a meeting tomorrow morning at 10:a.m. *(Paul Leister)*

Nov.17—3:00 p.m. A/D Swan came to back door and has talked to myself, Lea Sheppe and Omer Prud'homme re. results of staff meeting which resulted from I.C./Administration meeting. Proposals he agreed to were: ready to move 24 people to B-7 corridors and cells...would make one of the huts available for the I.C. and maybe 2-3 other prisoners ...would get bunks, showers, etc. installed in TV lounge to accommodate up to 30 people on a temporary basis...rest now in the

---

*In the period after the disturbances, Committee members were anxious about the very slow rate of removal of inmates from the Penitentiary gymnasium... what we find to be the most disturbing...is the virtual total lock-up on inmates in the B.C.Penitentiary. Those inmates in the gymnasium were kept locked up for two months without ever coming out into the yard.

When the Citizens Advisory Committee members...asked whether it was not possible to permit inmates in small groups to come out for open exercise...we met with the response that Security was required otherwise. Inmates...made it plain that they felt their confinement under such conditions was a form of reprisals...including inmates who had not participated in the September disturbances, were kept in...lock-up and the shops and other programs... remained closed. ("Submission to the Subcommittee on the Penitentiary System in Canada," made by the Citizens Advisory Committee of the B.C.Pen, Feb.15/77, p.16.)

gym would by that time be gone through transfers, etc....As soon as gym is cleared we get visits, yard, and start working on a permanent program...or so says Swan....However he threw another 'blackmail' trip at us—comes Friday if everyone in the gym tears down their tents, there can be visits this *weekend* ("to start with"). He didn't say anything about *weekdays. (Ivan Horvat)*

Nov.18—11:15 a.m. Mr. Swan came to the rear door of PTI area and he was in a rage. He said urine had been thrown on one of his officers and he was sick and tired of the situation in the gym and said if urine or anything else was thrown...a slug would be put into a rifle, or words to that effect. He was very angry and appeared to be very tired. He was asked not to make any rash decisions that would cause 70 men to be brutalized for the act of one person. He said he wants the gym cleared and quick.

Mr. Swan also said that Bob S. was raising hell in B-7 demanding 3-H and he (Swan) told him that if he didn't take the cell he'd go "upstairs." He also said when the politicians looked at the "mess" in the gym they were after his scalp and he had had his fill of the entire matter. *(Paul Leister)*

Nov.19—9:00 p.m. Mr. Russell called and asked if we were aware that the other back room has been broken into. He told me that they are aware of the inside door being barricaded, etc. I told Mr. Russell that we are aware of it now, and that there is very little we can do about it. It's done and that we weren't aware of any valuables being there. He said that this might extremely strain the present relations, to which I replied, "Sad but true," and that the sooner we are out of the gym the better. *(Ivan Horvat)*

Nov.22—2:10 a.m. A bomb exploded in the shower room.
Don't know what to expect. *(Ivan Horvat)*

Pipe Bomb, Fire Add To Pen Troubles

B.C.Pen gym set ablaze Monday as 65 inmates were being transferred from temporary accommodation in the gym... New Westminster Fire Chief Art Powell said, "We had to wait for a few minutes—for security reasons—before we could move in...."

—Province, Nov.23/76

Welcome to Prison Pigsty
Prisoners Made Their Own Pigsty

They brought the radio and press people into the B.C.Pen to see the mess—open house in a pigsty, but the SPCA wouldn't let you keep pigs in the gym. Vacated by 52 inmates Monday ...in the hey day of its use the gym floor had blossomed with tents like a hobo jungle as groups ...sought privacy or freedom from draughts. Ration boxes were erected around the tents.

Prison spokesman Jack Stewart...said the last *inmates could have been moved from the gym 2 months ago, but they refused to budge.* He said sections of the East wing are again liveable although water must be packed in because plumbing is still out of commission. The wing will be fully repaired by March. *Unnamed guard said, "It's impossible to deal with the Inmate Committee because no matter what you do for them they keep on making demands...."* Hit out at the Citizens Committee ..."Should be kicked out because committees just don't work in institutions like this."

—*Province*, Nov.22/76

Nov. 26. THIS LOG ENTRY MADE IN MY CELL

What had happened the morning after the bomb explosion—we (the I.C.) were called to a meeting and at our request RCMP supervisors Northorp and Neils and also Mary McGrath (C.A.C.) were present. Mr. Swan informed us that due to the bomb explosion, the previous plan of moving gym inmates to the TV lounge or the B-7 corridors will be scrapped and instead the men would have to move to...corridors of East wing.

We protested because that area has no plumbing, no heating and no showers, plus all of the windows are broken and the temperature gets below zero. Mr. Swan told us that's where they were going and that the move would start at 12:30 p.m.—one way or another. We told him that we would inform the gym population.

We went back to the gym, told everyone...[they] gathered their belongings and lined up at the door. They started leaving the gym one by one, as was asked by Swan. We asked to get some of us back to the PTI office where all our personal belongings were, in order to get together to move, but Swan said No—that we could get them later. (We never did.)

There were a little over 50 inmates in the gym, and when there were only 22 left, including the committee, the fire broke out in the back of the gym. Since everyone was lined up at the front of the inside gym door I asked the guard to open the door so we can go up the stairs and into the dome as there were only 22 of us left, and the smoke was becoming unbearable and the fire was spreading at tremendous speed.

THE GUARD RUSHED AWAY.

They threw some fire hoses into the gym but still wouldn't let us out.

Some of us made it to the side door and had to wait five minutes more until there were about 100 armed guards there and until they finished stringing barbed wire across the walkways before they would let Gordie out to pick up a flashlight so that we could check the gym and see if we were all there by the side entrance.

By now the gym was burning and visibility was minimal (none). Gordie and I made an attempt to check if anyone had fainted from asphyxiation and unable to make it to the door.

Everyone was out. *(Ivan Horvat)*

*   *   *

The *Columbian* offered quite a different account.

B.C.Pen Gym Turned Into a Cesspool

"It was quick action by the guards," said Brian Poxon, President of the B.C.Guards Union, that saved the lives of 20 inmates in the gym when fire broke out...guards quickly opened all doors so inmates could escape the gym then filled with dense smoke.

Graffiti found on gym walls, WE GET OUR WISDOM FROM OUR EXPERIENCE. WE GET OUR EXPERIENCE FROM OUR FOOLISHNESS.

—*Columbian*, Nov.24/76

However, when I discussed this episode two years later with men who had been in the gym that day, they described how in addition to getting everyone out safely, as well as themselves getting out without being burned alive, the I.C. also had to fight off the fury of those who were so determined to see the whole institution burn down that they were ready to kill anyone who interfered.

By coincidence, only one day before the fire emptied the gym, an MP was asking questions at Dorchester prison, New Brunswick:

Mr. John Reynolds (MP member of the Parliamentary Subcommittee on Penitentiaries): I notice in the report... that you have 308 [prisoners here] and yet your cell capacity is 385. With the capacity being strained at the B.C.Pen right now...I am just wondering—maybe you cannot answer, fairly—why a lot of inmates from B.C. would not have been transferred to fill up your empty cells.

Mr. J.L. Bennett (Regional Director, CPS Atlantic): We are in the process of doing that now.

Mr. Reynolds: ...can you tell us why they have waited so long to transfer them? Since you have this space, why was it not done just about immediately the riot took place, once it was ended?

Mr. Bennett: We will send a team consisting of 2 or 3 analysts out to B.C. and we will attempt to select what we call "normal associate" inmates....

Mr. Reynolds: You have to send your people? They do not have people capable in B.C. Region of defining who you would be able to use in your institution?

Again, why have they waited so long? I think that is an important question. Why could it not have been done? There has been a serious problem there, and it is still a serious problem. Why could not this have been done within days of happening?

Mr. Bennett: I believe a decision was made that they (B.C.) would attempt to deal with the problem at that institution, if they could.*

During these hearings, however, the guards indicated they

*Minutes of Proceedings, Issue No.6, Nov.22/76, pp.6,7.

would not budge from their position. As one witness from the PSAC union testified:

> ...we have a motion on our books that we will not jeopardize the lives of any officer, that we have the power to take whatever action we, the PSAC executive...deem necessary.... *We can and will run the institution, and if this means keeping them locked up this is what will happen.* *

*   *   *

Nov. 26. Will end the Log here because the communication access between the Citizens Advisory Committee members and the inmates has ground to a halt. We have repeatedly requested meetings with the Administration and/or the Citizens Committee.

To date—none.

The men in East wing are getting no yard, no hot water, no nothing. I hear disturbances from SMSU all day. Swan won't let us function, and he has suspended Gary Lake from Inmate Committee because of charge in outside court.

I can see that there will be more trouble here, before we even have the time to work out the consequences of [this] recent trouble. As I see it, the men have a right to be bitter; this riot was originally pre-determined and started by the guards in order to achieve their corrupt goals.

It backfired because they didn't expect it to work out as it did, and now we get the reprisals. (Ivan Horvat)

**Minutes of Proceedings,* Issue No.8, Nov. 23/76, p.51.

CHAPTER FOUR

What Happened To
The Memorandum of Agreement

Prison hostage taking, knifing, rape, suicide—these occur with a regularity that is as frightening as the conditions which generate them. Put anyone in a depraved environment and depravity will follow, since reactions are violent when there are no other alternatives. Concrete and steel will be demolished, and self-mutilations will increase.

But something new was being attempted at the B.C.Pen in the Fall of 1976. The protagonists were meeting at a negotiation table. For the first time it appeared that a crisis was going to be resolved in some other way—through mediation rather than through murder.

From this encounter emerged a *Memorandum of Agreement*, to be signed and honoured by all four parties. The remaining hostage would be freed, and there would be renewed efforts to make prison conditions more tolerable.

The prisoners' *Log* revealed how their dismay and anger grew as, one by one, the terms of the Agreement were ignored, and the C.A.C. involvement was weakened—one of its members even being ordered out of the institution. Most critical of all, the prisoners' 'temporary' interval in the gym was deliberately prolonged, making another disturbance inevitable.

Some publicity was given to the fact that within 48 hours of the signing of the Memorandum, the Commissioner of Penitentiaries in Ottawa received a set of demands from the PSAC (Solicitor General component), "that all legal means through the Courts to cancel the Memorandum. . .be taken immediately."

However, little publicity was given to André Therrien's reply of October 5, when he said that "the Agreement

1) is devoid of legal effect;
2) the basic reason for saying so is that it is clear the Agreement was negotiated under duress;

> 3) a subsidiary reason is that none of the purported parties, in particular the Inmate Committee, are legal entities; it is entirely a matter of CPS discretion as to whether the so-called Agreement is to be honoured in full or in part, or not at all.

> This basic principle requires that we develop...as many means as possible to resolve any such incident in a safe and peaceful manner for all persons involved...one of the main reasons why more than 40 incidents over the last three years involving approximately 100 employees have been resolved without loss of life.''

(What about the Mary Steinhauser 'incident,' among others, which was *not* resolved without loss of life?)

> ...we have decided to honour these terms contingent upon the fact that the inmates abide by their commitment that there will be no further unacceptable actions on their part. Failure to so comply will render the Agreement null and void.

What Therrien was really saying was: (1) the guards don't have to worry, because this document isn't legal and thus can be interpreted according to expediency; (2) what counts is to "resolve any such incident" rather than to explore its causes; and (3) the Agreement will end as soon as some "unacceptable" action occurs—which could include just about anything.

But as the Log has shown, the men were taken from the East wing to the gym, and crowded in upon each other without proper food, exercise, outside yard, or adequate health care, thus making it virtually impossible for them to "honour these terms."

It was *not* intended that it should be possible.

Less than two weeks *before* the hostage taking, the prisoners rushed off the following press release in their unsuccessful efforts to head off the explosion which, by that time, everyone knew was coming:

SIGNED BY OVER 200 PRISONERS

To the Public   Sept.14/76
Vancouver Sun,   B.C.Penitentiary,
Vancouver, B.C.   New Westminster.

Dear Mr. & Mrs. Public:

The Public Service Alliance (guards' union) claim working conditions at the B.C.Penitentiary are dangerous and have issued a ban on overtime and have demanded replacement of top management. Please allow us to add the following facts and one suggestion to the public record:

Facts

Just a few years ago, approximately 135 guards controlled security at the B.C.Pen when it housed over 700 prisoners and saw the presence of various visiting groups and other constructive rehabilitative programs. Today, 188 guards working massive overtime claim ''danger'' and the inability to control security for only 400 prisoners and no visiting groups, very little shop activity and almost no constructive programs of any kind.

The president of the local element of the PSAC and other old-line guards are executives of the union and have an iron grip control on that union. Any disagreement by younger guards is quickly screamed down by the old timers. Some of those same old timers are in positions of authority at B.C.Pen and are able to create turmoil by delaying recreation, visits, hospital calls, school classes, etc. (There is constant turmoil at B.C.Pen while the prisoners there are no different than at other maximum security prisons across Canada.)

Suggestion

Move Security (PSAC) beyond the fence and issue them whatever weaponry they feel necessary to prevent our escape into society's ranks. Issue each of them a *tank* if necessary, but move them out of the inner operations of the institution.

In that way, (1) they would not be exposed to the "danger" they claim exists; (2) the massive overtime they now work, amounting to millions of dollars annually across Canada, would bring a big savings to the public; and (3) the turmoil so necessary to justify the strengthening of their union would quickly disappear, to the public's satisfaction.

It was in this same spirit of meaningful criticism, accompanied by feasible alternatives, that the Memorandum of Agreement was studiously prepared. It outlined conditions for release of the remaining hostage, and it went on to propose the initiation of a serious inquiry into prison conditions.

Most of the clauses were flouted, postponed, or ignored—not unpredictably, when one recalls the warning contained in Bryan Williams' memo presented one week after the October 1 signing: "...we should...protest in...strongest terms at the present time because if anything happens I would like the inquiry or the public to know at a later date that it was not the inmates, not the Citizens Committee, but the Administration which blew the chance of a peaceful settlement." (to the C.A.C., Oct.7/76)

The *Memorandum of Agreement* defined itself as "the basis upon which the management of the B.C.Pen, the I.C. and the C.A.C. agreed to end the current situation within the penitentiary." How were the clauses of the Memorandum respected?

1. *Mr. Culbert, who is being held in the kitchen of the Penitentiary, will be released unharmed immediately.*

Mr. Culbert was released unharmed immediately after the Memorandum was signed.

2. *(a) The inmates with Mr. Culbert will turn themselves over to the RCMP who will have complete responsibility for their safe removal to an RCMP lock-up and transfer to another Federal Penitentiary.*

While they did turn themselves over to the RCMP and were transferred to other Federal Penitentiaries, the story did not end there. They were put into solitary confinement. After several months, when they were returned to the B.C.Pen, they found themselves again in the hole.

> (b) *The RCMP will take complete responsibility for the safe removal of men from the damaged areas of the Penitentiary. In performing this role, the RCMP will be observed by members of the C.A.C. and the I.C.*

The issue of transfer out of the smashed areas and later out of the crowded and volatile gym area was uppermost in every prisoner's mind. The RCMP were mainly to act as a buffer between the guards and the prisoners who feared reprisals from the more hostile members of Security.

Observing the RCMP, we noted they were taking pictures of prisoners as they moved from the East wing to the gym. The rationale was that this would prove to the public that no one had been physically abused by the RCMP. We countered that this could hardly prove "safe removal" since anyone could have been beaten up in the interim. Photographs should obviously record the *last* day of the RCMP surveillance if they intended to use them as evidence in their favour.

> (c) *The RCMP will take total responsibility for the transfer of all inmates being transferred from the B.C.Pen to other Federal Penitentiaries.*

When the first transfer took place on Oct.3, Mary McGrath and myself were on C.A.C. duty to observe. Only Mary was permitted to check the prisoners as they entered the vehicles. An RCMP officer wouldn't let me do the same although I was an accredited C.A.C. member. They treated me like any other member *only* until the hostages were released, but not a moment later.

> (d) *The RCMP will remain within the B.C.Pen for a period of two weeks and after the first week, will meet with Management, the I.C. and the C.A.C. to discuss any need for their presence.*

Although both C.A.C. and I.C. strongly recommended that the RCMP remain for at least several weeks more, within one week they were dismissed by the B.C.Pen, acting unilaterally. "Without notification to the Inmate Committee or the Citizens Advisory Committee, the RCMP were withdrawn en masse...."* One token officer remained on duty.

After removing the RCMP, the Administration then refused to allow prisoners into the exercise yard for the next two months, using the excuse that there wasn't sufficient staff to supervise them.

　　3. *Transfers*
　　(a) *All inmates within uninhabitable areas of the penitentiary will immediately be removed to habitable areas within the institution and receive necessary medical attention.*

The previous chapter demonstrates how this clause was violated. 200 men packed, literally on top of each other, in a small area, and kept in that condition for close to two months, with never a single moment of outside exercise, with food below average, and running a losing battle for adequate medication and medical care—this could hardly be considered "habitable."

　　(b) *Every case of an inmate requesting voluntary transfer from the B.C.Pen will be referred for decision to a Committee consisting of the Regional Transfer Board and the Citizens Advisory Committee.*

Voluntary transfer from the B.C.Pen, particularly for those who were in the gym, was one of the most important issues. With the C.A.C. working with the Transfer Board for the first time, the prisoners were especially encouraged.

However, the C.A.C. not only played a very minor role at these meetings, since they were relegated to mere observers, but as the weeks went by, they no longer even attended regularly.

　　(c) *All transfers will be to equivalent security in the institution to which the transfer is made. For example, a man in the general population will be transferred to general population.*

Minutes of Proceedings, Issue No.29, Feb.15/77, p.13.

This clause was not honoured. Stories (and in some instances the men themselves) came back from Matsqui and Saskatchewan Penitentiary in Prince Albert where they had ended up in solitary confinement.

By that time, the C.A.C. was no longer actively involved, leaving the B.C.Pen Administration free to disregard the Agreement. Prisoners only hold power when they hold hostage.

The prisoners therefore had no one to turn to for release from solitary where they found themselves, some for as long as eight months.

*   *   *

Lack of access to the public is the first cause of hostage taking. Problems relating to transfers are recognized as the second. To quote from the thirteen paragraphs dealing with the transfer of prisoners in the *Report to Parliament by the Sub-Committee on the Penitentiary System in Canada*, 1977:

One of the most imperious acts of the penitentiary authorities...is an involuntary transfer to another institution. It is common for an inmate to be moved suddenly, without notice, and without being told why he has been moved.

...a considerable source of anxiety to men who have much to lose...their lives, their good record for purposes of parole, their friends....

The inmates of another prison...may suspect him of [being]...an informer...a false rumour...could be the equivalent of a death sentence...in the absence of official reasons, rumour and conjecture dictate results.

...ordinary standards of decency require that a person be conceded the dignity of being treated as something other than an object to be manipulated according to whatever appeals to the absolute power and unfettered discretion of the Canadian Penitentiary Service. (pp.93-94.)

*   *   *

4. Reprisals
(a) There will be no physical punishment of any inmate involved in the incident.

When three months later a member of the I.C. is physically beaten resisting movement to the hole by the goon squad (composed of East Indians, in a move calculated to encourage racist reactions); or when 37 charges are laid on one prisoner, which include three incidents of 'walking too close to the wall,' it would have to be conceded that this clause was not respected.

(b) There will be no internal disciplinary charges laid until after consideration of the report of the public inquiry.

Administration disregarded this clause also. There were numerous instances when prisoners were placed in solitary (which is the ultimate 'internal disciplinary charge') immediately after they were transferred from the gym area. The Report was not made public until June 1977—eight months later.

(c) No double jeopardy. If criminal charges are laid arising from the disturbance no internal charges will be laid.

If prisoners were not to be simultaneously charged by inside Warden's Court and by outside legal process, why was the 'kitchen' hostage-taking group kept in solitary confinement until they went to trial in April 1977, and for another three months after that? (Again under Sect. 230(1)(a) which allows the Director to "Disassociate" a prisoner for an indeterminate period).

It was hardly a secret that double jeopardy was indeed taking place, but if neither the C.A.C. nor the I.C. could stop it, what hope had prisoners from their cells in the Penthouse?

Another reference was made to the reprisal situation when "The Members of Parliament urged any prisoner who was punished as a result of an appearance (at the 1977 Subcommittee Hearings) to write Parliament and action would be taken."* This instruction is farcical to anyone familiar with prison life, or with Parliament itself, for that matter. What action has *ever* been taken upon receipt of such a complaint?

*Cruel and Unusual, p.58. McNeil and Vance's valuable book.

A more accurate estimate was to be found in the submission by the C.A.C. to the Subcommittee:

> "Inmates...made plain to us that they felt their confinement under such conditions in virtual lock-up... [in the gymnasium for two months without ever coming out into the exercise yard] was a form of reprisal."*

5. *Possessions*
   All inmates, upon transfer, will be permitted to take with them personal effects, intact.

When prisoners were moved from the East wing to the gym on Oct.2, they brought their personal effects with them, in a pillow slip or a shopping bag. The fewer items they have, the more they treasure them. The pain and suffering is intense when prisoners return after a cell search to find their letters, pictures and personal things scattered all over the cell floor, often torn and destroyed. They have so few belongings that this becomes a catastrophe in their lives.

In a statement to Mr. Donald Yeomans, Commissioner of Corrections, from the Prisoners Committee of Dorchester Penitentiary, Sept.25/78 (following a prison disturbance), their Clause 2 begins, "...We want to be protected from the inhuman bondage being inflicted upon us and we want explanations for the following:

> How and why can these men, as well as all the men not taking part in the non-violent demonstration, be subjected to the following punitive actions directly after the sit-in:
>
> *a.* The confiscation of thousands of inmate hobbycraft and materials, personal cell effects, lamps, and dozens of hobby tables? No men were present during the confiscation, and none were given receipts or allowed to put their valuables into 'personal effects'?
>
> *b.* These items were taken from the institution by the truckload and burnt. They burnt loads of inmate hobby-

craft and personal belongings, most of which were paid for by the Inmate's Trust Fund monies, or his earned canteen allowances. Some inmates are suing the institution for the damage and loss of personal property, most of which was the result of many hours of personal toil. The inmates had approved permits, to work these hobbies.''

6. *Super Maximum Unit*
   Members of the Inmate Committee will be permitted to meet any inmates held in the Super Maximum Unit who they request to see, or who requests to see a member of the Inmate Committee. Such meetings will take place, either by the inmates from the Super Maximum Unit being brought to an office, or a member of the Inmate Committee being taken up to the Super Maximum Unit.

In Chapter 2, "The Eighty Hours," a first-hand account by one of its occupants shows what was happening in the Penthouse. We also read of the difficulties encountered by the I.C. when they tried to visit the hole, and to publicize their findings. Despite the intention of this clause, the Inmate Committee continued to be blocked from taking any effective action to relieve the paranoia, the "insanity, the fear, the violence" which characterize solitary confinement. Dr. Richard Korn, noted California Criminologist, goes on to describe its effects:

> ...when he is capriciously removed from the only society he has...for reasons he knows not, for a duration he knows not...he passes into a nightmare. He becomes a non-person...this process is foolproof...if you keep it up long enough it will break anybody...*it is a form of murder....*
> ...this process of breaking a man down to nothing results in inducing violence of a kind that no society can tolerate...Andy Bruce is the best possible lesson that solitary confinement can teach us...whatever violence Andy Bruce brought into the institution, it is nothing in

comparison to the violence that he sustains and will generate in the institution.*

7. *Public Enquiry*

> *The C.A.C. recommends that the enquiry be full and open with broad terms of reference to enquire into the particular and general causes of the disturbance at the B.C.Penitentiary, the resolution of the demands made by the Inmates, the implementation of the settlement and the future role of the B.C.Pen in the prison system. The enquiry should be in public and conducted by an impartial person with the report of the enquiry to be released to the public.*

The Solicitor General may have "responded by asking Parliament to establish the non-partisan subcommittee..."** and the members of this 11th appointed body since 1938 may indeed have felt "gripped by the conflicts of the system... nightmares...helpless...obsessed."† However, this was *not* the investigation called for by the Memorandum of Agreement, Clause 7.

The *broad terms of reference* were "limited to an examination of the prison system in isolation" (*Cruel and Unusual*, p.6) instead of relating the B.C.Penitentiary emergency to the recognized "crisis [which] exists in the Canadian penitentiary system."‡

The *resolution of the demands made by the inmates, implementation and settlement,* has yet to be treated seriously. Since all the decision-making remains with the Third Level—national headquarters— prisoners' *demands* are not a top priority.

The *future role of the B.C.Pen in the prison system* was best defined Sept.28/78 when its Administration, 'celebrating' its centenary, declared that it could last "another hundred years."

Minutes of Proceedings, Issue No.29, Feb.15/77, pp.29A:47,49.
**Cruel and Unusual,* p.3.
†*Cruel and Unusual,* p.5.
‡*Report to Parliament: by the Sub-committee on the Penitentiary System in Canada, 1977,* Recommendation No.1, p.2. Hereinafter, *Report.*

The *enquiry should be in public*—even the B.C. press had difficulty getting entry at times. But more important was the manipulation exposed at the Feb.17/77 hearing in Vancouver when an ex-prisoner with fourteen years experience was denied the right to speak at the Hearings because he had not made any prior submission. However, a self-professed 'ex-con,' Neil Burton, who had also failed to make any prior submission, was introduced by John Reynolds, MP. Allotted ten minutes by the Chairman, Burton used a full hour to support capital punishment, more "stringent discipline and punishment," and to deplore the "leniency of the system."

Nor was the enquiry *conducted by an impartial person.* A thorough investigation into the entire penitentiary system (of the scope of Justice Tom Berger's enquiry into the Native Indians' concern about the projected Arctic pipeline into their land) would have been more appropriate.

A committee of Canadian legislators, better known for their docile party allegiance, was not what the Memorandum envisioned. It was not until the end of 1978 that several MP's began to speak out.

"The suggestion that the government has accepted 22 of the 65 recommendations is false ...many of those they have alleged they have accepted they have rejected." Stuart Leggatt, MP (NDP)

"The government is deliberately avoiding the implementation of the penitentiary report... bureaucracy—not the politicians —is running this country." Simma Holt, MP (Lib.)

Mark MacGuigan, MP (Lib), Chairman of the panel, disagrees with the bureaucratic plot angle, but confirms that a majority of the former members of the committee are dismayed at the lack of action.

—*Sun,* Dec.28/78

On learning of the proposed enquiry's composition, many prisoners at the B.C.Pen wanted to boycott it, anticipating that its Report would join the many others still gathering dust, yet to be implemented. However, Fox succeeded in persuading the Inmate Committee that they should cooperate since, *this time* they would be 'dealing with the very law-makers who could effectively change the law,' which would in turn meet their demands.

Events have proven otherwise, as riots, hostage takings, stabbings and escapes continue in our prisons. The Sub-Committee Chairman, Mark MacGuigan, ("normally a man of restraint"), was later to express the view that if the Solicitor General, even with all-party support, was unable to change the system, "it was certain that changes would come from elsewhere."*

As I understand this remark, I would expect to see one of those changes come from the Native Indian section of the prison population. Status and non-status Indians comprise approximately 8% of Canada's population, yet occupy 40-60% (depending on the province) of its jails and prisons. Furthermore, "in 1976, 54% of all Native inmates were held in maximum security as against 31% non-Natives."**

The entire 44 Issues of these *Minutes*, available to the public, provide ample proof that racism permeates Canadian prison life. The racist tendencies in our society exist on both sides of the wall, and the prison establishment makes use of these. Scapegoatism of any kind serves to divide prisoners, and this strengthens the power of the Administration.

8. *It has been agreed that further meetings between the Management of the B.C.Penitentiary, the Inmate Committee and the Citizens Advisory Committee will continue to discuss outstanding matters.*

No such *further meetings* took place.

9. *The Inmate Committee, as presently constituted, will stay in existence until another Inmate Committee is duly elected.*

The election of another Inmate Committee, to be held within six

Cruel and Unusual, p.172.
**Robert Boyer, Commissioner of Métis and Non-status Indian Crime and Justice Commission. *Minutes of Proceedings,* Issue No.34, Mar.1/77, p.29.

months, was postponed pending the Hearings of the Parliamentary Subcommittee in February 1977, so that the present Committee could testify at it.

However, shortly afterwards, all the members of the I.C. (with the exception of Gary Lake) were transferred across country—some voluntarily, some involuntarily. Since then, there has not been another functioning I.C. Prisoners continue to be reluctant to step into this vulnerable arena. It required several elections over several years before Security would approve a new Inmate Committee in early 1979.

Harassment and hopelessness once again caused these prisoners to resign.

For that matter, the Citizens Advisory Committee is now exclusively comprised of Board Members of the John Howard Society. While this Society is part of the broad prison support organization in Canada, *appointed* Board members in a principally government-funded organization can hardly be regarded as representing the general community of "citizens."

In preparing its submission to the Parliamentary Subcommittee, the Citizens Advisory Committee held out great hope...

> As we understand it, the use of a formal Memorandum of Agreement (*whether it be legally enforceable or not*) was an unprecedented resolution of this kind of disturbance. Great importance was attached to its implementation in accordance with the terms and spirit of the Agreement and we feel that the Public Enquiry should look into this matter to ascertain whether the good faith upon which all parties signed the Agreement was carried over into the implementation.*

...hope which we can now see was nothing more than a forlorn sentiment.

*Minutes of Proceedings, Issue No. 29, Feb.15/77, p.29A:44.

The *Memorandum of Agreement* had failed. Therrien had as much as guaranteed it when he confirmed that "it is entirely a matter of Canadian Penitentiary Service discretion"—in other words, the decisions he and others at National Headquarters, the Third Level, were to take.

CHAPTER FIVE

Barred From Prison

Oct.6—The Grand Exit

It was now just five days since the last hostage went home. The Citizens Committee had been monitoring, for twelve hours a day, various activities: to see that the Pen was returning to 'normal'; to observe the movement of the 240 men from the destroyed East wing to the gym; to attend Transfer Board sessions for removing eligible prisoners to other institutions; and to continue meeting with the Inmate Committee still lodged in the PTI area overlooking the gym.

At 8:00 a.m. my four-hour duty period began. The Transfer Board was about to convene.

"Guess you're satisfied now you've given the inmates everything they asked for!" my escort jeered.

"Not exactly everything. But anyway, you have your two hostages safe and unharmed, haven't you?"

"We should've been allowed to do what we wanted to do in the first place," the guard persisted.

"And what was that?"

"Gas 'em!"

"And then what, after that?"

"There would've been *no* after that!"

It was still too early for the Board meeting. As my official ID-photo pass was not yet prepared, Jim Lazar (Living Unit Officer) took me to the gym area where I could talk with the I.C. I was still not allowed into the PTI area, so I had to talk with Gary Lake and others through the bars at the foot of the stairway. Six RCMP and Security guards were sitting at a table playing cards. No one bothered to search me, empty my purse, or use the metal detector.

Soon half a dozen prisoners had come to the gate to spell out their grievances. They needed garbage bags, toilet paper, clean laundry. A ton of putrid garbage at the exit gate had to be removed. And then six or seven letters were handed to me for mailing to families to assure them that everything was O.K.

Ms. Culhane turned to six RCMP and a Pen security guard and asked what the procedure was about letters. No one seemed particularly interested and she got a shrug in reply...then asked the police and security 'to please witness me accepting these letters and putting them in my outside pocket until I can drop them off at the V&C office.'

—Province, Oct.7/76

I didn't notice at the time that Lazar had quietly slipped away. Shortly, another guard came to take me back upstairs to the Transfer Board. There were many stories about the way prisoners were turned down without a chance to fully present and press their cases, so this was going to be interesting—to actually see for myself how the power play worked during direct confrontation between the Board and prisoners.

It was not to happen.

Just as the first prisoner was called in, a guard suddenly asked me to follow him—this time to Security. We entered a waiting-room opposite the office of Mr. Ev Berkey (Acting Director of Security). He came in, accompanied by another officer apparently to witness Berkey asking me if I had any prisoners' letters on me. They were hanging out of my pocket, clearly visible. I handed them to him and started to explain the circumstances, but could get no further than the first few words.

The prison controversy intensified Wednesday when Claire Culhane, a committee member, monitoring the clean-up at the B.C.Pen, was ordered to leave the prison for allegedly acting as carrier of inmates' letters. Prison officials confiscated a bunch of letters they said that they had seen being handed to Ms. Culhane by some inmates.

Jack Stewart (Information Officer) said letters handed in this manner are considered "contraband" and that...Ev Berkey had ordered Ms. Culhane to leave the prison and told her not to come back.   *—Sun*, Oct.7/76

My first reaction was just to sit down and refuse to move, confident that the accusation would be withdrawn if I had the opportunity to explain. However, there had been threats and innuendoes directed against the Citizens Committee in the past week; it was crucial that our group remain during this critical period—especially now that the Administration had sent the RCMP away. I realized they might use the letters to ban the entire Committee and thus weaken the prisoners' position.

I suffered the humiliation of allowing them to escort me out, but not until I made one more attempt to persuade Mr. Berkey to at least call Mary McGrath, who had similarly taken letters the day before. He side-stepped this, saying that he knew all about my 'making posters for the prisoners,' and that there were other 'incidents' which he wouldn't specify.

The Administration was prepared to go to any length to maintain their control. An inquiring public was, and is, not wanted in the Pen—under *any* circumstances. If we couldn't be frightened away, we would be put out, one at a time if necessary, by fabrications such as these.

Passing the PTI section I saw Omer Prud'homme (I.C.) standing at the upstairs doorway, facing the road. I signalled to him what was happening, pointing at my pocket. This particular escort refused to talk to me at all. However, he could hardly block his ears. I used our walk down the hill to elaborate on the details of the past hour. Berkey had ordered him to walk me to my car and make sure I drove off the grounds "never to come back."

At Mary's Legal Aid office, a five minute drive away, I described what had happened. She immediately called Berkey to say that the day before, she too had accepted letters for mailing from prisoners in the gym. Ken Parkinson, head of the *Visiting and Correspondence Office*, told her that since he had not yet provided the men in the gym with a mail drop, he would get back to her later. Leaving at noon, she instructed Parkinson to tell Vi Roden, her replacement, what to do with the letters. He told her to drop them off at the V&C Office at the foot of the hill on her way out. (The day before, I myself had directed her to the V&C as she was not familiar with the grounds.)

When Berkey could hardly support his position any longer,

"It was a ridiculous episode," Ms. Culhane told the Sun. "...another committee member had been involved Tuesday in an incident where the inmates had handed over letters for outside destination and it was apparently not uncommon for inmates to have committee members handle such communications."

—*Sun*, Oct.7/76

Mary went on to add, "Claire will return now, as she is our representative at the Transfer Board this morning." However, he persisted, claiming that there were "other incidents."*

I urged Mary to call Dr. Lipinski (C.A.C.Chairman) to deal with this serious infraction of our Agreement. While she was trying to reach him, we learned that Jack Stewart (Regional Information Officer) was on radio station CKNW.

...she will be allowed no further admittance to the B.C.Pen...action was taken after Ms. Culhane was observed receiving letters from inmates in contravention of penitentiary regulations...there was more than one incident in which Ms. Culhane was seen breaking prison regulations (but he would not elaborate.)

—*Sun*, Oct.7/76

As if that wasn't damaging enough, we next heard that Dr. Scott Wallace, MLA and C.A.C. member, was calling for my resignation. He had 'become increasingly disturbed with my pro-prisoner attitude during the negotiations of the past week.'

Telephone conversations with both Dr. Lipinski and Bryan Williams (lawyer member of the C.A.C.) confirmed my description of the letters incident, but unfortunately didn't produce any emergency meeting to issue our own press release, which I was insisting upon.

By noon, Colin Hoath of CBC-TV called and asked it he could have an interview. I explained that I would have to refuse, as the C.A.C. had agreed that only the Chairman was authorized to issue statements. (I didn't stop to wonder how he knew I was there). He argued that my refusal could imply guilt, and that since

*These preposterous "other incidents" are detailed in Appendix II, pp. 228-29.

the attack was personal, I should take the opportunity to clear myself. I was persuaded.

As he was packing up to leave, I told Hoath that there would probably be trouble, as I was breaking the Committee's rules. To my surprise he explained that he had called from Dr. Lipinski's office with his full knowldge. Why had Lipinski not taken the phone to assure me I *could* go on TV?

Later, on a radio station (CJOR) talk show, we heard this dialogue:

> "Look at today...Dr. Wallace, one of the Citizens Committee members, said that Claire Culhane was on the side of the inmates, very biased in her views... now it comes out that she was taking mail out of the Pen, and she has been asked to stay away," commented a caller.
>
> Pat Burns replied, "And quite rightly so."

Unfortunately, Pat Burns hadn't read from his copy of the I.C. press release of Sept.30 in which they were predicting this kind of personal attack:

> Throughout this experience we have been accompanied by a member of the Citizens Advisory Committee, Claire Culhane, who has been with us 24 hours a day from the very beginning...taken her duties seriously. However, *her present status of Prisoners Advocate is something which we feel may possibly at a later date bring on reprisals.*

The media continued to pander to the hysteria...

The volatile B.C.Penitentiary situation worsened Wednesday when a member of a Citizens Advisory Committee was banned from the prison...refused further admittance to observe transfer proceedings because she "illegally" attempted to pass on letters from inmates...visiting privileges were cancelled after she was "observed receiving letters...."

B.C.Conservative leader, Scott Wallace, a Committee member said, "It is time somebody spoke out...about Culhane's activities on behalf of inmates. We've lost a great deal of our credibility because we appear not to be neutral." —*Province*, Oct. 7/76

and to carry sinister insinuations . . .

Allegations that the B.C.Penitentiary Citizens Advisory Committee is linked to a national underground conspiracy to destroy Canada's prisons brought demands for apologies Wednesday . . . allegations were made in Ottawa by leaders of the Public Service Alliance of Canada. . . .

"I regret very much now that I didn't speak up earlier and call long before this for her resignation," Wallace said.

Lipinski told the Sun that Ms. Culhane's version . . . "is not in complete agreement with that of the security man . . . requires adjudication . . . Ms. Culhane's version . . . indicated it was very innocent and open."

—*Sun*, Oct.7/76

Wallace made a statement to the *Sun* on the same day, to the effect that he was "planning to contact Lipinski as soon as I can to suggest an immediate meeting of the Committee to discuss this issue and others that need to be clarified." But the 7:00 p.m. meeting had to be adjourned when a message was read to the eight of us present that 'No decisions are to be taken,' upon the request of four absent members—Lipinski, Roden, Leggatt, *and Wallace.*

Not one of these four had participated in the 80-hour hostage period.

It remained for the prisoners to place the incident in its proper perspective. They rushed their press release to the Solicitor General and the Commissioner of Penitentiaries, with copies to the media.

In it they established the important fact that I had indeed queried Jim Lazar, the Living Unit Officer, about the proper procedure for mail.

Mr. Lazar said he did not know what the procedure was but did not indicate she should not take the letters.

. . . the Inmate Committee wishes to state in the most emphatic manner that Mrs. Culhane, although firm in her stand against brutality and corruption, has never, at any time, entered into any scheme with any prisoner at this institution to violate the rules.

The Committee, representing

the general population, demands that the ban be lifted and an appropriate apology made to Mrs. Culhane at the earliest possible moment...the Committee in toto was absolutely amazed that a person of Dr. Wallace's reputation and intelligence would publicly air such statements without (1) proof of Mrs. Culhane's guilt, or (2) taking the matter to his own committee for resolution.

As for allegations that the Citizens Advisory Committee is linked to a national underground conspiracy to destroy Canada's prisons...this is an obvious lie ...the trouble throughout the penal system is not a 'conspiracy' on the part of anyone but only a symptom of the rancid corruption that runs throughout the system, especially at the union-institutional level.

—*Sun,* Oct.8/76

The meeting of the C.A.C. to issue a formal press statement denying the allegations and demanding a public retraction from the B.C.Pen was finally to happen Friday, Oct.8 at 5:00 p.m. Again, not everyone attended. Again, it was postponed—to Oct.11, following a morning C.A.C. meeting at Regional Headquarters CPS with Sol-Gen. Francis Fox, Commissioner André Therrien, and others.

No one on the Committee seemed to understand, or care, that five days after a person has been publicly slandered, the damage is virtually irreparable.

It was a strange weekend for me—strange, for one accustomed by now to spend the better part of each day with prisoners at the Pen. I was cut off from all contact but second-hand reports from those few C.A.C. members who were still going in.

I was determined to make the most of what would possibly be my last attendance at top brass sessions as a member of the C.A.C. When I learned that Fox had been to the B.C.Pen but had not met with the Inmate Committee (as his predecessor, Warren Allmand, always had), I strongly urged him to do so. Firstly, to discover what was happening to Ivan Horvat, who had been so heavily sedated that he had not been seen for three days. (Dr. Wallace agreed to go in to see him at 3:00 p.m.). Secondly, to avoid detracting from the I.C.'s credibility with the general population by seeming to ignore them. Others on the C.A.C.

spoke up in support and even joined me after the meeting to press the point personally with Mr. Fox. He not only remained unconvinced, but passed it off lightly with the suggestion that when he returned to B.C. at the end of the month, he *might* find time to see them.

I also read, and left with him, a written memorandum outlining suggestions for easier access to the B.C.Pen by the media, the lack of which constitutes one of the prime reasons for riots and hostage takings. If a regular monthly date was set for press conferences, the institution could profit by demonstrating to the public the improvements it was initiating; the prisoners would not feel pressured into hostage taking in order to make their grievances known and corrected; and the media itself could become a more creative social force by planning serious investigation of specific areas—programs, food, recreation, transfers—rather than always sensationalizing crises and fostering public fear.

Fox did not respond, then or later.

When this meeting ended, the C.A.C. moved off on its own to make some decisions about the slanderous attacks of Oct. 6.

It turned out that Bryan Williams had already prepared his personal memorandum on Oct.7, when he found he could not attend that first C.A.C. meeting. In it he had expressed frustration with the manner in which, once the crisis was over, prison officials were treating both the C.A.C. and myself:

> Mr. Murphy (CPS Regional Director General) indicated to me in my conversation with him that Claire Culhane had created problems and that our Citizens Committee lacked credibility because of some of her actions during the negotiations sessions. Mr. Peterson (Acting Director) told me in no uncertain terms that Claire Culhane's "chanting" sometime in August [August 10—National Prison Justice Day Vigil] had rendered her incapable of impartial judgment....
>
> I suggested to Murphy and Peterson that instead of the innuendo about Claire Culhane they name the specific objections they have in regard to her performance and put

them before our Committee and I promised that I for one would request that these complaints be considered, and if the specifics were found to be substantiated that I would press [her] resignation. No specifics were given to me except the "chanting" bit...and an episode when Ms. Culhane took considerable time in leaving the institution when requested to do so by Mr. Peterson. *I became convinced at that time that at the first opportunity which arose...the institution would find an excuse to keep Claire Culhane out of the institution.*

I am told that...Claire Culhane on one occasion very recently was specifically requested by Mr. Berkey to go down [to the gym] and "content the inmates."

I agreed (talking with Ed Lipinski) that we should establish independently whether Claire had been guilty of any kind of misconduct as suggested by Berkey and that if she was we should ask Claire for her resignation. *If she was not*, then as I put it, *the Administration would have to eat crow and permit her to come back into the institution.*

Berkey has now backed down on the letter-carrying incident but maintains that Claire Culhane should be kept out of the institution for 'other reasons'...I think we have reached a point where we cannot sit back without protest any longer....Berkey, Peterson and Murphy appear to be exercising judgment without justice...will not allow Claire in...will not revoke that order when the basis upon which those original judgments were made have both evaporated...it appears to me [she] has been turfed out for what now appears to be a 'phony reason.'

My personal copy arrived a good deal later.

In my own statement, I raised several questions:

I asked Dr. Lipinski what he meant when he said that my "version was not in complete agreement with that of the security men." Also, why he felt the incident required "adjudication." It was my understanding that "adjudication" applies to specific charges, while the charges against me were actually withdrawn within the hour. So, what was there to adjudicate?

I also asked him why he had presumably agreed to Colin Hoath of CBC-TV inviting me to be interviewed without first having advised me of the change in C.A.C.'s public relations policy. It was quite conceivable that I might have refused, and thereby lost even *that* opportunity to clear myself.

I asked Dr. Scott Wallace whether he felt he should have issued public statements calling for the resignation of a fellow member without first taking the matter to the Committee?

These questions, among many others, remained unresolved.

When the Chairman proposed that my resignation would be in the best interests of the C.A.C., I asked if *they* felt that the C.A.C. was fulfilling *its* obligations under the Letter of Understanding, and if not, where that responsibility lay? Regardless of whether I remained with the C.A.C. or not, its main emphasis, in my opinion, had to move from maintaining such a 'total impartiality' as to render it impotent, to more meaningful action.

Committees have been known to 'neutralize' themselves right out of existence.

In keeping with my original reason for joining the C.A.C., namely to offer my skills and experience in the area of prison reform, I accepted that my participation might now jeopardize the little progress that had been made. The prison population desperately needed outside support, now that the RCMP had been removed, and the C.A.C. was the only public group approved by the CPS. For that reason, only, I resigned.

However, to reduce the possibility of any challenge to the integrity of either the C.A.C. or myself personally, I did insist that the C.A.C. demand from the B.C.Pen officials a *public* retraction of their charges against me.

The retraction was requested in a phone call.

Within half an hour it was refused.

After the meeting, several members agreed to find a lawyer who (persuaded to waive his fee) would institute a libel action. One was found. Though our Committee was mainly composed of Members of Parliament, Members of the Legislative Assembly, University Professors, and lawyers, I was left to cover the court costs—out of my Unemployment Insurance, as my temporary teaching job had ended.

The prisoners felt differently.

When my libel suit against the B.C.Penitentiary was announced, Clarence Johns, a Native Indian prisoner, organized a collection for a legal defence fund. (I had been working with him prior to the disturbance, to get several of his Native brothers out to camp. Previously, they had been approved, but as so often happens, transfers of Native prisoners are set aside as others go ahead of them).

Six prisoners signed routine chits authorizing Personnel to transfer funds from their accounts to myself. The forms were returned without any valid reason. On further investigation we were told it was because I was not related to any of them.

Again, the staff were acting arbitrarily. A few months earlier, they had routinely approved the dispatch of $10.00 from a prisoner for some photo copying I had done for him. Obviously they were in a position to manipulate regulations.

Next, a tiresome round of correspondence, grievances and protests—ad nauseam. To no avail. The funds were never going to be released. All we had to do, I wrote to the Personnel office, was just continue this idiotic filibuster until these six men were either released, transferred, or died, for the story to end.

Less than a month later, five of the six were suddenly transferred to Dorchester Penitentiary in New Brunswick, in the traditional 'kidnapping' fashion—that is, with no opportunity to call their family or lawyers before being placed on a plane and transported 3,000 miles away.

Clarence was one of them. He did his best to reassure me in his letters from Dorchester not to feel responsible for their unrequested 'transfers.'

However, since that time there are prisoners who, on reaching Medium or Minimum institutions, are warned that continued correspondence with me will adversely affect their parole applications. According to the official explanation, one prisoner was returned to Maximum for 'displaying a negative attitude.' By coincidence, he had also put my name on his visiting list.

If there were any way to guarantee that no further reprisals would 'come down' on prisoners willing to testify in open court, I could name *seven* who could prove this statement.

Such assurances are neither offered nor trusted. This is hardly surprising in an environment where prisoners are 'set up' with *planted* contraband, for example.

In November 1977, representing the Prisoners' Rights Group at a conference in Victoria of forty-seven volunteer Justice Councils, I had the opportunity to introduce a Resolution:

> THAT in view of the information reported Aug.24/77 in *Vancouver Province* [originally supplied by myself] that "shivs" were being made in the machine shop at the B.C. Penitentiary by a person or persons other than a prisoner;
>
> And in view of the fact that the B.C.Pen is now reported to be partially closed to search for hidden weapons, including said type "shivs," items which therefore could conceivably have been deliberately placed in certain cells to incriminate their occupants;
>
> BE IT THEREFORE RESOLVED that this conference call for an immediate, full, open and public investigation into this very serious matter in order to try and diffuse the perilous tensions at the B.C.Pen.

Although the motion was passed, needless to say no such investigation ever took place.

*   *   *

First Sit-in at B.C.Penitentiary—December 15,1976

Majority of Prisoners Refuse to Eat

Virtually all the prisoners at the B.C.Pen...were on a hunger strike Tuesday...protest was to emphasize complaints about lack of proper bedding, the inadequate washing and toilet facilities and lack of exercise....

CPS spokesman George Moore couldn't confirm reports that the prisoners had demanded a $3 an hour minimum wage for any reconstruction work...strike began last Friday as a protest against living and sanitary conditions in the wrecked East wing where only superficial repair work had been done and where there are no cell toilets or running water.

...it was agreed that all

prisoners in the East wing would receive exercise...arrangements had been made to make 'superficial patchwork repairs' to the damaged auditorium for indoor exercise during inclement weather.

—*Province*, Dec.8/76

"No one can afford another hostage taking!"

Less than three months had passed, and again I was getting the grim message as I spoke with prisoners in the depressing visiting area.

On October 6, I had been ordered to leave the institution, but *only* in my capacity as a member of the C.A.C. When limited visiting was restored to the public early in December, I returned as a regular visitor. This fact needs to be emphasized: it was *not* because of the so-called 'contraband' letters episode that I was barred from every Federal prison across Canada.

The decision to bar me came later.

Meanwhile, the angry five-day hunger strike by the general population in support of the men forced back into the East wing—a significant gesture of consensus which the authorities should have known not to ignore—made it obvious that something had to be done to avert more 'smashing up' and perhaps another hostage taking. Keep in mind that the prisoners in the gym had been promised again and again they would never be sent back to that wing:

> Two members of the Citizens Advisory Committee at the request of the Inmate Committee and with the consent of the Administration, visited the East wing just before Christmas.
>
> The conditions there were truly appalling. The cells had no facilities whatsoever, although chemical toilets were available. There was no running water, and most depressing of all, most of the cells did not have any light. For most of the men the ony available light was that which filtered in from the outside through the polythene sheets which had been placed over window frames...plus the artificial light generated by a few light bulbs suspended from the ceiling.

The members visited every inmate...and their responses ranged from open hostility to complete and utter despair. That despair was made manifest over the Christmas holidays when a number of the inmates in the East wing slashed their arms.*

In spite of the C.A.C.'s awareness, trying to activate them was, once again, hopeless. This time I knew better than to waste much energy in that direction. In my opinion the C.A.C. was failing to make any substantial headway in helping the Administration solve the B.C.Pen problems.

The prisoners were again being kept isolated, unable to reach anybody—Administration or the public.

And again, things were coming to a boil.

In these circumstances, the *Prisoners' Rights Group* met and decided that if there was going to be another hostage taking it should be an outside volunteer one. It was the only way we could think of to bring the public in on it again—something the media would *have* to report. That things are terrible inside prisons is never 'news.' We counted on a 'voluntary hostage' act being news.

No one else in the group was prepared to be the hostage: those who wanted to were hindered by jobs and/or children, and those who were free to do so, refused. We worked out the following strategy.

I would call on the B.C.Pen Director with a list of issues. If he would not respond, I was to remain as a 'voluntary hostage' to serve as liaison with the prisoners and persist, without eating, for as long as necessary to resolve the situation and prevent another crisis from developing.

The *first* demand would be to summon any one of C.A.C. members Bryan Williams, Don Sorochan or Michael Jackson, to add to the validity of the discussion.

The *second* demand would be to change the wording from

---

*from the "Submission by the Citizens Advisory Committee to the Parliamentary Subcommittee," Feb.17/77, pp.16-17.

"movement and feeding" as it related to prisoners to that of "meals," as scheduled for the rest of the institution.

(Two years later, as a result of our consistent pressuring for language which "treats prisoners as people, not animals, as much deserving of respect and common courtesy as a non-prisoner," we were advised—Jan.4/79—by John Braithwaite, Deputy Commissioner of Communications of the Solicitor General Department, that he had been "assured by the Director of the B.C.Penitentiary that the revised institutional schedule will replace the word *feeding* by the suggested terms *breakfast, lunch* and *dinner."*)

The *third* demand was the immediate transfer of all men out of the condemned East wing—whether to corridors, TV lounge, or gym.

Fourth—visiting to be reinstated immediately, that is, two visits per week, one of which should be an 'open' (no partitions) visit.

Fifth—allow SMSU (solitary) prisoners a few hours daily into the general population.

Sixth—call to Ottawa to C.G.Rutter (Inmate Welfare) and to Inger Hansen (Correctional Investigator) to come out immediately to speak directly with the prisoners.

Seventh—call a press conference with Inmate Committee, SMSU, and any other areas as mutually agreed to.

Eighth—this press release to be delivered immediately to the Inmate Committee for internal broadcasting to offset any possible agitation caused by false rumours.

At 10:00 a.m. on December 15, 1976, with press release in hand, I and another PRG member called on Mr. Robert Swan, Acting Director at the B.C.Pen. Under the pretext that he hardly knew me as it was our first meeting, he proceeded to check my identity.

(Tacked on the wall above his head was a printed list naming the C.A.C. members with two lines prominently drawn through the names *Claire Culhane* and *RCMP Inspector R. Starek,* followed by the word "Resigned.")

Finally convinced of my identity, Mr. Swan heard out my reasons for being there. However, he refused to call the C.A.C. It became evident that there would be no useful dialogue. My companion left—as planned. She joined another member down at the monument area to display our posters calling for the transfer of the men from the uninhabitable East wing.

Police Carry Away B.C. Pen Activist

A prison activist... was arrested and carried out of the institution office by police Wednesday after she refused to leave.

Claire Culhane was charged with trespassing after she told A/D Bob Swan she wouldn't leave until eight demands for improvements in the Pen were met. New Westminster police were forced to carry her out of the building to a patrol car and later into the police station. Released a short time later, Culhane said she will picket outside the prison and go without food until Christmas.

Culhane carried a sign calling herself a 'voluntary hostage' of the prison administration. Explained this would be better than having desperate inmates take hostage again and had hoped her presence would lead to improvements in the prison.

Culhane called conditions in the East wing "intolerable" and said even the SPCA should be called in because it is not fit for the rats that inhabit it.

—*Columbian*, Dec.16/76

In the police station my purse was taken from me and searched, and a questionnaire was brought out. I later learned that only my I.D. had to be produced, since I had not been charged. However, in retrospect, it was worth having made the mistake—if only for the amusement it provided.

After the routine name, address, etc. was recorded, the interrogation went like this:

Officer: Nationality?

Culhane: Canadian.

O: Religion?

C: Do unto others as you would have them do unto you.

O: What! You mean, none?

C: No, I didn't say *none*. You asked me what my religion was and I answered: Do unto others as you would have them do unto you.

O: Racial origin?

C: Canadian. (I object to that question and consider it totally unnecessary in those circumstances).

O: Racial origin? (shrieked at me three times as I continued to answer 'Canadian' each time).

O: Are you Irish?

C: No, I'm not Irish. Just because I have an Irish name doesn't mean I'm Irish.

O: Racial origin!!! (again shrieked, this time bringing his face to within an inch of mine).

C: Well, if you must know, my mother came from Kiev (Ukraine) and my father came from Vilna (then part of Russia).

O: (Turning to his partner, triumphantly) That's Irish!

This exchange was matched at one of my weekly 'open fence visits' at the top of Cumberland Avenue alongside the B.C. Pen property. I would frequently stop to wave and shout greetings to the prisoners in the exercise yard, through three wire fences and across 200 feet of field.

An unmarked car pulled up and a police officer rushed out. "Get back in your car, you're trespassing on *public* property."

He was quite right. I was standing on the sidewalk. I refused to return to my car as long as he pointed his finger and shouted at me: "You *have* to get in, I'm the authority, you're only a citizen!" he added.

*   *   *

They then put me in a cell where, after waiting for 20 minutes, I requested that my lawyer be phoned to come and get me out. Within five minutes I was walking out the door and back to the B.C.Pen with friends who had been waiting. We had originally planned to hold a 24-hour vigil in front of the Pen on Christmas day. This seemed to be a logical way to spend the intervening ten days as well.

Others joined me from time to time as I maintained a ten-day 8:00 a.m. to 5:00 p.m. vigil, walking up and down in front of the prison with placards:

RESTORE OPEN XMAS VISITS
ONLY THE RICH CAN AFFORD JUSTICE
ABANDON SUPERMAX EVERYWHERE
NO MORE SOLITARY CONFINEMENT

From other such actions I had learned to use my time walking back and forth by offering views on the prison system to passersby, and learning from them. One former guard told me how he had warned a certain other member of the 'goon squad' to walk carefully. He said some who ignored his suggestion and persisted in their cruelty had paid the price. He himself had resigned before he reached that stage.

An electrician described his job at the new court house. He had installed a buzzer system in the courtroom, numbering the witness box #1, and going around the room to the Judge's bench, #10. His foreman instructed him to reverse the order, but the electrician insisted: "If there ain't nobody in that witness box, the Judge he ain't got no job!"

On their way to and from Matsqui to New Westminster Court every day, the busload of prisoners would cheer and wave clenched fists as they drove by. When it was a sympathetic driver, he would slow down.

Halfway through the vigil, Dec.20, I delivered a letter to Acting Director, Mr. Swan:

> ...of even greater urgency is the news that men are being locked up for 24 hours...with only occasional exercise periods; no library; no university courses; no recreation; no programs whatsoever. The latter two conditions had existed long before the recent disturbance.
>
> ...another 'confrontation' with the prisoners might well be disastrous for all concerned and something which dare not happen. We can and must avoid the experience of a Canadian Attica.
>
> The prevailing venomous attitudes and practices such as threats of using tear gas and numerous episodes of hosing down in SMU can only be viewed as fraught with danger...

must be replaced by... acceptance of the fact that prisoners are human beings and not animals, and that they must be accorded some opportunity to exercise a sense of dignity and self respect. If you take this away from them you must expect and do receive the inevitable reactions....

...immediate needs which must be met... decent living conditions... clean, warm and adequate housing, proper diet, responsible medical care, adequate recreation; meaningful work programs... surely not an impossible goal and surely failure to implement... has to be recognized as the basic cause of... the present disturbance.

The personal animosities which exist between individual guards and prisoners must be dealt with... it is absurd that prisoners must resort to hostage taking in order to effect transfers from an area where they obviously feel their lives are in danger....

In carrying out this... vigil it is my hope that... others may be encouraged to bring their views and influence to bear so that useful changes will begin to happen.

(On the same day I happened to receive an anonymous 'hate' note reading, "Claire: It is a sorry day for Canada that Hitler missed you, U.S. bombs missed you, but the P.L.O. won't.")

The Director was not about to consider any of these recommendations. I continued until Christmas Day.

Riot Cuts Activities for Yule at B.C.Pen

Except for what promises to be a sumptuous Christmas dinner, the festive season will pass almost unnoticed in the B.C.Pen this year... normal Christmas activities have been cancelled... no open visits... with the exception of the B.C.Pen all other Federal and Provincial prisons have been celebrating the Xmas season for the past week with visits and concerts being organized daily.

The lack of Xmas activities... has caused the Prisoners' Rights Group to mount a week long demonstration outside the prison calling on the authorities to allow open visits.   —*Sun*, Dec.23/76

Sixteen inmates inflicted super-ficial wounds on themselves in a bloodletting demonstration in the	B.C.Penitentiary East wing Christmas eve. —*Sun*, Dec.28/76

On January 12, 1977, I was served with a Summons claiming that I did "unlawfully trespass upon Penitentiary Lands." Trial was set for June 9.

The day of the trial began with a telegram from *l'Office des Droits Détenus* (Prisoners' Rights Office) Montréal, which "wholeheartedly supports Claire Culhane in her fight against the Canadian Penitentiary Service and her refusal to be intimidated by the Administration of the B.C.Penitentiary. We wish her success as we were successful in our trial against the Ministry of the Solicitor General."

Five of their members had been arrested March 15 in the Ottawa waiting room of Francis Fox and charged with "petty trespassing." On March 30 they pleaded not guilty, offering the following reasons for their sit-in:

1) The conditions of detention in the Special Correctional Unit (SCU) are intolerable and have so been judged by the Subcommittee of the Commons Justice Committee.

2) Despite the few changes brought about by Mr. Fox the situation at SCU remains basically the same.

3) In our opinion the Director of SCU, Mr. Pierre Goulem, and the Commissioner of Penitentiaries, Mr. André Therrien, are contravening Article 2 (b) of the Canadian Bill of Rights which states that: "no law of Canada shall be construed or applied so as to impose or authorize the imposition of cruel and unusual treatment or punishment."

4) In our opinion the Director of SCU...and the Commissioner of Penitentiaries...are contravening Article 1 of the Québec Charter of Human Rights and Freedom which states that: "every human being has a right to life, and to personal security, inviolability...."

5) In our opinion the Director of SCU...and the Commissioner of Penitentiaries...are contravening Article

4 of the Québec Charter...which states that: "every person has a right to the safeguard of his [her] dignity, honour and reputation."
6) Considering that..."every human being whose life is in peril has a right to assistance," [then] "every person must come to the aid of anyone whose life is in peril, either personally or by calling for aid, by giving him [her] the necessary and immediate physical assistance, unless it involves danger to himself [herself] or other persons or he [she] has another valid reason."

They informed the Solicitor General in writing of their intention to meet with him that day, understanding that Common Law gives citizens the right to petition an elected representative of the people. Yet the Solicitor General (who was free to see them that afternoon, according to his ministerial aid), accorded them the same kind of treatment as prisoners receive: "threats, arrests and accusations."

During the trial, Culhane, acting without a lawyer, read a prepared statement indicting the penitentiary system: "...and the respective governments which have funded it over the years which should be standing at this bar today, not myself...charge the Canadian Penitentiary Service in general, and the B.C.Penitentiary in particular, with gross mismanagement, unbelievable callousness and a less than human attitude in its dealings with prisoners and friends and families of prisoners.

"During the last hostage-taking incident...I saw men condemned to the most mindless form of treatment, robbed of their self-respect...lawbreakers incarcerated in the most lawless institution in the land where neither building, health, nor fire inspectors check and monitor the premises."   —*Sun*, June 10/77

I further stated: "while prisoners are expected to adjust to society's rules, little or nothing is said of the fact that on release [they] must re-enter a society which cannot provide employment for over one million...[I feel] compelled to ask if the Pacific Division of the CPS is addressing itself to this serious problem now that their staff has (in less than 15 years) increased from *6 to 112*...we must all accept our responsibilities to see that the community which we share is one that has room for all of us, prisoners, non-prisoners and ex-prisoners...I intend to use every non-violent means at my disposal to help abolish the present prison system and to help institute a moral, constructive and humane method of dealing with the community's problems *within the community*."

The same day, the *Sun* reported, "A one-day-hunger-and-work strike at the B.C.Pen ended quietly today as all inmates reported back to work."

It was welcome support. And at one point during the proceedings, even the Crown Prosecutor drew the attention of the Judge to this 'coincidence.'

The verdict came down the following week: Guilty. However, sentencing proved to be another problem. Judge F.K.Shaw hesitated, and finally named the fine—$25.

The maximum sentence was six months, $500 fine, or both. Imposing a prison sentence would have been complicated because at that time I was also barred from the Oakalla Women's Unit. How does one sentence a person to a prison which they are barred from visiting? Evidently they didn't want me inside under any circumstances—not even as a prisoner, much less a member of the *Prisoners' Rights Group*.

If the media had suspected the politics of the dilemma, they didn't say so. Instead, they featured: "Spokesman Fined $25.00." They did not note my refusal to pay. Nor did they note the Judge's further ruling, "no default," meaning that the fine was withdrawn. Eventually the *Sun* did carry my letter explaining why I had refused to pay.

...since my plea of not guilty has been entered on the basis that I was acting in my capacity as prisoners advocate...maintained that not only was I innocent of any wrongdoing, but that I had a moral responsibility to try to engage the prison administration in useful dialogue that particular week.

—June 23/77

*   *   *

Please be advised that Ms. Culhane was informed by the Visiting & Correspondence Department on December 21/76 on instructions from this Office, that her visiting privileges were cancelled at the B.C.Penitentiary as of and including December 15/76 for "Security Reasons" until further notice.

I am not prepared to give further explanation of this notice as it could affect the operation and security of this institution.

This letter was addressed to my lawyer on Jan.12/77. Neither A/Director Swan, nor anyone else in the entire System, has since elaborated upon the "Security Reasons." While the Dec.15 date coincides with my sit-in, it has never officially been linked to that event. By using the term "Security Reasons," without laying any specific charge for any specific crime, they made it impossible for me to defend myself.

This is exactly the same device as that used to keep prisoners in solitary indefinitely, under the Catch-22 of "Dissociation."

In the *Proceedings of the Third Canadian Conference on Applied Criminology* (March 1978), David Cole, LL.B., offered this observation on the "Rights and Responsibilities of Persons Arrested and on Remand":

Rough justice may be done but certainly the vast majority of prisoners and [others]. . . involved in this area do not regard the process as following the rules of natural justice and due process. (p.72)

The prison population reacted to the withdrawal of my visiting rights by getting 128 names on a petition. When they were not allowed to send it to me, I asked Mr. Swan what more peaceful, non-violent act can prisoners take than to put their name to a piece of paper? And when they can't even do that, what else is left? And if a disturbance should happen, whose fault would it be? Mr. Swan was unmoved.

Nonetheless, the petition eventually reached me:

To: Mr. Swan
From: B.C.Penitentiary Inmate Population
Date: January 17,1977

We, the undersigned, are asking for a re-instatement of visiting privileges for Ms. Claire Culhane. She has not been charged with any criminal offence, so there is no reason for her visitor's privileges to be suspended.

Others, who have broken penitentiary rules, have had their visiting privileges suspended for a definite period. Although Ms. Culhane was banned [as a C.A.C. member] from entering B.C.Pen, this does not mean there should be a suspension of visiting privileges.

This petition was followed by forty-four other individual letters from prisoners, as well as supportive letters from the Dean of Women at UBC, the Research Director at B.C.Corrections, Dept. of the Attorney General, and several lawyers. An application was filed on May 29/77 in the Federal Court of Canada Trial Division "for relief in the nature of a Writ of Certiorari...in the matter of the denial of visiting privileges...."

My lawyer called upon the Court to quash the withdrawal of my visiting rights on the grounds that the decision was "both arbitrary and unreasonable...and unfair under the cicumstances."

The affidavit emphasized that since I had become a "strong and persistent spokesperson for prisoners who lack the freedom and contacts to corrcct the many breaches of rules and regulations which affect them...it can be understood why my role is not likely to be one to curry favour with those in the administrative hierarchy of the Canadian Penitentiary Service, and who may thus find their decisions and actions challenged...."

The main thrust of our application was directed to the need for natural justice not only to be practised, inside and outside the walls, but to be seen to be practised. We were appearing before Justice F.U.Collier, who had recently been in the news.

...accused the Federal Justice Department of staging a 'distasteful spectacle' in a case before him...[he] was seeking, in effect, a ministerial ruling on whether the penitentiary inmates should have the right to take grievances to a civil court and represent themselves in the proceedings (Jack C. Magrath vs. The Queen). The Department of Justice, mindful of the *burgeoning prisoners' rights movement*, had attempted...to place obstacles before an inmate who is presenting his own suit.

... *until the advent of prisoners' rights*, Magrath's objections ...would have been handled through the usual grievance procedures within the institution. By bringing his suit into Federal court the inmate had shaken the system by subpoening fellow-inmates and causing a number of senior Canadian Penitentiary Service officials to spend three days in court.

—*Sun*, Sept.10/77

Since our own case was equally outrageous, and with the Department of Justice presenting a seemingly weak case, we really anticipated a favourable decision. However, on October 6, Judge Collier dismissed our motion, with costs, stating in his Reasons for Judgment:

> ...Ms. Culhane does not have any relatives, by blood or marriage, imprisoned in any Canadian institution. But she has apparently visited institutions and inmates in them in carrying out her self-appointed role....
>
> As I see it, a decision on security grounds, directing that a certain member...of the public shall not be permitted to visit the prison, or inmates in it, is an administrative decision which in its very nature does not require...the right to a so-called hearing. Nor does it warrant interference by this Court... *where it is merely asserted the decision was arbitrary, unreasonable or unfair.*

Perhaps Judge F.U.Collier has no relatives in prisons either, and perhaps he is among the alleged 95% of judges who have never set foot in a prison. But there are others who have.

After a single night at the Nevada State Prison...23 judges from all over the U.S. emerged "appalled at the homosexuality," shaken by the inmates' "soul-shattering bitterness," and upset by "men raving, screaming and pounding on the walls."

Kansas Judge E. Newton

Vickers summed up, "I felt like an animal in a cage. Ten years in there must be like 100 or maybe 200." Vickers urged Nevada to "send two bulldozers out there and tear the damn thing to the ground."

—"The Shame of Prisons," *Time*, Jan.18/71

Chief Justice Bora Laskin is another who has spoken out. In the matter of an appeal from a decision of the Inmate Disciplinary Board at Matsqui Institution, it had been held that the Federal Court of Appeal had no jurisdiction to review a disciplinary board decision which was not "required by law" to be made "on a judicial or quasi-judicial basis." (*Federal Court of Canada Trial Division*, T-4302-75, July 14/77).

David Cole—a well known Toronto lawyer, active in civil liberties and prisoners rights areas—in "Courts Must Monitor the Power of Prisons," comments.

If we allow that decision to stand, what does it say about us? ...that we are saying to prison custodians, 'Do with prisoners as you will only don't tell us what you do?' That we have so lost sight of basic human compassion that no one gives a damn about what happens behind the barred doors?

—*Globe & Mail*, Sept.15/77

Cole goes on to quote from the "scathing dissent" in which Judge Laskin expresses his own doubts.

...to assert that these carefully-wrought rules of procedure (Commissioner's Directives)... have no external force, that [prisoners] have no right to the benefit of the procedure because the penitentiary authorities have no duty to follow them...is much too nihilistic a view of law for me to accept.

—*Globe & Mail*, Sept.15/77

It was time for another sit-in.

*   *   *

Second Sit-In at the B.C. Penitentiary—July 29, 1977

Clarence Johns—the Native prisoner who had unsuccessfully tried to organize a collection in the gym towards my legal expenses when my libel suit against the B.C. Penitentiary was announced—had been transferred back to the B.C. Pen from Dorchester in June 1977. He was placed directly into solitary. He didn't even have time to gather up his personal belongings—belongings which were later alleged to have been lost in transit, but which we were able to trace through transportation documents to prove that they *had* reached the Pen. (He was eventually reimbursed $160 for his loss.)

Clarence's letters showed that he wasn't well and asked for someone to come and see him. I was barred from visiting, and when even the Native Court Worker, who has social worker status, was also denied access to him, I felt it was time for another visit to the Director's office.

On July 29, when it seemed sufficiently critical to make the effort to see Clarence myself, I called on Mr. Reynett, the new Director. I failed to persuade him to allow me a ten minute visit with Clarence—not even in his own office.

Again, I refused to leave.

Again, the New Westminster police were called in to remove me physically. But not before the arresting officer warned me that if I refused the director's order to leave, I would be charged with "assault." Mr. Reynett testified in his affidavit that he laid his right hand on my right arm, thereby creating the required physical contact which is then so often used in court to charge the 'offender' with the assault.

They must have reconsidered their strategy, for a week later the Summons spelled out the routine "unlawful trespass upon Penitentiary lands." This time, I was only held in the patrol car for half an hour as they took my I.D., and then they released me one block from the courthouse—"In case you have some photographers waiting for you. . . ."

Trial was set for December 29, 1977.

Once again I defended myself. The publicity which I sought was for the purpose of exposing and challenging injustices in the System, not to glorify myself, as some maintain. Specifically, I attacked the discriminatory treatment of Native Indian prisoners, and the persistent use of solitary confinement.

Judge W.S. Selbie was not impressed.

Prison activist Claire Culhane was found guilty of trespassing on B.C.Penitentiary property and fined $150.00...today.

She told the court she would not pay the fine and if a prison term resulted, it would be a "small price to pay."

She said she charged the CPS with trespass on *her* rights and on the rights of people in custody.

...in view of the fact that she had 'deliberately flown in the face of an earlier conviction'... Judge Selbie said he was fining her in the hope of deterring her from similar acts in the future.

—*Sun*, Dec.29/77

Once again, the media managed to distort the real meaning of my words, but finally did publish my correction.

"...a small price to pay *for the exercise of my rights as a citizen to speak out*" was the full statement. —*Sun*, Jan.6/78

On November 17, I appealed the original sentence imposed by Judge Shaw on my 'trespass,' requesting an absolute discharge. Two ironic 'precedents' were cited where,

> *July 1977*—members of three police forces (RCMP, Québec, and Montréal) had all pleaded guilty to charges of break-in at the offices of the *Agence Presse Libération du Québec;* and

> *September 1977*—an RCMP Corporal was found guilty of theft 'by conversion' of $11,000 seized in drug investigation.

All four had nonetheless been granted absolute discharge.

Judge M. Hyde was not impressed with my analogies. He dismissed my appeal, claiming that he was "not satisfied in this case that a discharge would be warranted, either absolute or conditional, because of the fact that *this offence*, however minor it may be, was deliberate, planned and not impulsive.''

The judiciary is not the only area in Canadian life where justice is travestied.

When a new Commissioner of Penitentiaries was appointed upon the death of Mr. Therrien, and *all* my communications to him regarding prisoners' affairs were ignored, an explanation was received and then forwarded to me:

> *Date:* Feb.14/78
> *To:* Mr. Mark MacGuigan, M.P.
> *From:* Mr. D.R.Yeomans, Commissioner of Corrections
>
> May I refer to your letter dated January 9,1978 concerning correspondence you had received from Mrs. Claire Culhane of Burnaby, B.C.
> *Our departmental position vis-a-vis Mrs. Claire Culhane is that we no longer answer her correspondence....*

By this time I had been effectively barred from visiting prisoners in the Federal system across Canada.

The same thing was to happen on the Provincial scene.

CHAPTER SIX

Oakalla

The Vancouver Public Library keeps a special newspaper file which deals only with "Prison Suicides." From this, and from other files on prisons, I have drawn a partial list of headlines concerning typical events which have taken place over roughly the last ten years at one institution—*Oakalla.*

*   *   *

HANGED SELF WITH BLANKET (Early 1970)
HANGED SELF WITH BEDSHEET (June 1970)
HANGED SELF WITH SHIRT (Aug. 1971)
HANGED SELF (Jan.6/72)
DROWNED SELF (Feb./74)
HANGED SELF BY SHOELACES (Mar.14/74)
APPARENT SUICIDE (Mar.26/74)
HANGED SELF WITH BED SHEET (Sept.24/74)
HANGED SELF WITH SHEETS (May 7/75)

OAKALLA RIPE FOR RIOT (*Georgia Straight,* June 19/75)
OAKALLA PRISONERS BOW TO SHOW OF FORCE (*Vancouver Sun,* July 2/75)
OAKALLA PRISONERS CLAIM PROTEST SIT-IN VICTORY (*Sun,* July 3/75)
SOLITARY CONFINEMENT "INHUMANE"—FARRIS (*Province, July 3/75)*
OAKALLA INMATES END SECOND PROTEST SIT-IN (*Province,* July 4/75)
TOUR BARES OAKALLA INDIGNITIES, FRUSTRATIONS (*Sun,* July 8/75)
MEETING TODAY TO DECIDE FATE OF OAKALLA "HOLE" (*Sun,* July 9/75)
OAKALLA INSTITUTION CELLS 'TO BE MORE HUMANE' (*Sun,* July 10/75)
OAKALLA MEETINGS END BUT 'NOTHING GAINED' *Sun,* July 18/75)

OAKALLA PLAYS PART IN HUNGER STRIKE (*Sun*, Aug.11/75)

HANGED SELF WITH JEANS (*Suicide File*, Aug.27/75)

OAKALLA PROBE ORDERED AFTER PRISONER BEATEN UP (*Province*, Mar.22/76)

UNCIVILIZED TO CURB PRISONER READING (*Province*, Aug.28/76)

SIX ESCAPE JAIL AS 100 INMATES WATCH (*Sun*, Oct.9/76)

OVERCROWDING SPARKS FEARS OF JAIL DISTURBANCES (*Sun*, Nov.5/76)

THREE INMATES ESCAPE OAKALLA (*Sun*, Nov.13/76)

PRISON SIT-IN GETS ACTION (*Prov.* Nov.23/76)

ACCUSED KILLS HIMSELF (*Sun*, Dec.23/76)

FIVE INMATES ESCAPE OAKALLA (*Sun*, Dec.28/76)

THREE MORE PRISONERS ESCAPE FROM OAKALLA (*Sun*, Jan.15/77)

METAL DETECTORS AT OAKALLA? (Jan.19/77)

MACDONALD CHARGES GUARDS VIOLATE PRISONERS' PRIVACY (*Sun*, Jan.22/77)

COVER-UP ALLEGED IN PROBE (*Province*, Jan.22/77)

PRIVACY 'NOT VIOLATED' (*Sun*, Jan.25/77)

DAY IN OAKALLA 'INTIMIDATING' (*Victoria Times*, Jan.26/77)

PRISON CHIEF LOSES SLEEP GETTING TO KNOW OAKALLA (*Sun*, Jan.26/77)

FORMER OAKALLA GUARD GUILTY OF POSSESSION (*The Columbian*, Mar.16/77)

2 OF 3 GRABBED AFTER OAKALLA BREAKOUT (*Sun*, Mar.23/77)

OAKALLA ESCAPERS CAUGHT TRYING FOR TAXI, HIDING (*Sun*, Mar.24/77)

PRISONER RECAPTURED (*Province*, Mar.30/77)

OAKALLA INMATE BOLTS TO FREEDOM (*Columbian*, Apr.12/77)

LACK OF MEDICAL ATTENTION IN OAKALLA 'SUICIDAL' (*Columbian*, Apr.12/77)

SPATE OF ESCAPES SPARKS SHERIFFS' SECURITY PROBE (*Province*, Apr.12/77)

ESCAPER NETTED WITH 2 OTHERS AFTER HOLD-UP
(*Province,* Apr.18/77)
ESCAPED OAKALLA PRISONER CAPTURED HIDING UNDER
BED (*Sun,* Apr.28/77)
GOVERNMENT MOVES ON OAKALLA PHASE-OUT (*Province,*
Apr.29/77)
NEW FACILITIES WILL PHASE OUT OAKALLA (*Columbian,*
Apr.29/77)
OAKALLA PHASEOUT STILL YEARS AWAY (*Sun,* Apr.29/77)
NO FUNDS TO HELP DECREPIT OAKALLA (*Columbian,* May
4/77)
GUARDS WARNING SHOT HALTS ESCAPE (*Sun,* June 23/77)
OAKALLA ESCAPERS STILL FREE (*Sun,* July 4/77)
LEAKY OLD OAKALLA, A PARADISE FOR BREAKOUT
CONVICTS (*Province,* July 7/77)
SEVENTH ESCAPER CAPTURED (*Province,* July 15/77)
SEARCH ON FOR EIGHT ESCAPERS (*Province,* July 18/77)
PRISONERS 'MORE HARDENED' (*Sun,* July 19/77)
ESCAPER'S MONTH-LONG JAUNT ENDS (*Province,* July
22/77)
PRISONER ESCAPES (*Sun,* July 27/77)
OAKALLA...STILL A PRISON OR JUST A LOW-RENT HOTEL?
(*Columbian,* Aug.13/77)
NEW OAKALLA LANDS STUDY "JUST A STALLING TACTIC,"
SAYS DAILLY(*Columbian,* Aug.18/77)
OAKALLA WOMAN INMATE JUST CAN'T BE CONTAINED
(*Columbian,* Sept.8/77)
ESCAPER WOUNDED AFTER PULLING GUN (*Province,*
Sept.10/77)
FIRE BREAKS OUT IN WOMEN'S SECTION OF OAKALLA
(*Sun,* Sept.15/77)
TREATMENT AT OAKALLA PROTESTED (*Province,*
Sept.28/77)
OAKALLA 'CRUELTY' CASE TOSSED OUT (*Province,*
Oct.25/77)
OAKALLA WOMEN'S SECTION SAID 'ALMOST SUB-HUMAN'
(*Sun,* Oct.27/77)

OAKALLA SEX SCANDAL INVESTIGATION SOUGHT (*Province,* Nov.10/77)

OAKALLA PROBE ORDERED (*Province,* Nov.17/77)

INSIDE 'HOTEL OAKALLA'—SEX, INTRIGUE (*Sun,* Nov.19/77)

PRISON CHIEF MUM ON 'BATTLE' (*Sun,* Nov.21/77)

FUTURE OF OAKALLA DELIVERS PRESENT SHOCK (*Province,* Nov.23/77)

DERELICT, ABANDONED BUILDINGS STAND OUT IN OAKALLA REAL ESTATE TOUR (*Sun,* NOv.24/77)

GARDOM WANTS RCMP PROBE OF OAKALLA CHARGES SPEEDED UP (*Sun,* Nov.28/77)

TOP TWO OFFICIALS AT WOMEN'S JAIL TRANSFERRED (*Sun,* Dec.2/77)

WOMEN'S JAIL STAFF WELCOME BOSS CHANGE (*Sun,* Dec.3/77)

GARDOM ORDERS "FULL" PRISON INQUIRY (*Province,* Dec.6/77)

'CHRISTMAS SPIRIT' MOVES 3 FLEEING PRISONERS (*Sun,* Dec.9/77)

TWO MORE ESCAPE FROM OAKALLA AFTER POLICE RECAPTURE EARLIER PAIR (*Sun,* Dec.12/77)

THREE WOMEN INMATES BREAK OUT OF JAIL (*Province,* Dec.28/77)

ESCAPER CALLS TO SURRENDER (*Sun,* Dec.28/77)

PROUDFOOT INQUIRY INTO JAILS FOR WOMEN TO START FEB. 3 (*Sun,* Jan.5/78)

WOMAN ESCAPES AGAIN (*Sun,* Jan.11/78)

WOMAN ESCAPER NABBED (*Sun,* Jan.23/78)

JAIL SYSTEM TERMED A VICIOUS CYCLE (*Province,* Feb.8/78)

WOMAN DUNKED IN SCALDING WATER IN 'JAIL JUSTICE' (*Province,* Feb.10/78)

OAKALLA INMATE SCALDING 'COVERED UP' AFTER PROBE (*Sun,* Feb.10/78)

GUARDS' JOB AT OAKALLA ISN'T EASY, INQUIRY TOLD (*Province,* Feb.16/78)

Cliques, 'Vicious Rumours,' Bared At Oakalla Probe
    (*Sun,* Feb.16/78)
Oakalla Guard Attacks Staff Training (*Province,*
    Feb.17/78)
Guard Tells Probe Of Poor Training (*Sun,* Feb.17/78)
Oakalla Officers Defied Jail Chiefs, Probe Told
    (*Province,* Feb.18/78)
Four Women Held In The Hole "Beyond Regulation
    15 Days" (*Sun,* Feb.18/78)
Oakalla Inmate Recaptured (Unlucky 'Six') (*Sun,*
    Feb.20/78)
Nobody Cares About His School For Women Inmates—
    Teacher (*Province,* Mar.1/78)
Escape-Bound Prisoners Don't Need A Hacksaw
    (*Province,* Mar.3/78)
Prison Nurse Tells Oakalla Inquiry Of Wrist-Slashing
    (*Sun,* Mar.4/78)
I Wasn't Allowed To Run Jail My Way, Ex-Warden
    Says (*Sun,* Mar.8/78)
Vitamins Could Halve Population Of Prisons
    (*Province,* Feb.27/78)
A Jail Escape That Never Was (*Province,* Feb.28/78)
Prison Probe Told Charge Laid In Welfare Fraud
    (*Sun,* Feb.28/78)
Same Ending For Escaper (*Province,* Apr.18/78)
Escaper 'Dangerous' (*Sun,* Apr.27/78)
Woman Escaper Recaptured In City (*Sun,* July 12/78)
Hanged Prisoner Identified (*Sun,* July 20/78)
Bomb On Towel Just Dummy (*Province,* July 22/78)
Police Hunt Escaper (*Sun,* Aug.2/78)
Inmates Stage Minor Riot (*Province*, Aug.14/78)
Guards Quell Rioters In Oakalla (*Sun,* Aug.14/78)
Women Continue Strike (*Province,* Aug.25/78)
Oakalla's Teresa Escapes Again (*Province,* Sept.12/78)
Prisoner Dies After Suicide Bid (*Sun,* Sept.25/78)
Prisoners Say Visit Ban Caused Suicide Bid (*Sun,*
    Sept.26/78)

OAKALLA TO CLOSE: NEW CENTRE ANNOUNCED (*Vancouver Express,* Dec.22/78)

WOMAN HOSTAGE AIDED BY AGE (*Vancouver Express,* Dec.29/78)

OAKALLA MUST GO, SAYS INQUEST JURY (*Vancouver Express,* Jan.12/79)

FREQUENT CELL CHECKS ADVISED (*Vancouver Express,* Jan.15/79)

OAKALLA HUNGER STRIKE ENTERS 4TH DAY (*Columbian,* Jan.29/79)

OAKALLA INMATE FLEES (*Columbian,* Mar.10/79)

UNION WANTS FIRED OAKALLA PRISON GUARDS TAKEN BACK (*Vancouver Express,* Mar.23/79)

OAKALLA GUARDS REINSTATED BUT 'STILL PAYING' SAYS UNION (*Vancouver Express,* Apr.20/79)

OAKALLA: CONDITIONS ARE BAD AND GETTING WORSE (*Kinesis,* April/May, 1979)

LEGAL BOOKS IN PRISON INADEQUATE CLAIMS ACCUSED (*Georgia Straight,* May 9/79)

GUARDS OPEN FIRE (*Columbian,* May 11/79)

GUARD STABBED THE DAY BEFORE ALLEGED ASSAULT (*Columbian,* May 30/79)

OAKALLA INMATE ESCAPES (*Columbian,* June 14/79)

OAKALLA EYED FOR INCOMING WOMEN INMATES (*Sun,* July 4/79)

OAKALLA INMATES REFUSE FOOD (*Columbian,* July 5/79)

*   *   *

Lower Mainland Regional Correctional Centre (LMRCC), better known as Oakalla, is the largest of five provincial Correctional facilities in B.C. for those serving a 'deuce less one' (two years less a day). It includes maximum security cell accomodation for 701 prisoners and a pre-release dorm for 22. It is located in Burnaby. The site is large and impressive with a view towards the north mountains. A lake is situated on its edge.

There is also a female institution on the same site, known as Oakalla Women's Correction Centre (OWCC). Accomodation is provided for 73 in dorms, rooms and cubicles. A panabode hut and two other buildings are not being used, despite the overcrowding and public criticism.

In July 1977, I received an anonymous letter from a former employee at Oakalla:

Dear Ms. Culhane,

. . . The writer will now relate some events that occurred at the above institution, which still cause me to be nauseated whenever I think of them. The writer until now has not had the courage to mention the incidents to anyone.

On a certain night. . .the writer was on duty in the South wing of the above institution when a minor disturbance broke out on the third tier of the wing. Two guards who were assigned to the above tier made out reports against three inmates. I cannot recall who two of the inmates were, however the third inmate was one J——. The above guards, rather than investigating who was causing the disturbance, merely threw all of the inmates' names into a box and drew the above inmates' names from the box and sent them to the hole.

There were also cases where if an inmate wrote a letter that the guards did not like, the guards would ensure that the offending inmate did not receive any mail from the outside merely by throwing away any incoming mail and not mailing any outgoing mail. The above happened on more than one occasion while I was employed by the above institution.

During the same time frame three male guards of the institution, attached to the women's unit, were brought under internal investigation for having sexual intercourse with women inmates and also for performing illegal "skin searches" of the above inmates. The above incidents were witnessed by the female staff of the institution who, to their credit, reported the incidents to their superiors. The writer has no knowledge of whether any action was taken against the male guards who were involved either by internal proceedings or by outside court.

The writer hopes that the above information will be of some use to you in your struggle to acquire better living conditions for the inmates of the various institutions.

Yours in Struggle for those who are wronged.

Not the naked reality of the B.C. Penitentiary which I saw first hand—not my research and reading on the subject—not my tours of prisons and personal contact with many prisoners—not any of these experiences shake me up like this sordid, grubby, miserable, hopeless mess called Oakalla.

Your visiting privileges at Oakalla have been discontinued until further notice. I have taken this decision because I believe that to continue your visiting privileges at this time would not be in the best interests of the institution. (from E.W. Harrison, Regional Director, B.C. Corrections, March 10/78)

Judge Patricia Proudfoot: We all know the name Claire Culhane?

John Eckstedt, B.C. Corrections Commissioner: Yes.

Proudfoot: She apparently has been barred from visiting in Oakalla?

Eckstedt: Yes.

Proudfoot: The problem that Ms. Culhane has is that she isn't given any specific reasons. Do you know anything about this and have you been involved in it at all?...do you see any reason why, if she hasn't been, Ms. Culhane can't be given specific reasons?

Eckstedt: I see reason why she can't. Yes. I'm not sure if, in this specific case, they apply but there are often reasons why we don't or cannot or choose not to inform people of why they're being excluded or barred from an institution.

In her case—I have asked for and received...all of the documentation with all the letters from all the directors and all of the descriptions of incidents, and all of the things that are involved in that decision. The Minister has asked for a specific report on that in order to make a decision about whether or not and to what extent Ms. Culhane has been informed of the details of the decision concerning barring her from the provincial institutions.

Proudfoot: . . . would it be wise—to sit with her and tell her why not, rather than have this build-up of: 'I don't have any reasons. . . if I have done something wrong why don't you do something about it?. . . if I have done something on security or if I'm just suspect of this, then charge me with an offence,' and not have the people inside. . . with this awful nagging of: 'why is Ms. Culhane barred from the prison . . . people like Ms. Culhane are helpful, and they don't have any reason to feel that they shouldn't be allowed in institutions.'

Eckstedt: Yes. Yes. We are looking at it, as I say, we are going to be discussing it with the [Attorney General].*

On April 17/78 Garde Gardom, Atty-Gen., informed me:

. . . I have determined that this recommendation is made by both Management and supported by the Union and after having the file examined. . . I am not able to justify my interference with their decision.

*   *   *

Three years earlier (April 1975), as an instructor in the department of History at Capilano College, I was invited to offer a course at Oakalla Women's Correction Centre. When the College's budget for this course ran out, I continued voluntarily. I had become deeply concerned about the women prisoners, and wanted to support their interest in Women's Studies.

Transcript of Hearings, Royal Commission on Incarceration of Female Offenders, March 2/78, pp.3861-63.

Of course, prisoners in both men's and women's units at Oakalla struggled with Administration for improved conditions.

In the summer of that year, the male prisoners staged a protest to draw attention yet again to their demands, even though they had been told "time and time again that in jail we have no rights":

—*We Demand Our Rights Be Given To Us—Freedom of Speech, And To Be Treated As Human Beings.*

—*We Demand The Right To A Proper Educational Program And Better Educational Facilities.*

—*We Demand The Right Of Job Training.*

—*We Demand Privacy In Our Visits, In A Dignified And Relaxed Atmosphere.*

—*We Demand That Isolation Be Abolished.*

—*We Demand Staff Training That Recognizes Prisoners As Human Beings.*

—*We Demand The Right To Be Represented, To Call Witnesses Of Our Own Choice, And To Be Judged By Persons Independent of the Prison Administration.*

—*We Demand To Be A Part Of Decision Making Process.*

About 130 (male) inmates at...(Oakalla) continued a non-violent "sit-in" on a prison sports field...as officials considered their 8 point demand for better conditions. The prisoners, part-icipating in an annual sports day, refused about 3 p.m. to return to their cells at the end of the events and began the demonstration—the second of its kind this year.

In a written statement of their demands, the inmates maintain the prison "is very outdated and there is very little being done to better it..." they are not armed and have emphasized the protest is non-violent. "We're trying to keep it non-violent and they're playing with shotguns"...refer-ring to 12 armed guards walking around the...sit-in area and 14 more milling nearby.

—*Province*, July 2/75

To this list were added the following demands from the women prisoners, who never had any Sports Day, were rarely even allowed outdoors except for brief periods in their tiny 'play-pen':

— *We Demand That A Complete Investigation Of Medical Facilities And Staff Incompetency Be Made By An Unbiased Medical Expert.*

— *We Demand A Better Staff Training Program And Screening Process.*

— *We Demand Better Recreational Facilities.*

— *We Demand That More Time Be Taken With Each Individual In Order That Their Choice Of Transfer Is Given More Consideration.*

...about 23 staged a sympathy move with a sit-in in the women's gym during Tuesday evening and again Wednesday morning.

— *Province*, July 3/75

Having heard that the *Prisoners Union Committee* (PUC), a small group of prison activists, were supporting the sit-in from the roof of a bordering private garage, I joined them. We did it mainly to witness any violence that might take place, and to provide moral support, the same kind that was coming in waves of chants from the women's gym: "We're with you! Hold firm!"

After twenty-one hours, the 130 men won three concessions before they were herded back into their cells: a media tour; meetings between their Inmate Committee (accompanied by the PUC) and the Administration; and no reprisals.

"To be honest, we're warehousing people here," Oakalla Warden Henry Bjarnason admitted after a day long media tour of the prison Monday...[this] comment was superfluous. The frustrations that staff endure and the indignities that inmates suffer in the 63 year-old institution were evident.

— *Sun,* July 8/75

Representing the *Capilano Review*, I participated in the media tours of both men's and women's units. Although we were told that we would be allowed to see everything and talk privately with anyone, it didn't quite work out that way.

In the South wing of Oakalla, once described as 'a throwback to colonial days when Oakalla held people in custody for the Sheriff of New Westminster,' we were not allowed to make any contact. On other occasions the guards were adamant about standing right next to us. Despite this, prisoners were quite willing to be quoted by name, and poured out their grievances. They fully realized that the listening guards would, more than likely, take it out on them later for their stories to us. One prisoner shrugged when I warned him about being overheard.

"I know I will probably 'get it,' but I'm coming out soon. So what difference does it make? At least I have the chance to tell people from the outside what it's really like in here. I figure it's worth it."

Another prisoner shoved three hand-written pages into my hand urging me to step aside and read it into one of the media's tape recorders, and then return it to him. It took only three to four minutes to follow his well-conceived plan.

In Westgate B wing, we were shown a small classroom with ten desks crowded upon one another. The students expressed their desire for more courses, larger facilities to accomodate all the others who also wanted to upgrade their schooling. But, at the top of their priority list, was the demand for better treatment of their nun-teacher who, they claimed, "has 75% of the staff treating her like a dog because she tries to do things for us."

The Hospital Unit, we were told, provided many benefits—free dental care, eye glasses, prosthesis, and rhinoplasty (plastic surgery on nose). However, time did not permit any examination of charts to verify the actual number of treatments—which, as a trained Medical Record Librarian, I was particularly anxious to look into.

We were shown a former 'padded cell' which a guard claimed was no longer needed. "We now use chemical controls," he boasted. He was, in fact, inadvertently exposing the more 'scientific' methods which are now being used in B.C. institutions to dehumanize prisoners.

In addition to segregation areas in the main buildings, we saw the "hole"—under the old cow-barn. A five by seven foot cell, encased by heavy plexiglass, installed within another bare cell, was furnished only with a mattress, a bucket for toilet use, a naked bulb burning round the clock, and a vent in the ceiling no larger than a grapefruit.

Daytime, the occupant told us, is distinguished by two sparse meals.

Nightime, by two glasses of water.

Oakalla Is To Have A Better 'Hole'

Although Atty-Gen. Alex Mac-donald has said the present isolation cells...a group of 5 x 7 cells under an old barn...will be phased out within three weeks...

prison guards who met him on Wednesday said there now is no talk of abandoning isolation as a necessary form of discipline.

—*Sun,* July 10/75

The Women's section, while smaller and less grim in its general appearance, produced even more complaints.

"The clinic is a laugh...we get a hot two minute interview with the doctor and that's called medical attention...one doctor prescribes for withdrawal pains, but the other doctor won't."

The class room had space for only six. The tailor shop offered exceptionally good training, but "materials, staff and money were lacking" (Justice Proudfoot, *Report*, p.92); work programs for women fitted the traditional stereotypes: laundry, kitchen, hairdressing, with pay ranging from thirty-five cents to $2.00 *a day*.

And, not only did the women have their own solitary confinement unit in the basement of the building, but they, too, were taken down the hill to the old cow barn to share those very special quarters.

Telegram

The Hon. Mr. Garde Gardom,   Sept.16/77
Attorney General of B.C.,
Parliament Buildings,
Victoria, B.C.

We represent T.B., inmate LMRCC, presently held along with three other women in cell underneath old cowbarn. These small cells have wet concrete floors and walls, no sanitation facilities, are infested and smell of manure. Client is kept in these conditions 24 hours a day with only mattress on floor, a bucket, and a blanket at night. We understand a directive against use of these archaic conditions was issued from your office about 2 years ago. Client in this cell three days this date. Appreciate your immediate reply this situation.

Douglas E. Moss,
Barrister & Solicitor
Vancouver, B.C.

Further to this prisoner's predicament, we learned of several other similar instances. What follows is an exchange of correspondence, as found in the Proudfoot *Report,* between the Prisoners' Rights Group and the Director of the Oakalla District, H. Bjarnason:

1977.

Oct.20: Would you kindly explain why three women...T.B., C.A., and M.C. were detained for thirty days in isolation cells? (PRG).

Nov.4: This was answered in our previous correspondence. (Director).

Nov.11: This question was not answered...under section 2.26(e) of the Gaol Rules and Regulations, it says: "...confinement to isolation cells on a regular or restricted diet for a period of up to 15 days...." Why are women sometimes assigned to 30 days? (PRG).

Nov.18: I am unaware of any inmate being sentenced to 30 days in segregation. If you would supply me with the names, dates, etc. I will investigate this further. (Director).

Nov.24: On Sept. 15/77, C.G., C.A., T.B., and M.C. were

taken to the isolation area under the old cow barn. They were returned to the isolation area in the main building within 36 hours when they were consigned for 30 days in isolation, but were released in 25 days with the remaining 5 days held in abeyance, depending on their future behaviour. (PRG).

Dec.15: . . . following are my findings:

    C.A. sentenced 10 days isolation
    C.A. sentenced 30 days isolation (concurrent)

    T.B. sentenced 5 days isolation
    T.B. sentenced 30 days isolation (concurrent)

    M.C. sentenced 15 days isolation (definite)
    M.C. sentenced 15 days isolation (indeterminate)
    M.C. sentenced 21 days isolation (indeterminate)

    C.G. sentenced 15 days isolation (definite)
    C.G. sentenced 15 days isolation (indeterminate)
    C.G. sentenced 5 days isolation (consecutive)

Under the Gaol Rules the Warden has the authority to award [sic] a sentence up to and including 15 days isolation and if the charge is of a serious nature. . . may request the Director to authorize an award of up to 30 days confinement in isolation. (Director).

Not only are these 'findings' confusing and open to misinterpretation, but more pertinent to our correspondence, Bjarnason admits 'awarding' *more* than 15 days in each case. The PRG persisted:

Dec.19: Would it be possible to have the dates included in your listing [to verify whether these sentences applied to the September 1977 incident]? Also, under what specific regulation may the Warden request "up to 30 days"? Is this in the Gaol Rules. . . or in some other set of rules? (PRG).

1978.
Jan.3: I believe the information which I already supplied in this regard is sufficient, and that no further correspondence is required. I consider this matter closed. (Director).

As late as January 1979, twenty women were again placed in solitary confinement under the old cow barn. The Regional Director explained on a T.V. program that there was no other place to keep them, while admitting the area was not very pleasant.

Though correspondence with the Administration was rarely satisfying, talking with the women after they came out of Oakalla was something else again. Like the men, the women had pasty complexions (too much starch in their diet and too little fresh air and sunshine), matched by their dulled, bored attitude. But, 'Mary' was different. She was keen to know what was going on in the outside world, where she would be able to fit in, and most particularly, how she would be able to help break down the public apathy about prison life.

She once told me about losing 40 days of her 'good time' (three days per month deducted from total sentence for good behaviour) for insisting on accepting my visits. She shrugged it off as being well worth it, with the casual air of one who had become accustomed to coming and going from Oakalla.

Womanly Comforting Not Lesbian—Inmate

The way 'Mary' (not real name) saw it, there's a difference between lesbianism and one inmate's comforting another.

"...it is a very lonely and isolated feeling when you are in jail, when you are upset...crying or something...even just to be able to lie beside somebody, to know you have somebody there, that's very, very important."

—*Province*, Nov.20/78

Some of her stories were amusing; others were not. She described how, on admission, one had to scramble for a sheet, pillow, blanket, towel and even toothpaste and soap, until one learned how to play the game; she told the story of L.L. whose illness was ignored until the day the Sheriff refused to take her to court as she looked so ghastly. Only then was L.L. rushed to hospital where intestinal obstruction and toxemia were diagnosed and surgery performed. (I recall L.L. showing us her scars the evening she attended one of our Women's Studies courses).

A few months later L.L. hanged herself with her dressing gown belt.

'Mary' was keen to expose Oakalla. As soon as she was released, she called me to put her in contact with the media:

> *'Mary':* But you've got to understand you are in an unusual setting. Now, say we were high. . .a woman guard would come to me and say, "O.K. . . .you are going down to the digger until you straighten out." *Now* the way it is, the men [guards] come and as soon as the girl sees a man she automatically cringes up, and they don't just come in ones, they come in threes. So you know you are not going down without a fight. . .it is going to be physical violence because there is no way. . .you know. . .three guards and one girl.

> *Interviewer:* You mean that the guards will beat that woman up?

> *'Mary':* Well, they have to drag you down to isolation now, don't they?. . .and in three different shifts there are three different rules. . .

> *Interviewer:* Is there anything to that (talk about sex between inmates and guards) to your knowledge?

> *'Mary':* I have seen a male staff go into a woman's room after 10 p.m. lock-up, and stay in there for a while, and things like that. . . .

> *Interviewer:* Isn't there any rehabilitation program or anything going on there?

> *'Mary':* No, there is none at all. . .we just sit around. I have been lucky because I play piano and they give an 'idiot pass' to the gym and just lock me in there.*

When she completed a later T.V. interview, Mary was delighted to have had the opportunity to tell it all. "I'll sure have to watch my back," she admitted, "but it's worth it."

---

*C.B.C. "Good Morning" radio program, Nov.8/77.

I dropped her off at the St. Regis Hotel in downtown Vancouver where she was to meet a friend. She promised to call me when she returned home that night.

...Three days after the broadcast, 'Mary' (26) was found dead in a hotel room in Vancouver, apparently from a drug overdose.

—*Province,* Nov.21/77

"Apparently from a drug overdose" is the way the media so often reports the finding of dead bodies of ex-prisoners.

No inquest.

No police investigation.

And the family, more often than not, are persuaded to authorize an immediate cremation.

Who is doing any research on unreported, unresolved deaths of ex-prisoners?

B.C.'s Purse Strings 'Too Tight For Investigations Of Several Deaths'

Inadequate provincial funding for coroners has meant several local deaths have not been investigated as thoroughly as they should have been, says Vernon coroner, Dr. Graham Spiller.

—*Sun,* June 21/78

Early in August I was informed that my regular Women's Studies class was cancelled. The Director learned that I had been participating in the demonstrations at the B.C.Pen protesting the murder of Mary Steinhauser. He withdrew my teaching privileges. Next he withdrew my visiting rights, though he gave no official reason.

The B.C.Human Rights Branch of the Department of Labour helped me later to recover my visiting rights. This was limited to visiting only the Doukhobour women prisoners, as Mr. Burns, the Director, admitted they hardly needed my help to carry out their protests. (The Doukhobour women, members of a religious sect living in the interior of B.C., were known to disrobe and set fires

**B.C. Pen.
and Okalla**

UNDER THE OLD COW BARN: Solitary Confinement at Oakalla. The plastic pail serves as toilet. Reading matter allowed in the cell is limited to a Bible and religious pamphlets. The view consists of a concrete wall.

—*Vancouver Sun photo*

THE TIGER CAGE: Isolation unit at Oakalla. Note the "toilet" bucket at prisoner's feet, the abscence of bedding, and the grotesque lighting effects created by the shadows of the bars. —*Monday Magazine photo*

PRISONERS' RAGE: row of smashed cells in East Wing, B.C. Pen.

—*Vancouver Sun photo*

AFTERMATH: Fire in the gym, B.C. Pen—*Vancouver Sun Photo*

THE DOME: B.C. Pen. —*Vancouver Sun photo*

EAST WING, B.C. PEN: Totally demolished 29 September, 1976

—The Columbian photo

as their way of protesting). They viewed their 'crimes' as minor when compared with those of the son of a visiting prison official who was a high-ranking officer in the American Army in Vietnam. "Your son is burning people," they told him. "We just burn our mattresses."

Eight Doukhobour women were housed in a separate hut at the foot of the hill, away from the prison population. My first visit ended abruptly when a call from the Gatehouse ordered me out.

The women were accustomed to entertaining their guests for the full afternoon: preparing their own meals with food brought by relatives, they served up big bowls of borscht. They protested this order angrily. But, we were allowed to sing one song before I had to leave. With linked arms, standing in a circle, we went on verse after verse after verse. The phone kept ringing. The matron kept shouting to me to leave, trying to make herself heard above the singing.

Thus began my relationship with these women whose religious convictions were matched only by their determination.

A year later some of them were transferred to the Kingston Prison For Women, Ontario. I received an anguished letter from P.C. who was refusing to accept her release without her companion—the oldest woman in the group, who had been in jail almost continuously since Sept. 1974. Sixty-three year old M.A. was not due to leave for another six months. These women had been carrying out many protests, including a seven-month fast (from Nov.1975 to May 1976), and were very ill. A broad campaign, initiated by the PRG, succeeded in obtaining a Special Executive Clemency Order, signed by the Governor General, and the two women were flown home to B.C. on April 12, 1978. M.A.'s husband wrote:

> Thank you so much from us all, relatives and friends...she arrived just skin and bones, and that's no lie, but with very good spirit, very happy to see us all and to be free.

Within another two months, five of the Doukhobour women were in the news. Again they had been sentenced to Oakalla. This time I received a communication from them describing how five

matrons overpowered them, holding them down forcibly while the
doctor did an internal search for matches.

After waiting outside Oakalla prison most of Monday, prison activist Claire Culhane succeeded Tuesday in delivering a letter to Marie Peacock, Director...protesting the treatment of five Doukhobor women being held in solitary confinement.

Culhane said she was dragged away from the Oakalla gates by police officers...after Peacock had refused to accept the letter. But with TV cameras waiting... the prison director [early the next morning] rolled down her car window to accept the document.

—*Sun*, June 21/78

In fact, they were protesting the use of *toothpaste* as a vaginal
lubricant. Jail doctor Robert Schulze (who is now called Dr.
Crest, I am told) was not identified by the media, but Mr. Kent,
Director of Inspections & Standards Department in Victoria,
made a statement.

...an investigation had determined that a jell-type toothpaste rather than a surgical jelly had been used as a vaginal lubricant

...it's mildly antiseptic...not harmful...but the imagery of it was inappropriate....

—*Sun,* Aug.25/78

Much publicity is given to the Doukhobours' protest practice of
disrobing and burning. But, one never reads about the reasons for
their persistent refusal to take the stand and swear an oath. They
sent me a copy of their creed:

> Thou shalt not swear by thine own life, not by the head, the
> heart, the eye, nor the hand; not by the sun, the moon, nor
> the stars. Not by the name of God, not by the name of any
> spirit good or bad. You shall not swear by anything for in an
> oath there is no gain. A man whose word must be propped up
> by oath of any kind is not trustworthy in the sight of God or
> man. The man of worth just speaks and men know that he
> speaks the truth.

As news spread about my involvement with the Doukhobour women, many prisoners wrote me describing their experiences with this sect—always with praise and respect for them as fellow prisoners. Even the women in Kingston Prison For Women, who initially had been quite hostile towards them, mainly because they did not understand their principles, began to secretly leave vegetables (from their own plates) by their cell doors, as a gesture of support.

Finally, after visiting with these women for several months, I received permission to visit other women at Oakalla. But even routine visits became complicated beyond belief. Just phoning for an appointment to visit often ended in a hopeless tangle. Although the caller is supposed to be able to overhear the prisoner's response, this is what sometimes happens:

Caller: May I have a visit with 'Joan' today?

Staff: Just a minute. . . [as she supposedly calls 'Joan' on the intercom. Silence, as outside line is cut off]. . . Sorry, 'Joan' says she doesn't want to see you today.

Only later would one learn that 'Joan' had never even been called.

Mail, which was supposed to be entered in the Register, also very often just never 'arrived.' No trace—even when I delivered it by hand so the postal system couldn't be blamed for non-delivery. Once, when I took the time to identify which staff had received my mail from me and on which specific day, the letter was later 'found' in a drawer. These incidents may appear unimportant and trivial, but prisoners' only contact with the outside is through their visits and correspondence. When they find themselves cut off, they begin to panic. When they react, they then lay themselves open to charges of "abuse."

At least at Mission Medium Security Institution, the censorship of mail was more overt, as disclosed by the following absurd exchange of correspondence between a prisoner, the director, and myself:

Mar.4/77: I just thought I'd drop you a line to say hello and to let you know that I'm alive and well out here in the boondocks. I haven't heard anything from 'up front' about getting you cleared for visiting yet. Which is not unusual for this place. (We are like mushrooms in here; they feed us shit and keep us in the dark). You would think that at least they'd have the courtesy to tell me yes or no. (Prisoner).

Mar.13/77: Good to hear from you and learn that you and all the other garden specimens are doing so well. We once had a donkey in Ireland which we kept in the backyard, and the 80 year old widow neighbour also used to stand by anxious to pick up the droppings to fertilize her rose garden...(my reply).

Mar.22/77: Your correspondence of Mar.13 to J.A. is herein returned. Paragraph 1 of your letter requires some clarification because we are unable to determine exactly what you are wanting to communicate. Yours truly. (Director).

Mar.25/77: In order that my communication be delivered to J.A., I will attempt to clarify the first paragraph as requested...There had been a reference to the cultivation of mushrooms which require darkness and fertilizer for their growth. My comment was simply intended to be humorous, and in so doing I recalled a true incident which took place when I lived in Ireland many years ago, where fertilizer was a very vital component and expensive to obtain. That is the sum total of the first paragraph which you were unable to comprehend. (my reply).

Ottawa has recently introduced a new twist into their correspondence regulations. Previously, when I sent newspapers or magazines to prisoners, staff would open and review them to determine if they were in the best interest of the prisoner and the institution. Now, the same items are returned to me *unopened,* with the notation *Not permitted: Return to Sender.*

Formerly, correspondence was governed by Sect.2.21 of the CPS Regulation which determined that:

No reading material, of any description shall be permitted in an institution if it is calculated:

    a) to bring into ridicule or contempt any religion or faith
    b) to promote controversy between members of different religions or faiths, or
    c) to affect adversely the good order of administration of the institution.

As if (*c*) were not a sufficient catch-all for anything the authorities might wish to exclude, they have now added to the existing hundreds of Divisional Instructions, D.I. 830, Sect. 2(b), (sub.1):

No article or goods may be sent in to inmates in any institution, nor may outside persons make payments or subscriptions with the intention of having articles or goods subsequently delivered to inmates in institutions. . . .

It would appear that the authorities fear the prisoners may be keeping themselves informed about the outside world, the same world that they are expected to 'adjust to' upon release.

By this time the Prisoners' Rights Group (PRG) was publicizing its Three Goals and its Three Dont's.

The first goal is to help prisoners help themselves. Mainly, this refers to finding them a good lawyer, sorting out their personal and family problems, helping them deal with inadequate or incompetent medical attention—and often to just writing and visiting with someone who has absolutely no one who knows or cares where they are. As we are not a funded group, it is made clear that we cannot raise bail or offer financial assistance of any kind, and now no such demands are made.

We move into other related areas, whenever we can, that help to establish that prisoners are people who should be accorded their human and civil rights.

About 160 prisoners at Oakalla have registered to vote in the Dec. 1975 provincial elections—the first time that balloting will be held in a B.C. penal institution. The Provincial Elections Act guarantees the right to vote for prisoners being held on remand, and for those serving sentences for summary or minor offences. [Only those under sentence for indictable offences are barred from voting]...but these rights were never exercised until it was brought to the attention of the Chief Electoral Officer and the Atty-General's department....

—*Sun*, Nov.13/75

In this instance it finally required a personal visit to the NDP Premier to convince him of the need to guarantee *every* eligible B.C. citizen the right to vote before polling booths were, for the first time, set up in Oakalla.

But another ambitious project we undertook did not meet with the same success. We had learned of research which revealed the effects of diet on behaviour, how in some instances food allergy or malnutrition can unbalance mental processes, leading to violent behaviour. In other cases, "hypoglycemia"—also called the 'nasty personality disease'—can cause a person to become irritable, irrational, afflicted by a vague sense of dread, and frequently violent. Researchers were indicating that there were examples of hypoglycemia-associated crimes, including 'motiveless murders,' assaults, sexual offences, and other violations. We forwarded these reports to the Administrator and his hospital staff, including a recent statement by a police chief of Fairfield, Ohio.

"If crime could be reduced, even by a small degree, by exploring the effects of food, then we should by all means explore these possibilities. We couldn't do much worse than we are with the more orthodox approaches to crime prevention."

—"Food & Your Health," *The Whig-Standard,* Kingston, Ontario

We approached the Oakalla Administration with a pilot project for two prisoners who would cooperate and monitor their diets for two weeks to see if there were any corresponding changes in their self-acknowledged erratic behaviour. After months of debate and argument, the Administration finally agreed. However, the two prisoners offered to us to enter into this simple experiment were promptly disqualified: one because the kitchen staff didn't like him and therefore wouldn't permit him to prepare his own tray in the kitchen; the second prisoner was on remand (awaiting trial) and therefore not eligible to participate in *any* prison program. Since, unlike other citizen groups, the PRG had never been accorded the right to visit with prisoners, both the Administration's cooperation and the pilot project stopped here.

The second goal of the PRG is to help educate the public as to the true nature of the Canadian prison system. Beginning June 1977, we have been producing a weekly half-hour cable television show, *Instead of Prisons.* There are now seven outlets, including New Westminster where the B.C.Pen is located. Soon, too, Matsqui and other prisons will be able to watch it.

When the Oakalla Inmate Committee learned that other prisons had cable hook-ups, they tried to get it extended into their area, from the old Warden house up the hill. PRG obtained a professional estimate from an independent technician—$3,000 to $5,000. When the Inmate Committee placed their formal request, the Director brought in *his* estimate—approximately $21,000. By coincidence, the amount in the Inmate Welfare Fund at that time just happened to be $21,000.

We also participate in the annual *National Prison Justice Day* —August 10—twenty-four hour vigil which includes fasting and work-stoppage inside and outside the prisons across the country. This is in memory of those prisoners who have died 'unnatural deaths.' The Millhaven prison population had initiated this day of protest in 1976 after two of their numbers had died in solitary. Guards, who disliked being disturbed by the flashing lights, had tampered with the panic-button wiring, leaving the men to die unattended in their cells:

> *Stuart Leggatt, MP:* What I want to ask is why there are not panic buttons now?...the reason I asked was because of the death of Eddie Nalon in this institution.
>
> *Warren Richardson, Pres. PSAC-Millhaven:* I cannot comment.*

*Minutes of Proceedings, Issue No.23, Feb.2/77, p.9.

The following recommendation was made by a Coroner's Jury, May16/75, serving on the inquest into the death of Edward Nalon:

> That the emergency signal systems in each cell, and the time clock which assures regularity in range patrols, be made functional, with steps taken to provide that they remain functional.

Two years later, the signal system still "had not been made functional." This time it was Bobby Landers who died unattended in his cell.

The PRG's third goal is to join with the growing movement to abolish the present uneconomical, counter-productive, and in many instances brutal and inhuman prison system. Our ideology is based on economic and social justice for all, concern for all victims, and reconciliation within a caring community, since we believe that crime is mainly a consequence of the structure of society.

We support community-supervised programs, a moratorium on new prison construction, and all other realistic alternatives which promote *decarceration*—decreasing the number of people imprisoned—and *excarceration*—getting people out of prison.*

When my "visiting privileges at Oakalla [were]...discontinued until further notice...in the best interests of the institution" it served to curtail discussion with guards as well as with prisoners. I often talked with guards, especially those engaged in turnkey duties. Some were receptive and willing to discuss alternatives to the present system. I would ask them if they would not prefer to take the responsibility of supervising one or two prisoners

---

*In Sweden "sanctions involving loss of liberty (are)...avoided wherever possible...do not improve...adjusting to a life in freedom...widespread view and supported by experience that better results are obtained...by correctional care outside institutions...more humane and a cheaper form of care than institutional." (*Fact Sheets On Sweden,* published by the Swedish Institute, in Sweden, Dec. 1977, Classification: FS 62 d Oeq)

outside, on the street—to find them a place to live, a job or training, stay by them, as it were, for as long as required—and draw their salary in that way? I never encountered a negative reaction. They would admit it seemed far more useful.

Such a program would probably need twice the personnel presently employed, so there would be no fear of loss of employment if and when the prison were shut down. For that small percentage of prisoners who are not yet ready for community programs, a treatment centre could be maintained to offer more intense supervision and social help, but with none of the present excesses which demean both the 'keeper and the kept.'

The PRG also has *Three Dont's:*

Don't B.S. Us—tell us the whole story so we don't get left with 'egg on our face' if and when we get to the top brass with your grievance. (At this point had they planned to Bullshit us they would drop their grievance and change the subject.) We do *not* find ourselves manipulated as the authorities would have it appear. We are *not* bleeding hearts exploited by prisoners. The whole system, not just one part of it, is based on exploitation.

Don't Expect Anything—so you won't be disappointed and reject future help offered by anyone else. We are not in any position of power to make promises or guarantees. We can only contact lawyers, doctors, family, and friends, as well as write and call Adminstration as you ask us to do. We will continue to write and visit you (where possible) as long as you wish. And that's all we can promise.

Don't Even Call Us—if you can't take the extra heat that will more than likely come down on you. We are hardly the most popular group with the authorities.

Prisoners usually approach the PRG after they have tried every other way to deal with their grievances, but with so little success that, by that time, they feel they have nothing to lose.

However, as we have seen with 'Mary' and others, the heat can also come down even after the prisoner is released. When inquests are not held for 'unnatural deaths,' we can draw disturbing conclusions.

At a meeting of the Citizens Advisory Board of B.C. Corrections—a committee set up to operate in the provincial prison field and which we had been invited to join—in the fall of 1977, PRG reported stories about sexual misconduct and demoralization in the Women's unit at Oakalla, which prisoners and staff were describing to us. Quite predictably, at the first opportunity, the PRG was asked to withdraw from the committee.

Shortly afterwards, these same charges proved sufficiently valid to require official action:

> The Royal Commission of Inquiry into the Incarceration of Female Offenders established under Order-in-Council 3632, dated Dec.5/77, was set up naming Patricia Proudfoot, Justice of the Supreme Court of B.C. as Commissioner.
>
> [This Commission] resulted from various allegations made public by the media... of irregularities in the operation of OWCC, including sexual misconduct between male and female inmates.... *(Report,* p.1).

Several significant points were made in the course of the hearing:

> *Judge Proudfoot:* ... it should be a legitimate and realizable aim to ensure that the programs and way of life at an institution give individuals who wish it some opportunity to make progress. Institutions should not, if possible, contribute to a further erosion of the inmate's personality... should not contribute to a deterioration of behaviour and lifestyle. Boredom and lack of challenge were two problems that appeared to us to pervade the day to day life. (*Report,* p.10).
>
> *Dr. John Eckstedt, B.C. Commissioner Corrections:* ... in my view one of the problems we have is that we really don't

know what we are doing and that has to do with the lack of social and political mandate. (*Report*, p.8).

Other facts were completely ignored when it came time for the Commission to formulate recommendations:

> ...[the Commission] was bombarded with opposition to the plan [Compulsory Heroin Treatment Program which] inmates assure us...cannot succeed, while citizens groups express real fears about the infringement of civil rights.... (*Report*, p.118).

While damaging testimony regarding solitary confinement was also brought forward, the Commission did not even mention it in their 57 Recommendations:

> ...cruel and unreasonable confinement. The sense of deprivation that takes place [causes] irreparable damage. It simply serves to isolate a person and destroy their ability to deal with their problems. I think this type of isolation reacts on both parties, it acts on the party who has the authority to relegate others to such a situation, as well as the victim. (C.Culhane, in *Report,* p.76).

Two issues which *were* incorporated in the recommendations could provide a basis for necessary changes:

> This Commission could never get a satisfactory answer as to why the panabode was closed—probably the most successful program in operation. (*Report*, p.121).

> *Recommendation 43:* The panabode [halfway house] program at OWCC be re-opened. (*Report*, p.120).

The other recommendation deals with what is still one of the most disregarded rights of prisoners, their correspondence:

"Mail censorship is a complete waste of time." (H. Bjarnason, Director).

". . .very little contraband ever arrives by post." (Ms. Powers, Matron).

". . .it isn't something that's necessary, and yet perhaps should be done randomly." (Ms. Peacock, Local Manager).

. . .also evidence that the whole procedure is time consuming—an important factor when there is a constant reference to staff shortages.

Ms. Culhane and Ms. Jodouin also had a good deal to say in their evidence. . .content of the letters to inmates was being used to taunt, tease or threaten. . .no concrete evidence . . .but not beyond the realm of possibility.

. . .no rationale whatsoever for the opening of outgoing mail.

. . .at one time the Deputy Director retained three letters written by an inmate. This cannot be tolerated and should be resolved by discontinuing censorship of mail. (*Report*, pp.132-133).

Recommendation 49: All censorship of mail ingoing and outgoing stop forthwith. (*Report*, p.126).

One of the last recommendations (No.54) stated that "Dr. Jewett's Citizens Ad Hoc Committee monitor the implementation of the recommendations of this report. (*Report,* p.151). However, Dr. Jewett has since publicly stated that Attorney General Gardom has denied her Committee the authority to fulfil its commitment.*

When reference was made to reprisals, the Judge supported Commission Counsellor, John Hall, that no one need fear reprisals for any testimony presented at the Hearings. But I insisted that such an assurance was utterly meaningless.

Reprisals do not come neatly packaged and labelled. Reprisals

*T.V. Program, *Instead of Prison*, produced by PRG, Channel 10, Feb.10/79.

happen weeks and months later, most commonly in the form of charges laid for otherwise negligible acts, or for some thing which would previously have passed unnoticed.

Reprisals could be taken against me, I even suggested, for publicizing the true nature of reprisals.

Sixteen days later, notices went up in every wing at Oakalla that I would *no longer be permitted to visit any prisoner at that institution.*

The Commission feels compelled to comment on the visiting of Ms. Claire Culhane of the Prisoners' Rights Group within OWCC. It has been drawn to our attention that she has been barred from that institution and, accordingly, is no longer able to visit inmates there.

This Commission does not criticize the Corrections Director for taking this type of action, if warranted. However, this Commission does condemn action such as this being taken without giving the individual affected an adequate explanation. Once again officious action of this type can only bring the administration into disrepute. Ms. Culhane is *entitled to know why she is barred from OWCC.*

Dr. Eckstedt, after some prodding, appeared to agree with this proposition when he appeared before the Commission.

It is the sincere hope of the Commission that this matter and any further similar situations will be dealt with in a judicious manner. (*Report,* pp.129-130).

Since no one was prepared to deal in a "judicious manner" with my being barred from visiting at Oakalla, I was left to deal with it in a 'judicial' manner.

On Sept.16/78, in the Supreme Court of B.C. under Registry No. A781199, the following petition was filed—myself as Petitioner and the Atty Gen. of the Province of British Columbia, and Edward Harrison, Regional Director, as Respondents:

Petition

...applies to the Court for an order for relief pursuant to Section 2(e) of the Judicial Review Procedure Act (SBC 1876 Chap.25) reviewing, setting aside or quashing the decision of the Regional Director...made the 9th and 10th days of March 1978 discontinuing the Petitioner's visiting privileges ...and for an order compelling the Respondent...to comply with the rules of natural justice and to act fairly and justly in the circumstances by providing the petitioner with the detailed facts, circumstances and reasons, upon which his decisions were based and an opportunity to respond thereto, and for an order prohibiting the Respondent...from discontinuing the Petitioner's visiting privileges....

The petition was dismissed by Justice G.G.S. Rae, Oct6/78:

...in my view the Respondent's submission...is sound, without permission or licence of the Crown, the Petitioner would be a trespasser. That permission or licence which the Petitioner once had is revocable at common law, at the will of the licensor. No authority is required for that simple proposition. What the Crown gave by way of licence or permission it had the right to take away, and the Respondent in acting as he did in withdrawing permission, did so in his capacity as a servant of the Crown...acting...in a purely administrative capacity....

Although he ruled against her, the judge did go on to make this point: "Perhaps one may say in general that anything which contributes to enlightenment of the citizenry in the field of crime, punishment and the use of prisons as part of the process of punishment, has something to be said in its favor."

Looking very closely at that statement, reading between and through and over the lines, it would seem to contain some slight, indirect approval.

—June Sheppard,
Edmonton Journal, Mar.9/79

I have appealed this decision. The date has been set for November 2, 1979.

Meanwhile, riots, suicides, hostage taking, escapes and violations of Gaol Rules and Regulations by prison officials continue to take their toll of men and women doing 'hard time' at Oakalla.

Picking Off The "Radicals"

Newly formed Unit 8 presently holds four women...placed [there] because they were either assertive with guards or acting for ostensibly political reasons, i.e. doing consciousness-raising among prisoners, laying complaints or attempting to free themselves.

No official statement as to why they have been moved to Unit 8 has ever been given...they are kept segregated...denied privileges previously held...handcuffed at all times while being escorted between their cells and to and from other areas...cannot have 'open visits'...access to the library (what remains of one), gymnasium or the outdoors.

In short, Unit 8 is a form of solitary confinement, with the same exception of the work schedule. Clearly the administration sees any self-assertive behaviour as a threat to the 'peace and good order of the institution,' and will go to any measure to ensure total control.

—"Oakalla: Conditions are Bad and Getting Worse," *Kinesis,* April/May 1979.

CHAPTER SEVEN

A Prison Within A Prison

Protective Custody Unit (PCU)

In the Memorandum of Agreement signed at the B.C.Penitentiary, there is no clause dealing with the prisoners in the Protective Custody Unit for the simple reason that the Inmate Committee did not represent that section.

Who are the men in this Unit who are kept separate from the general prison population, presumably for their own protection? They are those convicted of sex offences (skinners). They are those labelled informers (snitches). And they are those who have asked to be moved into that Unit, believing themselves to be in physical danger from other prisoners.

We can compare PCU with two other structures in our society.

Governments must maintain a spy system, euphemistically called "Intelligence," in foreign countries. No government, we know, can exist in the modern world without its Intelligence Department.

Secondly, no police force can function effectively without its undercover agents. Police also need to recruit informers to provide information for conviction of those involved in criminal activities, or as also happens, to convict innocent people.

The prison also depends on its spies and informers, since the hostility between Custody and the prison population, as well as between prisoners themselves, must be constantly reinforced if the Administration is to maintain its control over the institution.

Protective Custody Units set the stage and provide the actors for this tragic drama. No prison system can function without its PCU, or its equivalent.

Twenty years ago, the biographers of Agnes MacPhail (first Canadian woman Member of Parliament and well known prison reformist) also commented on this tendency:

In some institutions a corrupt "spy" system using favoured prisoners kept the air vile with suspicion and hostility.*

A letter from an ex-prisoner (dated Dec.5/78) gives an insider's version:

> L.R. is in PCU against his own will. When he was admitted he asked to be put into population but after being told he would be killed (Administration told him this) he consented to go into PCU—not fully realizing the implications behind being put into that environment. Since he's been there, he repeatedly asked to be put back into population, but to no avail. You might ask, why this sudden interest—especially when I tell you I didn't know this fellow from Adam. The answer is he is not an isolated case.
>
> There are a lot of youngsters, who upon entry, are virtually scared into PCU by the Administration. They've never done time in a pen before and when confronted by these solemn-looking people and told they will be raped, killed, etc. they check in, out of fear—not realizing that once in there they are branded by the population a "dead man"—inside and outside those walls.
>
> Now the second question you may pose is "to what advantage is this to the Administration? and why would they mark a man 'Judas' if he wasn't?" The reason the Administration puts a man's life in jeopardy is: these people (the ones who aren't dangerous sex offenders and informants of known calibre) are used to infiltrate *all* of the Medium and Minimum institutions where there are no [official] PCU's— 90%, 60% and 30% are not necessarily accurate proportions, but they are very close figures.... When an informant becomes known at one institution, he is just packed off to another, if not in one province then to another.

---

*In Margaret Stewart and Doris French, *Ask No Quarter: The Story about Agnes MacPhail* (Longhams & Green: Toronto, 1959), p.202.

*And they will continue to inform on threat of being sent
back to Maximum where there is a PCU.*

This is the only way authorities can successfully run these
institutions, and that's why they are clamoring for more
candidates for PCU. How long do you think they could run
one of these places smoothly if they had no PCU element
there? Why do you think the Penitentiary Service goes to
such great lengths in their continuous efforts to recruit these
people? Because they need them.

If they did not have them, then all the institutions in
Canada would be run as tight as Maximum Security is,
because they couldn't afford to run them any other way.

I think we're going to have to face reality here and state
that at least a few Members of Parliament are aware of this
travesty of justice, this wanton sentencing of young men to
death, this murder!

Don't forget there are 25 more prisons being built and they
need the troops to man the PCU's.

I think it's about time the Canadian public was made
aware of the greatest "horror" story in penitentiary history.
But how do you make them aware—how can you obtain the
necessary facts and figures—only a very special inquiry will
obtain these results.

When supposed responsible citizens are given the power to
virtually mold men into the lowest form of life, then one
must ask oneself "how can we judge these victims of the
hierarchy?"

I know you may have a hard time digesting what I am
writing and I'm the first to admit that most of those in PCU
belong there—but there are more than a few who don't.
*About 10 or 15 years ago there was no such thing as PCU in
Canadian Penitentiary System. Now there are over 1,000
men in them.*

January 18, 1979, prisoners at Dorchester Penitentiary, New
Brunswick, called for the total dismantling of their PCU.
Recommendation #1 of their Factum reads:

(*a*) PCU within this institution has always been a problem to the main population. Recently it has been increased in six months from 40 to 80 residents. Administration does not discourage men from going there but rather they encourage the move, even for minor problems.

(*b*) As a result of this unit, the population has suffered many cutbacks and losses to the already small number of facilities, e.g. removal of 3 trailers to PCU and added work load to staff and liaison officers drawn to supervise the unit.

(*c*) The PCU draws from the budget for activities, films, equipment and special needs. The population suffers the resulting shortage in most areas.

(*d*) The losses only encourage recruitment of this unit. It should be relocated in order to restore the morale necessary for co-existence of main population.

If these indictments are discounted because they originate with prisoners, read what a Special Projects Officer employed by the CPS reported to the Parliamentary Subcommittee.

Dr. Carole Anne Searles, Criminologist, commissioned to do a study on sexual offender treatment, went to Minnesota Security Hospital (USA) which has an excellent program:

At the end of the year [1975] we presented our findings and recommendations as to how a treatment program could be implemented in Canada for these fellows.

Since then the only thing that has happened is an increasing of the population of sex offenders. In 1974 it was something like 495, and as of this morning [Mar. 11/77] to my knowledge, it is 892 . . . .

Nothing has been done since the submission of the work group's report. . . all we are doing is holding them until they can get released and then do their own thing over again.

Mr. Halliday, MP: You mentioned having sent a report, I

believe to Mr. Therrien, back in June 1975? Is that
correct?

Dr. Searles: That is correct.

Mr. Halliday: Was this report implemented or not?

Dr. Searles: No.

Mr. Halliday: Did you have recommendations in your
report?

Dr. Searles: Most definitely. This was the report that was
worked on by the CPS, National Parole Service and
National Parole Board, explaining how a treatment
program could be implemented in Canada, right down
to the last detail, including budget. Everything had
been worked out.

Mr. Halliday: What has been, to your knowledge, the
outcome of that report? What has happened to it?

Dr. Searles: Nothing.

Mr. Halliday: Were you given a reason why nothing had
happened?

Dr. Searles: Lack of funds? Maybe the public not ready for
a treatment program for sexual offenders yet.

Dr. Mark MacGuigan, MP (Chairman): How many people
are involved in the CPS in treatment of sex offenders?
How many people at Headquarters, for instance, like
yourself?

Dr. Searles: Nobody.

Mr. Halliday: To what extent is the Ministry or the CPS
funding research in sex offenders?

Dr. Searles: To my knowledge, there is no funding going on
for sex research.*

The Subcommittee concluded its own findings on PCU with
this criticism:

Minutes of Proceedings, Issue No.39, Mar.11/77, pp. 4,5,9,23,25.

What happens to men in protective custody is intolerable. Corrective action now is required. (*Report,* p.140).

Yet it ignored Dr. Searles' blunt advice with its weak *Recommendation No.57:*

A small number of maximum security institutions should be used exclusively for inmates who require protective custody. Each such institution should have a section designated as medium security.

Perhaps they forgot that hostage takings occur in PCU's as well, as happened only one year before at the B.C.Pen.

...the first involving inmates who are held in the prison's Protective Custody Unit (PCU).

Protective Custody inmates, who rely on security staff in prison to protect their lives from other inmates were not considered a high security risk to guards' safety, but the rules may be changing following Sunday's 14 hour incident.

...the number of such inmates has increased at B.C.Pen and other maximum security prisons to such an extent that entire wings of prisons are set aside for protective custody cases, creating dangers among the protective custody inmates themselves.

—*Province,* Apr.27/76

As recently as May 29/79 prisoners at the B.C.Pen learned that during the period of their transition to the new Kent Institution, PCU would gradually outnumber the general population. As the Pen becomes a huge Protective Custody Unit, PCU will eventually take over *all* the job positions.

When PCU prisoners take over kitchen staff duties, serious problems will arise. (Recall how, when the men were in the gym, the guards taunted them with the prospect of being fed by the PCU).

Some of the possibilities are that the remaining general population would be on increased or total lock-up to ensure a peaceful take-over; that general population would go on a hunger strike to protest being fed by PCU; and that consequent tensions could lead to isolated violence or a general riot—partly in protest, and partly in the hope that such action would speed up transfers to Kent.

A PCU-staffed kitchen could create a volatile situation. Many already fear that Kent could become a replica of Millhaven, where the premature reception of prisoners proved disastrous.

Obviously, since PCU blame the open population for their less favoured conditions, they could use their kitchen job to 'pay back' by tampering with the food. On the other hand, the Administration don't have to worry about *their* food being contaminated since the food they eat is prepared by staff hired from the street. Shouldn't *all* prisoners have the same assurance?

The solution is clear. As general population working in the kitchen are transferred, their jobs should be filled by staff hired from outside, instead of by PCU.

Part-time help is more economical than million-dollar riots.

The Protective Custody Unit serves an important political function within the prison structure.

In order to maintain their authority, Third Level penitentiary officials—many of them ex-military Intelligence—must preserve, among other controls, the PCU.

Established power thrives by keeping people divided who are subject to it. For example, PCU's are breeding grounds for racism. At Oakalla, East Indian prisoners tend to be directed automatically upon admission to the PCU wing. At the B.C.Pen, when East Indian guards are selected for the 'goon squad,' again racist tensions are sure to intensify. An already high level of racism outside is perpetuated inside.

The system exploits the complexities of sexism as well.

Deprived of their outside sex partners, and confined for long, unwholesome periods of time, prisoners sometimes turn to whatever sexual release they can find. The Administration is able to use information about such intimate relationships to further coerce and thus compel participation in the 'spy' system.

Ostensibly, administrations set up Protective Custody for the protection of certain categories of prisoners against the physical threat of others. But the real intent is to divide the prison population to a degree that prevents them from being able to cope with the hopelessness of their incarceration.

How else explain placing someone in the cell next to the brother of the man he was suspected of having 'fingered.' Appeals from the Prisoners' Rights Group to Oakalla's Director, warning of the potential revenge, were ignored for months. They were finally separated, fortunately, before a fatal stabbing.

A prisoner's life is also precarious in general population. If the guards by-pass *his* cell while searching the rest of the tier, he can be suspected of having done something to earn the guards' favour. If he is lucky he will be able to convince his cell-mates that he was being 'set-up.' If he is not so fortunate, and the guards succeed in sowing suspicion against him, he faces either 'toughing it out' without being stabbed, or taking 'protection' in PCU.

Inevitably, *there are now PCU's within PCU's*—literally, a prison within a prison within a prison. These are for prisoners who must be protected against each other, even within that Unit. This is a logical proliferation of a process designed to produce people who, if they are to survive at all, will feel compelled to inform, to intimidate, to use and to fear each other—ad infinitum.

CHAPTER EIGHT

The Third Level

A major reason why prisoners go to such extreme measures as self-mutilation, riot, and hostage taking is their need to communicate their problems to both the prison authorities and the public. The prisoners resort to such radical methods because there is no adequate vehicle within the system which prisoners can use to make their complaints or "grievances" known.

At present there is a Grievance Procedure for prisoners who feel they have been "unfairly deprived of that to which [they are] entitled...or where [they have] been dealt with unfairly in any other way."* Prisoners obtain forms, if they are able, and fill them out, if they can read and write. They then submit the complaint, and it is filed at three successive levels:

    1st—*Institutional*
    2nd—*Regional*
    3rd—*National*

Failing to get any satisfaction at the First Level, the prisoner can appeal to the Second, and so on to the Third Level. When even Ottawa won't co-operate, one can appeal to the Correctional Investigator (Ombudsperson), obtain the necessary forms, and initiate yet another round of correspondence.

These procedures are available, at least in theory, to all prisoners. However, many do not know this. Even when the authorities agree to repair the breakdown in this crucial means of communication, the proper information and forms still don't always filter down through the many levels of bureaucracy to reach the prisoner at the bottom.

The *Annual Report* for 1976-77, p.22, confirms this:

> A number of inmates complain that grievance forms are lost after they had been delivered to staff.

Annual Report of the Correctional Investigator, 1976-77, p.1.

...a number of grievances simply are abandoned because inmates are not aware of the procedures.

" . . . security guards refuse to give me [these forms] upon request. Thank you for your help."

If the complaint somehow manages to get through to the Ombudsperson, the score* is still abysmally low:

category of complaint	received	resolved
transfers	238	11
miscellaneous	219	10
medical/dental	110	12
temporary absences	95	1
visiting and correspondence	73	10
dissociation (solitary)	70	24
disciplinary proceedings	67	9
compensation	61	7
information on file	15	4
grievance procedures	10	1

Rectification of complaints actually investigated is only 16.3%.
And from C.G.Rutter, Director of Inmate Affairs, Ottawa, we learn how:

Inmates feared retribution for grieving. And this is a fact. I know this. Do not ask me to prove it. I know. So many things happened that [are] so coincidental to things that did happen after an inmate grieved.**

Clearly a great many things stand between prisoners and those who could do something to solve their problems. Not the least of these is what seems to be the absolute discretionary powers of the bureaucrats, as the following shows:

*These are the most recent figures available. The 1977-78 Report, presented to the Solicitor General Dec.1978, is known to include some criticism of the CPS. As of July 1979, the Report has not been released to the public.
**Minutes of Proceedings, Issue No.3, Nov.3/76, p.16.

Inmate Grievance Presentation
             1st level no.   *2nd level no.*   *3rd level no.*
FPS No.   *Name*
Inmate No.   *Institution*

Details of Grievance:

On May 9, 1978 I submitted a Mrs. Claire Culhane to the
V&C Office to be placed on my visiting list. I received this
request back and was informed she would not be allowed to
visit me. As she has not broken any regulations in the
course of our past visits in both LMRCC and the
B.C.Penitentiary, I fail to see why she was refused, unless it
is for her political beliefs, which do not come near to
breaking rules of V&C offices.

Corrective Action Requested:

To have her name placed on my visiting list and have her
"allowed to visit with me." Also to have the reasons for
this refusal sent to myself and also to her. Also, a written
apology to myself and to her, sent by the party or parties
involved.

June 23, 1978   Signature of Inmate

Eleven days later, the prisoner received this reply:

1st Level

Institutional Reference   *Date Received*   *Signature of Asst. Director*

Remarks:

Your grievance has been forwarded directly to the Third
Level, since all matters pertaining to Mrs. Culhane are dealt
with by our National Headquarters.

   Decision:
        ☑ *rejected*   ☐ *upheld*
   Reason:

        4 July 78   Signature of Institution Director

A "reason" could not be supplied by the First Level since Ottawa had taken responsibility. On April 19, 1979 the same prisoner wrote me that when he saw the first "remark," he was told, "It's going up to Level 3, bypassing 2." He enclosed the second version with the comment, "The next time I saw it, it is as you see it now":

Remarks:

I have now been informed it is my decision to permit or deny visits by Claire Culhane. I have decided Ms. Culhane will not be placed on your visiting list.

I have this grievance form in my possession. The original "remark" has been whited out with Liquid Paper and the second remark is typed over it. But this literal *cover-up* was rather inept: one can plainly see the last two words of the original—"National Headquarters." The trickery is quite visible.

In January 1979, when I had re-opened the matter of my visiting rights with Ottawa, the Commissioner informed me that the Third Level had little to do with the decision, and that he expected "each Director to use his discretion wisely in the application of regulations, and should a Director allow you visiting privileges, I would not normally expect the decision to be reviewed."

Feb. 22, I sent a copy of the above grievance to Ottawa. It had confirmed just the opposite: that "all matters pertaining to Mrs. Culhane are dealt with by our National Headquarters." Yet he assured me, March 22, of each Director's autonomy. No reference was made to the enclosed grievance form.

May 1, the B.C.Pen restored my visiting rights. Shortly, three other institutions did the same. However, the alleged "security reasons" for having barred me for two and a half years have never been spelled out, and are still in effect elsewhere. June 1, 1979, the Director of Mission Medium Security prison says, "the basis for this decison is that your visiting would not contribute to the secure and effective operation of the institution."

How can one defend oneself against such an abstract charge?

Nonetheless, the alleged "security reasons" have never been defined.

The absolutism of the power structure is a fact of life. Since losing my day in court, no other avenue exists to restore my visiting rights. They depend, and evidently still do, entirely on the 'discretion' of one individual.

While, obviously, *I* can live with this, imagine what the same procedure means to men and women in solitary confinement for years on end, who are imprisoned unjustly, serving vastly excessive time, suffering from medical/dental/psychological severities, or spending endless years thousands of miles from their homes, and so on—with even less hope for due process than I have.

A high degree of deception must be practised not only by those who give the orders but also those who carry them out. For example, we are told that a 'bread-and-water' punishment diet no longer exists. We've come a long way! Now the steward can claim that what they're serving is: 8 oz. oatmeal porridge, ¼ oz. salt, 1 oz. sugar, 4 oz. milk, 2 slices dry toast, 8 oz. black sugar-free coffee—*for thirty breakfasts.* 8 oz. bowl of soup with 3 slices white bread and water—*for thirty lunches.* 8 oz. boiled potato, 4 oz. meat or fish, 4 oz. vegetables and 8 oz. black sugar-free coffee—*for thirty dinners.*

It wasn't until Inger Hansen officially protested for the fourth time that a lack of bulk and Vitamin C might result in physical deterioration, that this Punishment Diet is no longer "awarded in conjunction with punitive dissociation."

But who is to know if this directive is being followed? Who is there to check where only last year people *were* ordering this diet, and others *were* automatically obeying? The new directive does not necessarily mean things have changed.

A pattern emerges. The blatant disregard for maintaining even the appearance of truth persists in every area of prison life.

*   *   *

Usually, exposés of the "shocking reality of life behind bars" manage only to astound, agitate and infuriate. They appeal mainly to emotions. Seldom do they draw political conclusions by examining the prison system as a function of the state—an instrument for class, racial and national oppression. Ironically, the publication of prisoners' autobiographies and other harrowing descriptions of prison life by reformists are *not* a threat to the Establishment, insofar as they only describe what exists—and by now, we know what exists. What *is* a threat is any truly political analysis which proves that prison conditions are not unique, positioned as they are in the increasingly controlled society in which we live.

Taking into account the 'legal' violence applied to prisoners, it is important to recognize how recurring violence is generated which is then used to create the image of the dangerous person who must be caged for the protection of society. But it is really society which is 'dangerous.' Latin American Bishops, meeting at Medellin, avoided "...comparing or identifying the unjust violence of the oppressors, who support this 'iniquitous system,' with the just violence of the oppressed, who are forced into the position of having to use violence if they are to gain their freedom."*

Society is based upon an unequal distribution of power and opportunity, disguising its discrimination against the poor and the powerless. It uses prisons as an instrument to create a criminal milieu that the ruling class can control. The existence of a just system of criminal justice in an unjust society remains a contradiction of terms. No society can call itself civilized as long as one section has the power to brutalize another section. Eventually this brutality infects the whole of society and turns back upon itself. An example is the high rate of marital breakdown among guards.

The Prison System

The prison as we now know it has been described as a product of the Industrial Revolution, which created a need for cheap labour, and which used the captive criminal to its own advantage.

*Alain Gheerbrant, *The Rebel Church In South America,* (Penguin, 1974), p.163, and the General Conference of the Latin American hierarchy, signed by 920 priests.

Even the legitimacy of slavery was not seriously challenged until the late 18th century. As modern states were drawn into imperial wars, more repression was required to control the ensuing economic and political chaos.

The use of prisons as a means of ensuring social control is fundamental to all societies. Outrages practised against prisoners, which some find so appalling, should not be so difficult to comprehend: they are consistent with prison structures which certain governments use to retain power. Those who are labelled as 'threats to security' become the incarcerated symbols used to strengthen the state's authority.

> In prison we are governed and controlled by the same attitudes that govern and control the lives of people outside the prisons, the attitudes are more to the extreme...we are forced into resisting force.*

Penal institutions are a microcosm of the violent world which generates them, where each day over one billion dollars is spent on an arms race calculated to destroy us all. Trying to separate the violence of the prison system from this reality is like trying to separate our sale of Candu reactors ($10 million kickbacks included) from nuclear warfare—a political naiveté which Canadians can ill afford.

When the illegal activities of the RCMP came to light, editorials somberly pointed to the repressive direction which our government was taking. In order to maintain its power, like any other 20th-century nation, it must control the military, the police, and the prison system. *Any person or group daring to criticize and expose these functions has to expect, and will receive, the full brunt of authoritarian vengeance.* Only an informed, determined, massive public support of civil and human rights—particularly of prisoners, who are supposed to be deprived of only their *legal* rights—can redirect this system's values.

Thus the police, whose role is allegedly to protect and serve the

*John Clutchette (one of the Soledad Brothers), quoted in Angela Davis, *If They Come In The Morning*, p.153.

people, become, in the words of Angela Davis, "the grotesque
caricature of protecting and preserving the interests of the
establishment and serve nothing but injustice. It would be unable
to do so were it not sanctioned and supported by the judicial
system."*

Why Do We Tolerate Prisons?

A carefully prepared Report on Crime and Punishment in
America gives one answer:

> If social factors cannot be controlled or predicted, the
> relevance of individualized treatment is decreased and may
> be negligible...a prisoner detained to prevent crimes that
> could be avoided by social reforms may bear a greater
> resemblance to a scapegoat than to either a patient or a public
> enemy...to date our society has largely ignored this
> dilemma.**

The combination of serious economic stresses in Canada today
with its multi-racial population creates an enormous propensity
for scapegoatism. Instead of analyzing, in its proper historical
setting, the economic crisis gripping the western world, many
Canadians continue to blame the 'drunken, lazy Indians'—
'welfare bums ripping off the system'—'scab immigrants'—
'aggressive women'— and, of course, 'cons'— the ex-prisoners
who compete for jobs with law-abiding citizens.

The Minister of Finance recently predicted that the worst is yct
to come, as unemployment will remain unsolved right into the
1980's. He adds that "when people start reacting against those
cutbacks, it will strain our institutions in new ways."†

We can conclude two things. Firstly, Canadians who do not
grasp the real basis of our deteriorating economy might vent their

---

*If They Come In The Morning, p.39.
***Struggle For Justice* (New York: Hill & Wang, 1971), p.41.
†*Vancouver Province*, Aug.25/78.

frustrations on the nearest 'scapegoat.' Secondly, the twenty-four projected new prisons are to ease the anticipated "strain [on] our institutions"—that is, to receive those who will no longer accept the poisoning of their water, air, health, and their very lives, those who will no longer accept living below the poverty line, and those who will no longer tolerate injustice and degradation anywhere in Canada, *not even in our prisons.*

Scapegoatism, and particularly its racist element, flourishes in our society, and nowhere more visibly than within our detention centres. Yet a Parliamentary Subcommittee, which sat for months listening to a stream of bitterness from Native Indian prisoners, allotted one half of one Recommendation to the Native issue:

> *Recommendation 61:* At least one separate institution should be provided for youthful offenders on a selective basis. There should be at least one wilderness camp for Native peoples and other residents accustomed to life in remote areas.

A deliberate and contemptuous indifference towards Native prisoners may not have been intended. Nevertheless, this Recommendation does reflect a remarkable capacity to accept, without protest, the disaster of a race of people other than one's own.

In a lighter vein, the ability to accept the unacceptable also appears in a failure to demand a national amnesty for every man and woman doing time for forgery, when Sol. Gen. Francis Fox, himself guilty of that offence on his own admission, was not even charged. In a statement to the Ontario Legislature, Atty-Gen. Roy McMurtry said, "to launch a prosecution would be to bring disproportionately harsh consequence to a person of good character who had already suffered greatly...(emphasizing)... the decision would have been the same for anyone regardless of status."*

Fox had resigned from the cabinet after admitting he had had an affair with a married woman who became pregnant and that he

*Province, Feb.24/78.

forged the husband's name on a document when the woman entered the hospital for an abortion. Fox was grateful when he learned he was reprieved.

"The most important thing in my mind is that there is more in life than strict justice." — *Province*, Feb.25/78

What Can We Do?

The first essential is to recognize the *class* nature of the prison system, in which 95% of prisoners are and will continue to come from the socially and economically deprived class—victims of a threatened, frightened and crisis-ridden capitalist economy—and to that extent they are political prisoners.

Some prisoners realize the political nature of their imprisonment. We ought to be equally aware of the relevance of prisons to the total economic system, and how they are set up to maintain a so-called criminal population which the Third Level class has the power to abuse and control. As an ex-prisoner put it, "It's not a crime to be hungry, but it is a crime to steal...sometimes you don't have much choice."*

The Quakers describe the remaining 5% classification of prisoners—the white-collar, upper class criminal—the species which is rarely, if ever, included in criminology studies:

> Crime is no respecter of wealth, power or class; the prevalence of unprosecuted middle and upper class violation is...a phenomenon...labelled white-collar crime...unbiased statistics...would probably show that the proportion of criminals in various segments of a population increases with wealth and power, and it seems certain that the loss caused to victims of such "rich" crimes far exceeds that of the usual lower-class criminality.**

Traditional prison reformists—in spite of their unquestionable

Minutes of Proceedings, Issue No.10, Nov.25/76, p.73.
**Instead of Prisons*, p.188.

sincerity and motivation—easily deceive themselves into thinking that their painstaking efforts will fundamentally change the prisoners' lot, that at long last brutalities will end, and that prison will become a reasonably respectable segment of a reasonably respectable society—regardless of deficiencies, errors and aberrations.

But that is not how many prisoners view it: "When pressures for reform lead to demands to relieve 'overcrowding' by adding new cells or bed space, the result is inevitable: the coercive net of the justice system will be spread over a large number of people, entrapping them for longer periods of time."*

And Jessica Mitford writes: "Tactical questions that nag at many political activists engaged in the struggle to improve prison conditions and advance prisoner rights...their very achievements may tend to confer legitimacy on the prison and thus help to perpetuate the system...It becomes imperative to distinguish between two types of reform proposals: those which will result in strengthening the prison bureaucracy, designed to perpetuate and reinforce the system, and those which to one degree or another challenge the whole premise of prison and move in the direction of its eventual abolition."**

Reformers must ask themselves whether their 'reform' would improve conditions but at the same time reinforce the system, or would it, instead, help to shift power relationships, thereby creating a potential for basic changes. A useful guideline is whether the reform will result in as few people in prison as possible and for as short a time as possible.

This is not a new and radical approach. As long ago as 1914, Julian Hawthorne wrote calling for "...nothing less than that penal imprisonment for crime be abolished." Readily admitting that he could "hardly escape the apprehension that the mass of public opinion will dismiss this as preposterous and impossible," he goes on to say, "nothing is more certain in my opinion than that penal imprisonment for crime must cease, and if it is not abolished by statute, it will be by force."†

*Struggle For Justice, p.25.
**Kind and Usual Punishment, p.201.
†"The Subterranean Brotherhood," cited in Instead of Prisons, pp.13-14.

Fifty-five years later, "the almost total abolition of juvenile prisons in Massachusets occurred because of a rare combination of personal creativity and the power invested in that person by the Legislature. Dr. Jerry Miller, Director of the Department of Youth Services, managed in only three years to empty all but one juvenile prison by transferring the young prisoners into a variety of community alternative living situations...Miller believes 'swift and massive change' is the only sure way to phase out institutions...slow phased winding down can mean no winding down and often insures they'll wind up again."*

Effective actions such as these can be initiated while guarding against being coopted into the system, or frustrated to the point of giving up.

More insidious is the new 'big lie' technique in which Cabinet Ministers are specializing these days. I refer particularly to the number of old prisons which are 'scheduled to be phased out.' Once the headline has accomplished its goal, the public is counted upon to forget about it, and another pause takes place in real phasing out. This in turn provides a convenient smoke-screen behind which new prison construction proceeds.

For example, "in the Pacific region alone there were 269 empty cells out of a total capacity of 1,527" as well as 1,837 empty cells across Canada. Yet the prison system continues to expand.

Canadian Correctional Service announced last week it would expand Mission Medium Institution by 20% within the next year. Expansion comes as part of the federal government's massive $280 million 5-year construction plan, ostensibly designed to save tax dollars.

...with the addition of the living unit (to contain 35 or 36 inmates) will come also the addition of 97 staff members....

—*Fraser Valley Record*, Dec.16/78

Cutting back on Government spending could well begin here. When asked whether there was in fact a declining number

Instead of Prisons, pp.16-17.

of prisoners within the Pacific region, Dr. Tony Parlett, Regional Coordinator of Education and Training, agreed: "...we can look at the declining student enrolment figures and apply them to the inmate situation...trend noticeable in past 6 or 7 months."

However, he was looking to the "effect of the compulsory heroin addiction treatment program, sentencing procedures, etc." to determine whether the trend would continue. In spite of a forseeable decline, the government goes on building the prison empire.

...current Correctional services forecasts have the Medium security population figures for the Pacific Region at 852 by next year, 866 by 1982 and 894 by 1983.
—*Fraser Valley Record,* Dec.16/78

But the most myopic analysis of all is the announcement by Jean-Jacques Blais, Sol-Gen., that the prison construction plan would save $225 million in capital costs and $60 million annually in operating costs.

In light of the declining prison population, it will save *nothing* since it is unnecessary construction. One doesn't save money by spending less than what one didn't need to spend in the first place.

But there *are* several areas where effective changes *can* be initiated. First, the use of prisoner "volunteers" as subjects of experimentation for large scale medical research must be exposed and halted. The Nuremberg Judgment ruled that

> voluntary consent...is absolutely essential...that the person...should have legal capacity to give consent...be so situated as to be able to exercise free power of choice... should have sufficient knowledge and comprehension of the elements of the subject matter involved so as to enable... understanding, enlightened decisions.*

Current prison conditions obviously do not provide such preconditions. Prisons are useful *as they are.* An official at Wyeth

*Kind and Usual Punishment, p.167.

Laboratories says, "almost all our Phase 1 testing is done in prisons...if prisons closed down tomorrow the pharmaceutical companies would be in one hell of a bind."*

Secondly, the legalization of all drugs to eliminate the blackmarket trafficking and drug-related crimes whose victims flood our prisons requires not only a campaign for legalization, but also the unmasking of possible political intrigues. For example, the Pentagon could be viewed as using the international drug trade to establish political control over its client states, much as it used the 'foreign aid programs' in the last decade. Were the drug trade exposed, this would help deprive the prison system of one of its main sources of 'merchandise'—prisoners.

After receiving considerable evidence regarding the use and misuse of drugs, prescribed and otherwise, the Subcommittee presented the following trivial Recommendation (No. 54):

> The Penitentiary service must keep adequate records of the drugs dispensed to inmates so that control may be extended over the amount of medicine employed.

Six months later, a National Advisory Committee publicly proclaimed the "chaos" in the Medical Health Care Services Branch of the CPS. They attributed it to "lack of policy and an administration set up that puts major medical decisions in the hands of 'health care officers' with little or no training."**

Governments and prison bureaucracies must be subjected to relentless public pressure. It is alarming to read the passage in *Cruel and Unusual* (p.166) which refers to the Subcommittee's "cautious and side-long glance [at Canada's drug laws] politically, even discussing this approach as an alternative is dangerous."

Also trade unionists should be more aware of the parallels between their campaigns for higher wages and better conditions, and those of prisoners against slave wages (75 cents to $1.75 per

Kind and Usual Punishment, p.170.
**Province*, Dec.21/77.

day average) and primitive living conditions in certain institutions. A significant slogan that grew out of the holocaust of Attica in 1971 was *Abolish Attica—Create Jobs—Economic Conversion of Alternative Jobs for Guards.* *

While trade unions oppose convict labour as a threat to trade union standards and as potential strike breakers, they should also turn their attention to prisoners' demands for proper job training accompanied by authentic trade papers. As the Canadian government moves to imprison militant labour leaders and activists (viz. Canadian Union of Postal Workers), bonds of solidarity between the labour and prisoner movements would add to a mutual political awareness.

Fire fighters, too, for their own personal safety as well as others', should be supporting prisoner demands for adequate fire protection equipment, and frequent, regular, responsible government inspection (which is virtually non-existent at present). Twenty-one prisoners died needlessly on June 21/77 in a St. John, N.B. jail house fire. And we read at the conclusion of Chapter 3 how it nearly happened at the B.C.Pen.

Further, more thought should be directed to our political and social attitudes towards prisoners. Those 'leftists' who tend to dismiss prisoners as "lumpenproletariat" ignore the fact that

> . . . as long as we maintain our capitalist society we are going to have those who refuse, or who are unable to participate in this society gone mad, and many of these people are going to end up in prison. . . While most radical organizations openly claim support for the prison struggle, few have gone much further.**

Everyone concerned with civil liberties must address themselves to the renewed threat of the re-introduction of capital

Attica: The Official Report of the N.Y. State Special Commission on Attica, p.xl.
**Terry L. Huston, prisoner at San Quentin, "Prisons: a Marxist Position," *Monthly Review,* N.Y., Nov. 1973, p.29.

punishment. Already returned in thirty-five states south of the border, the death penalty is historically identified "...as an instrument of repression against opposition, racial, ethnic, religious and underprivileged groups...has never been known to have a special deterrent effect."*

Amongst those who have been sentenced to twenty-five years before parole in lieu of the death penalty, the feeling is that the rate of suicide and 'unnatural deaths' amongst their numbers will run so high by the time their 25 years have been served, that the death penalty, in truth, still exists. Nonetheless, it is the *political* aspect of this law, that no repressive 'police-state' government can rule without, which is the ominous feature.

The *Inmate Bill of Rights*—as ratified by the General Assembly of the Canadian Federation of Civil Liberties and Human Rights, May 1978—deserves wide circulation. The Bill's eighteen recommendations begin with a call for immediate implementation of the United Nations Standard Minimum Rules for the Treatment of Prisoners (to which Canada is a signatory) in their entirety. Such documents, if applied, could radically improve current prison policy.

It is quite evident that the larger the prison population the CPS can maintain, the higher the budgets, the more overloaded the bureaucracy, and consequently the more grants and contracts are spread around the legal, medical, pharmaceutical, academic and other professions. The Criminal Justice system, with its judges, administrators, police, probation and parole officers, can also be expected to resist changes which may diminish their budgets and their influence. By the same token, within each of these categories lie many opportunities to encourage and organize changes which will eventually contribute to a shift in the power structure.

The above proposals are not made solely for the benefit of the prison population, but also to expose the government's use of the

*See Appendix III for full text of *Declaration of Stockholm*.

prison system to control the civil population as well. There are presently fifty-four federal prisons in Canada. Nine more are under construction, with fifteen more to come. Within four years there will be *seventy-eight* federal prisons in Canada. *WHY?* Especially when all this additional construction persists in spite of present and predicted decline in prison populations.

Furthermore, pressures must be exerted to open up prisons to concerned communities, and to end the state of incommunicado so dearly loved and indispensable to the Administration. When prisoners are prevented from communicating with us, we must find ways of publicizing this denial. We must do the same when prison activists are banned from visiting and when their mail is interfered with.

Attempts are already being made to silence those who are still free to speak out. It is paramount therefore that everything published on this subject in the time remaining should contribute to decisive analyses and plans of action. An unyielding solidarity with those already in prison is a good place to start.

The treatment of prisoners in Canadian institutions is indeed "cruel" but it is not "unusual." Every punitive act tests not only their capacity to survive, but our capacity to permit such suffering.

—When the system moves on in its semantic game to rename solitary confinement with terms such as "disassociation" or "Special Handling Unit," as described in the *Toronto Star,*

...one of the cruellest inventions of the Canadian Penitentiary Service and should be abolished.

In her final report as federal prisons Ombudsman, Commissioner Inger Hansen lays it on the line. The conditions in the special handling units and solitary confinement sections of prisons, she says are deteriorating. Time hangs heavier and contacts between human beings are con-

stantly being reduced.

The evidence is clear: Special handling in Canadian prisons means specialized mishandling. The units should either be made more humane immediately or abolished completely. No matter how dangerous an inmate may be, he neither deserves nor needs this kind of treatment.

—reprinted in *Vancouver Sun,*
July 5/78

—and when the director of Millhaven, where one of the Special Handling Units is located, "agrees that not all men held in the SHU need to be there. . . feels that an SHU may be necessary for a very small number of inmates but would like to see the unit removed from his prison,"* but when they nonetheless continue to operate so that "after one visit we realized that the conditions there were really unbearable. . .23 hours a day in their cells. . . I went into one and could only remain for about three minutes. . . I was afraid I would faint,"†

—then it is time to examine the choice which must be made by prisoners and non-prisoners alike. The one which, by calling attention to the lawlessness of our prison bureaucracies, but *not* challenging their very existence, means we are helping to preserve them; *or,* the one which utilizes the abundance of existing information and energy to challenge the whole rotten prison régime, with specific alternatives.

Abolition of the prison system is but one facet of the struggle to abolish the whole capitalist system. It is an integral part of the strategy to build a free and open society where community problems will be dealt with *in the community.* Prisons, as presently conceived, will no longer be needed. Estimates vary, according to who is making them, but probably 70-90% of those now incarcerated could safely, economically and usefully be transferred to community-supervised programs, and the remaining 20% or so who are not ready for such a move could then be placed in treatment centres where the best medical, nutritional, and psychological attention could bring them back to a safe level.

Not a single new prison needs to be built. There is an overabundance of them now. New prisons built and waiting to be filled should be converted into community centres. Patrick Gillespie, of the guards' union at Dorchester, also felt that "there should be ways set out to prevent people from getting to jail rather than making unlimited resources available once they have gotten

Liaison, Vol. 4, No. 7, Aug. 1978, p.26.
†Gilbert Décoste, Citizens Advisory Committee, of the Centre de Développement Correctionnel, Québec, *Minutes of Proceedings,* Issue No.14, Dec.8/76, p.49.

into jail.''* When that happens, prisoners won't have to be telling us:

> . . .we are taught sloth. . .we are unlearning to work. . . unlearning to love. . .being taught how to hate easily.**

I am convinced that it is not possible to remain indifferent to the sight of another human being encaged. You are either responsive *to* this human degradation, or you are responsible *for* it. In one way or another, you *are* accountable—whether to your conscience, or to the judgment of your peers who care. A conscious and organized ten percent of an angry, fed-up citizenry could begin to change what appears to be a formidable, entrenched establishment. In their domain, environmentalists have already accomplished a great deal by organizing and by publicizing truths which affect us all. The same can be done with prisons.

And yet, in this nuclear-dominated age, when we all face possible extinction, how to deal with the question: why worry about prisoners when every available resource and skill is needed just to preserve the planet? The answer, as I see it, is that by trying to abolish the present prison system we challenge a social/political/economic order which must preserve and expand its prisons to confine *anyone* who dares resist it—trade unionists, nuclear protestors and political activists all qualify as potential 'criminals.' Those who choose these areas of resistance face reprisals. However, in Canada-1980, such risks must be taken.

As usual, a prisoner provides us with a fitting climax:

> The PSAC. . .issued a press release in which it requested that the RCMP make an enquiry in order to find an agitator, someone from the outside who was cooperating with the inmates to criticise and to try to change the penitentiary system.

*Minutes of Proceedings, Issue No.8, Nov.23/77, p.27.
**Minutes of Proceedings, Issue No.12, Dec.7/76, pp.37-38.

What I can't understand is that one should ask the RCMP to find an unknown person among 20 million people across Canada.*

They don't have very far to search. That "unknown person" is speaking out from pulpit, platform, and press in growing numbers and with gathering force.

Minutes of Proceedings, Issue No. 13, Dec.8/76, p.35.

Epilogue

No objective examination of the best prison system can avoid the conclusion that it is primitive, coercive, and dehumanizing. No rational, let alone scientific appraisal of treatment or rehabilitation programs within the prison setting, can assess them as anything but a total sham. The best efforts of correctional personnel are doomed to frustration and failure, whether measured by recidivism rates or any other reasonable standards of "progress."*

*   *   *

Conferences, symposia, commissions, hearings, enquiries—these take place regularly across this country to deal with the "Incarcerated Offender" and what can be done for them, for the system, and for the personnel, whether in federal, provincial or municipal detention centres.

There is a general consensus that the system is riddled with injustice, and that is the reason these sessions are held so frequently—to try to find the answers, plug the holes, and above all to keep it functional so the thousands of jobs do not disappear. The prison empire must not be allowed to collapse upon itself.

And while everyone is worrying about their individual priorities, the daily degradations go on. Innocent people continue to serve time for lack of a conscientious lawyer, or because of a lost transcript, or because someone fouled up registering an appeal on time, or for any score of reasons.

Other people do 'life' three thousand miles from home, when they could be doing it so much better where they could at least have their weekly visits.

Others are victims of medical crimes, not merely incompetence or inefficiency. The files are full of examples.

And then, of course, there are those who are consigned to the living hell of solitary confinement:

*Emmanuel Margolis, Senior Officer, *Connecticut Bar Journal*, Vol.46, 1972, p.3.

A hallucination, a waking dream, a dream you are having with your eyes open and that is very frightening. That is what madness is. . .you have to make sense of it [but] how do you make sense of something that is crazy.*

Working towards the ultimate goal of "as few people in prison as possible, and for as short a time as possible," I'm wondering if it isn't time for a *People's Tribunal* to close the gap between expectation and performance, between all the enquiries and the actual prison scene. The following scenario is offered as a possible action beyond continuous rounds of talks. It will need the active support of many people, but I do believe it can contribute to significant change in the prison history of Canada.

If it succeeds in releasing *one* innocent person, in providing necessary medical attention to *one* person, in transferring *one* person back to their home base, or getting *one* prisoner out of solitary (or SHU, or whatever it will be called next) then it will have been worth all the effort. By establishing *one* precedent, we will have opened the doors to more.

The idea is to find several volunteer community people to act as mediators, whose reputation and integrity are respected by both sides. Arrange for them to visit every prisoner who has a genuine injustice to report. There would be no legal jargon to decipher, no complex or contradictory 'grievance procedures' to unravel. Prisoners will tell their story, and mediators will question them until they are fully satisfied with the validity of the complaint. This process depends on having inside access to the prisoners. Should this be denied, a substitute 'court of last resort' could be set up at the prison gates. There, friends of prisoners, "advocates," would present their case for them to the mediators.

This would be a new kind of enquiry. It would not be government-funded. There would be no secret hearings, and *all* the findings would be released to the public. Funds would come from supporters' donations to cover minimal travelling and technical expenses. Families and friends of prisoners would surely

Minutes of Proceedings, Issue No.29, Feb.15/77, p.29A:50.

offer accomodation in their areas, so no extravagant hotel bills need be incurred.

The second unique feature would be the setting of a one year time limit, from the date of the first presentation, for some positive response from the authorities. For example: release of *one* innocent person, transfer of *one* person back home, empty solitary confinement of *one* victim. If due justice is not rendered, then the People's Tribunal should plan to announce, well in advance, a public, non-violent, social action open to everybody. If the authorities still refuse to act, then a second and a third action should be planned—any social change requires on-going actions.

This would not be a subversive action, but an open attempt to introduce some justice into a prison system where little or none exists. It would aim at making the government accountable, and in a democracy that means answerable to *all* the people, inside and outside the walls.

This idea was offered at a workshop on "Sentencing" at a recent conference on the "Female Offender" (Vancouver, Jan. 19/79). Inger Hansen, one of the panellists, commented that the idea would suggest that the courts are not doing their job properly. Agreed. Robert Francis (Law Faculty, University of Calgary) described his own experience as a legal member of the committee of Warren Allmand (former Sol-Gen.) for the abolition of the death penalty in 1976. When Francis "vehemently opposed the 25 year alternative sentence," he was unofficially dropped from the committee by not being notified of the time and place of future meetings.

The third panellist, Judge Ray Blais, Provincial Court, North Battleford, Sask., examined the idea carefully, posed some questions, and then asked:

"Do you think it will work?"

"I don't know, I really don't know," I answered. "I just know we have to do *something* to deal with all the shameful unfairness we *know* exists in our prison system. Unless you have a better idea, I am offering this one."

That's as far as the idea has gone.

Obviously there will be many thorny questions to overcome: whether *anything* exists in the entire criminal justice system which can rescind a sentence passed by a court of law; whether the Penitentiary Act itself can be successfully opposed, and so on.

The courts, legislature, and even the penitentiary system often act with unprecedented speed and force when it is a matter of destruction of *property*. I submit that we must find ways to act with equal speed and force when it is a matter of destruction of *human beings*.

With the publication of *Barred From Prison*, I hope that others will join in setting this idea in motion.

> For all practical purposes, imprisonment means the caging of human beings either singly or in pairs or groups.... If there were the slightest scientific proof that the placement of human beings into boxes or cages for any length of time, even overnight, had the slightest beneficial effect, perhaps such a system might be justifiable. There is no such proof; consequently, I should think that a massive attack on the constitutionality of the caging of human beings is in order.*

*Gerhard Mueller, "Imprisonment and Its Alternatives," *Instead of Prisons,* N.Y., 1976, p.40.

Postscript: To Whom It May Concern

This is to certify that Claire Culhane, a member of the Citizens Advisory Committee of the B.C. Penitentiary, has been sitting with us, the Inmate Committee, since approximately 2 a.m. this morning and has observed every *peaceful attempt we have made to have the simple opportunity to expose the insidious corruption in this institution; and the criminal, intentional manner we are used over and over again by ambitious and evil men to further their greedy aims and political aspirations.*

At the moment, this letter is being written because of the political corruption in this region and we honestly feel this mess may end worse than ATTICA.

We trust Claire Culhane, and if it should end as Attica ended, or worse, we feel certain she will take the facts to the public.

The only problem we see is, will the public listen even to her?

Signed:
Inmate Committee, Sept. 28, 1976

Appendix I

Stiff Courtroom Security For Pen Inmates Hearing

Police security was extraordinary Tuesday when seven B.C. Penitentiary inmates appeared in New Westminster court to have charges read against them in connection with a riot and hostage-taking that began Sept. 28.

All spectators were ordered searched—all three of them: two reporters and a photographer.

Four penitentiary guards stood on either side of the docket as the prisoners were led in, handcuffed and shackled. Four policemen stood elsewhere at the ready.

—*Province,* Nov.24/76

STATEMENT OF THOMAS MASON SHAND

Mr. Shand: Your honour, I should like to read a statement that I prepared and hope that the court would understand that I am not referring to this courtroom or to any individual in this courtroom, that I am talking when I talk of courts across Canada. These are my own personal feelings and I hope that my own personal feelings won't have any effect on the sentencing of these other individuals. I'm saying something that I think has to be said. I would hate to see someone else persecuted for what I said. I have made the statement myself. I have had no help in its preparation. It's my statement. If it's all right with your honour I should like to go ahead with it.

The Court: Surely.

Mr. Shand: I have pled guilty to all these charges after spending seven months in solitary confinement. I have come to realize the futility of preparing a proper defence against the charges laid. If I thought I stood even a slight marginal chance of receiving a fair and impartial trial I would take this case to high court. But as other inmates before me have found out all they can expect and receive from the courts of this land is ridicule and degradation.

Here I stand before this court chained like some wild beast, with a heavy guard around me to emphasize my alleged dangerousness. One can only wonder for whose benefit all this show of security is. I can assure the court it certainly doesn't benefit us, the accused. I should like to ask you, sir, how can any judge or jury ever be expected to believe any defence we may put forward with this ominous cloud cast over us. We stand before this court depicted as animals not capable of functioning in any other way than the way you have portrayed us here. How can anyone ever give us the benefit of the doubt when the courts have gone to such great extent to take any doubt away from us there may have been.

I am going to try and explain to the court how all this came about even though I know you have made up your minds as to what happened and what kind of people we are. Truth no longer enters into this case. If it did others would be standing along side of us. They would not be inmates, they would be penitentiary officials charged with inciting to riot and conspiracy. But as we have seen by other court actions this will never happen because the sacred white [cow] must be protected at all costs. I should like to now try and explain to the court why we had to resort to taking hostages.

As most of you must know by now the riot was simmering for the better part of three days before it became full scale. In these three days prior to the major riot not one thing was done by the Administration to curb the impending riot or to alleviate the tensions that then existed. The only party trying to get things back to an even keel was the Inmate's Committee who were met with opposition and open hostility by the Administration at every turn. On the subsequent day of the riot we were working in the kitchen while a full scale riot was in process in the East wing. It had been going full blast for some two [days]. I still, to this day, do not understand why we were permitted to be out of our cells when such an explosive situation existed. One can only conclude that the Administration wanted the ensuing events to take place.

We were made to understand that custody was in the process of getting ready to rush the East wing with tear gas and clubs to subdue the rioters. We knew there was also the possibility of great loss of life to our brothers because many of them were quite prepared to die for their cause. There was no doubt in our minds as to the seriousness of the situation. Things had deteriorated too far to hope for a peaceful settlement so when we were asked to take hostages we did because it was the only thing left to do.

We then took Walter Day and Wayne Culbert hostage thereby creating a Mexican-standoff. I should like to state here and now that at no time during the 27 hours Walter Day was held or the 81 hours imposed on Wayne Culbert was either one subject to ridicule, physical abuse or idle threats. They were both treated as best as the situation allowed and every precaution was taken to insure their welfare and safety.

Another myth I should like to try and dispel is that, contrary to popular belief by the prison Administration and committee investigating prison violence, the inmates did, in fact, everything in their power to stop the riot and hostage taking long before they were ever conceived. All their pleas and requests fell on deaf ears from the Solicitor-General's office right on down the line.

It is my own opinion that had the Committee acted in any other way than they did there most certainly would have been some loss of life and they would have been derelict in their functions and duties as elected members for the inmate population. There has been great ado made of the hostage takers and the rioters, and virtually nothing is said of the hostage *makers* and the riot *creators*, which can only be compared to cattle being blamed for stampeding and the cause of the stampede being left unchecked, so that there may be other stampedes.

The Solicitor-General's component of the Public Service Alliance Association has such overwhelming powers that they are able to create a disturbance or a hostage taking in any maximum security penitentiary in Canada at any time they so desire. They can and have done this many times in the past and will continue to do so in the future unless drastic measures are taken to curb their awesome power. They are able to create incidents to justify higher pay and tighter security measures. What they are in fact doing is asking for a 24 hour day lockup for all prisoners in maximum security institutions, thereby eliminating all the dangers to themselves. And at the same time they ask for a high-risk pay when there is no longer a high-risk factor involved. All this is done at the expense of the inmate who is manipulated into situations, and the public who must bear the brunt of this form of blackmail where the hidden message is, "Give us what we want or we will set the animals loose."

It is fantastic when you consider that just 17 years ago it cost Canadian taxpayers 27 million dollars to run the prison system which today costs ten times that amount. With what result? Is the crime rate down? No. Are related training programs improved? No. As a matter of fact they have disappeared for the greater part of our maximum security institutions, leaving a large part of the population idle.

The only winners of today's prisons are the guards who get higher pay and the outside contractors who build more slaughter houses. The losers are you, the public, who get nothing in return for your investments, and the inmate who will one day be coming back to your society to thank you for all you have done for him. He will probably be so thankful that the next time you try to send him back for a trade and psychiatric treatment he will probably try and kill you to prevent you from doing so.

It is my honest opinion that each and every one of you knows the injustices that are committed against the inmates in your prisons where they are held. I include the more than 100 deaths which occurred in the past five years in the Federal prisons of which more than 80 have been attributed to suicide. But you know better, and so do I: nothing has been done to seek out the real reasons for these deaths or the perpetrators who committed them. Yet you sit back and wonder why there is no longer respect for the laws of the courts of this country.

In a way, the courts and the people who make the laws of Canada are more criminal than the people they send off to prison. You have powers and authority collectively to do something about the deplorable conditions which exist in our prison system. You have created a mammoth monster which you no longer have control over, and if you still have, it is very little or not applied. I speak again of the Solicitor-General's component of the Public Service Alliance of Canada.

All I'm able to say in my defence is that had there been a more peaceful way to bring about the cessation of hostility we would have tried that way first. When inmates in prison can no longer negotiate peacefully to have their complaints and grievances heard by Ottawa and the public, then they will do it violently because they know you understand violence. Sometimes we are forced into situations in which we do not necessarily want to participate, but circumstances surrounding that situation give us little or no chance, or choice, but to participate.

Thank you, Sir.

The Court: Thank you Mr. Shand.*

*New Westminster, B.C., April 25, 1977.

Appendix II

There were actually seven "other incidents" referred to by A/D Ev Berkey and Information Officer Jack Stewart. These reasons for banishing me from the B.C.Penitentiary were kept secret until Jack Stewart, at the *Examination for Discovery*, was obliged to respond to the lawyer's questions.*

1) *"It had been reported to Mr. Berkey that Ms. Culhane had on several occasions applauded vigorously to statements being made by the members of the Inmate Committee to the rest of the inmates in the auditorium."*

No comment.

2) *"She was reported as having said to the Inmate Committee that she would assist them by producing signs with slogans on solidarity that could be hung in the auditorium, which such slogans would say 'One for All and All for One.'"*

Comment: "Dangerous stuff."—H. Poulus, attorney for Culhane.

3) *"It was reported that she was overheard in conversation with a member of the Inmate Committee at which time guards' names were mentioned in connection with letter bombs."*

Comment: See page 65 for an accurate description of that episode when the words 'letter bomb' were used by a member of the Inmate Committee to jokingly describe the breakfasts being served in brown paper bags. No guards' names were mentioned.

4) *"There was a report from an officer that Ms. Culhane was seen to be in a less than lady-like position with Inmate Horvat, in view of the general inmate population. Specifically, that Mr. Horvat was seated and Ms. Culhane was resting her upper body and arm on Ivan Horvat's thighs."*

Comment: In order to hear a prisoner calling up to me from the gym floor, for a moment I had to lean over Horvat, who was seated on the window-sill.

*As cited in the transcript of the *Examination For Discovery* of J.R. Stewart, No. C765545 of the Supreme Court of B.C., Jan.13/78.

5) *"There was a report from an officer at the front gate of the institution that Ms. Culhane had been told not to take a basket of fruit into the institution. After she was escorted up the hill, he noticed that the basket of fruit had gone."*

Comment: When I was denied permission to take in a basket of fruit from the mother of a prisoner, I left it with the officer at the gate. It was no longer there when I returned four hours later.

6) *"A personal conversation I [Stewart] had with a staff member of the B.C.Penitentiary who reported to me that either one day or two days prior to Ms. Culhane being sent out of the institution, that he had observed her and a member of the Inmate Committee passing a folded piece of paper."*

Comment: While I have no recollection of such an incident, had it indeed been observed, the normal procedure would have been to immediately charge us with misconduct and seize the "folded piece of paper" as evidence. No such action ever took place.

7) *"There was one further report that I [Stewart] am aware of that does not relate to a specific incident. It is an RCMP report expressing concern about the security aspects of Ms. Culhane's involvement with inmates in the auditorium."*

Comment: Where innuendos replace specific charges, no defence can or need be made.

Appendix III

DECLARATION OF STOCKHOLM
11 DECEMBER 1977

The Stockholm Conference on the Abolition of the Death Penalty, composed of more than 200 delegates and participants from Africa, Asia, Europe, the Middle East, North and South America and the Caribbean region,

Recalls That:

—The death penalty is the ultimate cruel, inhuman and degrading punishment and violates the right to life.

Considers That:

—The death penalty is frequently used as an instrument of repression against opposition, racial, ethnic, religious and underprivileged groups,

—Execution is an act of violence, and violence tends to provoke violence,

—The imposition and infliction of the death penalty is brutalizing to all who are involved in the process.

—The death penalty has never been shown to have a special deterrent effect,

—The death penalty is increasingly taking the form of unexplained disappearances, extra-judicial executions and political murders,

—Execution is irrevocable and can be inflicted on the innocent.

Affirms That:

—It is the duty of the state to protect the life of all persons within its jurisdiction without exception,

—Executions for the purposes of political coercion, whether by government agencies or others, are equally unacceptable,

—Abolition of the death penalty is imperative for the achievement of declared international standards.

Declares:

—Its total and unconditional opposition to the death penalty,

—Its condemnation of all executions, in whatever form, committed or condoned by governments,

—Its commitment to work for the universal abolition of the death penalty.

Calls Upon:
—Non-governmental organisations, both national and international, to work collectively and individually to provide public information materials directed towards the abolition of the death penalty,

—All governments to bring about the immediate and total abolition of the death penalty,

—The United Nations unambiguously to declare that the death penalty is contrary to international law.*

*Amnesty International, Conference on the Abolition of the Death Penalty.

Index of Names

(*Note:* Inmate Committee names are not listed from Ch. 3, *The Log.*)

*　　　　*　　　　*

A CHECKLIST OF PULP BOOKS:

BOMMIE BAUMANN:
Wie Alles Anfing:
  How It All Began

LEO BURDAK:
Gearfoot Wrecks

BRIAN CARSON:
A Dream of Naked Women

TOM CONE:
Three Plays

CLAIRE CULHANE:
Barred from Prison

JANET DOLMAN & ROBERT NUNN:
Mankynde

C.W. DOLSON:
The Showplace of the County

DAN DOUGHERTY:
The National Hen

ROGER DUNSMORE:
On the Road to Sleeping Child
 Hotsprings, 2nd Edition
Laszlo Toth

KEN EISLER:
Inchman

L. L. FIELD & M. B. KNECHTEL, EDS:
Elbow Room

RAYMOND FILIP:
Somebody Told Me I Look Like
 Everyman

D.M. FRASER:
Class Warfare

AUGUSTIN HAMON:
The Psychology of the Anarchist

ALFRED JARRY:
Ubu Rex (Translated by David Copelin)

CHRIS JOHNSON:
Duet for a Schizophrenic

MARY BETH KNECHTEL:
The Goldfish that Exploded

JOHN KULA:
The Epic of Gilgamesh as
  Commissioned by Morgan

BETTY LAMBERT:
Crossings

MARK MADOFF:
Paper Nautilus
The Patient Renfield
Dry Point

CARLOS MARIGHELLA:
Minimanual of the Urban Guerilla

ROMAINE MURPHY:
The Molly Bloom Poems

ROGER PRENTICE & JOHN KIRK:
A Fist and a Letter

NORBERT RUEBSAAT:
Cordillera

BRIAN SHEIN:
Theatrical Exhibitions

JOHNNY TENS:
Tenth Avenue Bike Race

CHARLES TIDLER:
Whetstone Almanac
FLIGHT: The Last American Poem
Anonymous Stone

TOM WALMSLEY:
Rabies
The Workingman
Lexington Hero
The Jones Boy
Doctor Tin

ANTHONY WILDEN:
The Imaginary Canadian

MARK YOUNG:
Brother Ignatius of Mary

PLEASE WRITE:
Pulp Press
Box 3868 M.P.O.
Vancouver, Canada V6B 3Z3

FOR A DESCRIPTIVE CATALOGUE